F.V.

A BEGINNER'S GUIDE TO THE MMPI-2

$\mathcal{A}$ BEGINNER'S GUIDE *to the* MMPI-2

James N. Butcher

American Psychological Association

Washington, DC

First printing January 1999
Second printing July 1999

Published by
American Psychological Association
750 First Street, NE
Washington, DC 20002

Copies may be ordered from
APA Order Department
P.O. Box 92984
Washington, DC 20090-2984

In the U.K., Europe, Africa, and the Middle East, copies may be ordered from
American Psychological Association
3 Henrietta Street
Covent Garden, London
WC2E 8LU England

Typeset in New Baskerville and Futura by EPS Group Inc., Easton, MD
Printer: Sheridan Books, Ann Arbor, MI
Dust jacket designer: Kachergis Book Design, Pittsboro, NC
Technical/Production Editor: Amy J. Clarke

Library of Congress Cataloging-in-Publication Data

Butcher, James Neal, 1933–
      A beginner's guide to the MMPI-2 / James Neal Butcher
         p.   cm.
      Includes bibliographical references and index.
      ISBN 1-55798-564-2 (acid-free paper)
      1. Minnesota Multiphasic Personality Inventory.   I. Title
   BF698.8.M5B86   1999
   155.2′83—dc21
                                                                                           98-41100
                                                                                                CIP

British Library Cataloguing-in-Publication Data
A CIP record is available from the British Library.

Printed in the United States of America

Contents

Exhibits and Figures

Preface

Writing a "brief" introduction to the Minnesota Multiphasic Personality Inventory–Revised for Adults (MMPI-2) is a very challenging task. The MMPI-2 is the most widely researched (over 200 articles a year) and broadly used personality assessment instrument in psychology. How can a brief introduction to the interpretation of this personality inventory do the topic justice? What can be said in a 177-page book without neglecting important topics and applications and being seen as superficial? What types of material could provide the beginner with a clear idea of the essence of what the MMPI-2 is and does?

When Margaret Schlegel from APA Books asked me to consider writing a short introduction to the MMPI-2, I naturally balked because I thought that this book could not be written without appearing superficial or negligent in coverage. However, as I began to see the task more clearly, as one of simply introducing the MMPI-2 to a nonprofessional audience, the idea began to have great appeal—why not an overview for nonpsychologists (physicians, attorneys, etc.) who desire an easy and quick overview and do not have time to invest in one of the available full texts on the topic? This book is different from other texts, in that it assumes little in the way of a psychology background and presents all that is needed for a basic understanding of how the MMPI-2 works.

For roughly 35 years, I have taught the MMPI and MMPI-2 to graduate students and professionals in psychology who have not been exposed to the instrument in their training. I have also had the occasion to provide brief overviews or "mini-workshops" on the MMPI-2 to lay audiences, such as jurors, personnel managers, police and fire chiefs, and so forth, who have needed to know "a bit" about the test but not in great depth.

In the assessment courses and introductory workshops that I teach, I have typically used a "quick immersion" technique to provide pertinent background to familiarize the student with the basic concepts and measures quickly and briefly so as to get them involved with the clinical interpretation of cases as soon as possible. For example, I usually begin the course with an intensive reading assignment (e.g., within the first week of the term) to familiarize them with the measures on the MMPI-2—using a descriptive textbook to provide students with a broad picture of the MMPI-2, how it was developed, how the scales work, and what the various scales and profile patterns assess. Then, the remainder of the term can be devoted to an in-depth coverage of specific topics, such as using the MMPI-2 in treatment planning and in forensic evaluations, with a great deal of focus on case interpretations. This is the way psychologists really get to know the MMPI-2: by seeing how it actually works with a broad range of patients with different symptoms and behaviors.

This introductory book follows that quick immersion model by providing all of the basic information that is needed to give the beginner an appropriate general framework. My goals in this book include the following:

- To provide a readable (nontechnical) introduction in a brief format for the person who needs a "quick overview" of what the MMPI-2 is and does.
- To explain how the test was developed to describe and predict behavior in a broad range of clinical settings.
- To illustrate with case material how an individual's responses to the 567 MMPI-2 questions result in test scores and patterns that match his or her behavior.
- To introduce the reader to the variety of scales on the MMPI-2 and a strategy for drawing information from them.
- To demonstrate how the scale interpretations can be integrated into a clinical evaluation and how the results of MMPI-2 evaluations can be communicated to others through a report.

Beginners should have, with the information provided here, a basic understanding that will enable them to pursue more effectively the broad knowledge base available on this topic.

I would like to express my appreciation to several people who contributed to this book project in different ways. Margaret Schlegel provided me with the idea for the book and the encouragement to develop it; Ted Baroody was extremely helpful in providing feedback about what worked and what did not work in the initial manuscript; two reviewers

provided valuable input into the "nuts and bolts" of the material included in the book; and Linda Fresquez was helpful in typing portions
of the text, particularly in making some of the typing changes that I
received from reviewers. Finally, I would like to express my appreciation
to my wife Carolyn L. Williams and daughter Holly Krista Butcher for
their support during this project.

James N. Butcher
Minneapolis, MN

A BEGINNER'S GUIDE
TO THE MMPI-2

A Well-Traveled Path: MMPI Use and Administration

A countless number of psychologists and psychiatrists have traveled the path to learning the Minnesota Multiphasic Personality Inventory (MMPI) interpretation since Starke Hathaway (see Figure 1.1A), a psychologist, and J. C. McKinley (see Figure 1.1B), a psychiatrist, took those first steps to bring objective clinical assessment into clinical settings in the late 1930s. Hathaway and McKinley's work—aimed at obtaining veridical (i.e., truthful or accurate) information about their patients through their patients' own symptom descriptions—initiated a long tradition in objective clinical assessment.

MMPI-2 Background and History

Hathaway and McKinley were, of course, not the earliest personality researchers to use self-report procedures in an effort to obtain personality-based information about people. The use of self-report methods dates back to the end of the 19th century when Francis Galton explored ways of having people rate themselves on personality factors. The use of self-report questionnaires gained a wide following in the 1920s and 1930s shortly after Woodworth (1920) developed the first personality questionnaire, the Personal Data Sheet, during World War 1. Personality questionnaires proliferated after the war, and psychologists showed great ingenuity in developing measures to assess various personal qualities, such as hope, will, or temperament. Most of the early inventories were rationally derived questionnaires compiled from

Figure 1.1

Starke Hathaway (A) and J. C. McKinley (B).

vaguely defined theoretical constructs, without much regard paid to questions as to whether the measures were valid or accurate.

Hathaway and McKinley brought a different perspective to personality assessment—the empirical method—and with their effort, an important tradition in clinical assessment began. The MMPI came just in time to see service in World War 2 and to become a standard assessment vehicle in the broad expansion of clinical psychology in the boom years following the war.

The Empirical Method: Scale Development Based on Validation

Hathaway and McKinley (1940, 1943) considered it important to develop measures that would both assess important clinical problems and validly portray their patients in an objective manner. Because they were working clinicians, they had confidence that patients could and would describe their problems honestly through self-reports if only the proper conditions could be arranged for them. These two clinicians provided a psychometric framework through which these symptom reports could be objectively appraised. Several important points need to be understood about Hathaway and McKinley's strategy because these factors made the MMPI different from other personality evaluation instruments of the day and infused the instrument with qualities that gave it the stamina to survive the test of time.

In developing their inventory of problems, Hathaway and McKinley broadly sampled clinical charts as well as the psychiatric problem research literature to obtain a comprehensive sampling of symptoms, beliefs, problems, attitudes, and so forth as their initial item pool. They started with a pool of over 1,000 items, which they reduced down to a little over 500 items for the initial data collection, testing *normals* (people from the community not under a doctor's care) and *clinical patients* (those in treatment who had clearly defined symptoms). They wrote the items at a low reading level (sixth grade), such as "I have never been in trouble with the law" and used a test administration format that would promote cooperation with the individuals taking the test. They had each item typed on a card; people taking the test were asked to read and decide whether a statement applied to them and then to place the card in one of three designated slots in a box—*true, false,* and *don't know.*

Hathaway and McKinley chose a method of scale development that was based on demonstrated empirical validation. Instead of deciding in advance as to which of their provisional items measured which personality characteristic, the authors chose to base their scale membership on obtaining items that actually worked to separate the clinical group from the normal population. This approach, referred to as *criterion keying test construction,* involves selecting items for scales by identifying those that discriminated a clinical (criterion) group from a group of normals (see Exhibit 1.1 for an outline of this method). The clinical groups were chosen on the basis of standard clinical criteria of the day, as a beginning point in defining the authors' scale meanings. Once the scales were derived and validated against external criteria, they were not considered tied to their developmental criteria. That is, they were shown to have meaning apart from their initial definition and to have construct validity, as described by Cronbach and Meehl (1955). The effectiveness of an empirical scale in personality assessment is dependent, in part, on the extent to which highly similar cases were used in the formation of the criterion groups. If the test constructor is careful and meticulous with respect to the inclusion of appropriate cases, then the scale is likely to be more valid for discriminating other similar cases.

Exhibit 1.1

Empirical Clinical Scale Development Based on Actual Item Validity

The Original MMPI

- Items for the clinical scale on the original MMPI were selected on the basis of their ability to empirically discriminate between a well-defined clinical group (e.g., depressed patients) and a sample of normals.

- Initially, items were selected from various sources, such as clinical cases, textbooks, and previous tests, to address clinical symptoms pertinent for describing personality.

- MMPI items were administered to a large group of individuals (724) who were not under a doctor's care, namely, the Minnesota normative sample. The responses of these individuals serve as the normal reference sample.

- Several homogeneous clinical groups were gathered to serve as the criterion or clinical group: hypochondriacal, depressed, hysteroid, sociopathic, paranoid, psychasthenic, schizophrenic, and hypomanic patients.

The MMPI-2

- The traditional clinical scales of the original MMPI were kept in their original form to maintain continuity with the original instrument. Additional validity research was conducted to verify the accuracy of the revised MMPI-2 norms in detecting problem behaviors.

- In the MMPI-2 (the revision), the scales were normed on a nationally representative sample of normal individuals (1,138 men and 1,462 women).

- Scales are interpreted on the basis of their empirical relationships or personality correlates. A high score on a particular scale indicates the likelihood that the individual possesses the characteristics known to be associated with that scale.

- In addition, several new scales were developed for the MMPI-2 (e.g., the Superlative Self-Presentation Scale [S], Addiction Proneness Scale [APS], and the Marital Adjustment Scale [MDS]) to assess specific problems using the empirical scale construction strategy.

Hathaway and McKinley attempted to obtain the most homogeneous cases to maximize the diagnostic similarity of the cases included.

Hathaway and McKinley used a general normative sample in their scale development work, which was considered a good estimate of normal personality and mental health problems, although this sample was, according to today's standards, relatively small and overly narrow—it was based largely on individuals living in Minnesota who were not under a doctor's care. For the times, however, the sample was considered a good representation of "people in general."

Hathaway and McKinley also began a tradition of approaching a test protocol with a degree of skepticism, until the individual's cooperativeness had been assured. They recognized that not all people taking the MMPI are fully cooperative and honest in their approach to the items. They also recognized a need for control scales to evaluate an individual's approach to the items. As seen in chapter 2, the need to appraise a client's test-taking attitudes carefully has been greatly expanded in the present form of the instrument, the MMPI-2.

Finally, Hathaway and McKinley began a tradition of empirical research—the development of a sound empirical database—which has continued into the present. A personality assessment instrument based on empirical scale validation requires a substantial supporting research base, as found with the MMPI and its successors.

Is There a Theory That Underpins the Use of the MMPI-2?

The man in the cartoon shown in Figure 1.2 appears to be providing an apt description of the original MMPI. There is no preferred theoretical "party line" that MMPI-2 users follow in interpreting test profiles, but the instrument works in practice. Psychologists do not have to swear allegiance to a particular theoretical orientation or school of psychology to incorporate the MMPI-2 into their clinical practice; the inventory is used by cognitive–behaviorists, behaviorists, psychoanalysts, and even nontheoretical practitioners. The only thing resembling a theory underlying the MMPI is that MMPI-oriented psychologists (often referred to fondly as the "Multcult") tend toward rigorous empirical analysis. The description often attributed to MMPI users is *dust bowl empiricists* (a term referring to the arid period of drought in the 1930s during which little was thought to come to fruition but what did emerge was solid and lasting) because of their scientific skepticism and proclivity to disbelieve anything that has not been substantially verified by research data.

Success of the Empirical Approach

Hundreds of articles on the original MMPI clinical scales attest to the success of the empirical method at both describing patient behavior and acquiring loyal adherents who want a reliable and valid means of typi-

Figure 1.2

Dunagin's People/By Ralph Dunagin

2-4

"Sure it works fine in practice, but the theory's no good!"

fying patients' behavior and problems. Within a few years, the MMPI had surpassed in usage all other clinical assessment methods (Lees-Haley, Smith, Williams, & Dunn, 1995; Lubin, Larsen, & Matarazzo, 1984), had gained recognition as the premier personality research instrument (Butcher & Rouse, 1996), and had been translated over 150 times and became extensively used for research and application in 46 other countries (Butcher, 1985). Moreover, many other researchers have developed additional scales to address other clinical problems, for example, to assess ego strength, immaturity, or drug abuse potential. These scales are often referred to as the *supplemental scales*.

A Revision of the MMPI: The Development of the MMPI-2

Over time, the MMPI began to show some signs of aging, and by the time it reached its 30th birthday, some interest was emerging for conducting a revision of the original instrument. In a retrospective review of the status of personality assessment, Hathaway (1972) lamented the lack of progress in the field because the MMPI approach had not been superseded or improved on to that point. In the same book—which was devoted to a discussion of whether the MMPI should be revised—both Butcher (1972) and Dahlstrom (1972) were positively inclined toward modifying the original MMPI to make it a more up-to-date instrument. Several problems and limitations of the MMPI were detailed in this book. For example, several noted personality researchers (Warren Norman, Jane Loevinger, David Campbell, and Paul Meehl) expressed opinions about a revision therein. By this time, clearly the original items were somewhat dated in terms of the language used in the questions, and there were a number of nonworking items on the instrument—items that were not incorporated into the widely used scales and others that were found to be objectionable. Moreover, the MMPI was used for frequent applications (e.g., suicide assessment, substance abuse assessment, treatment planning) for which no items existed on the inventory. Furthermore, the norms for the test were considered in need of modernizing because they were thought to be overly narrow, in part because they consisted of a small, somewhat provincial sample of normals from Minnesota. Butcher (1972) noted some interest in redeveloping the norms using a more diverse population.

Changing an instrument that still worked reasonably well and served as the standard for clinical personality assessment was not, however, an easy matter. A full decade passed before the test publisher (University of Minnesota Press) responded to the need for a revised version of the MMPI and appointed a committee, with James Butcher, W. Grant Dahlstrom, John R. Graham, and Auke Tellegen to conduct it.

The instrument underwent a major revision during the 1980s, and after substantial data collection, two revised versions of the inventory were published: The *MMPI-2* (for adults) was published in 1989 (Butcher, Dahlstrom, Graham, Tellegen, & Kaemmer) and the *MMPI-A* (for adolescents) was published in 1992 (Butcher, Williams, Graham, Archer, Tellegen, Ben-Porath, & Kaemmer, 1989). The redevelopment research and the revision of the MMPI took place over a period of 10 years and involved testing over 15 thousand individuals from the general population and from various normal and clinical groups. The following factors characterize the revision and provide basic information as to the structure of the MMPI-2.

1. *Revision and modernization of the MMPI item pool.* Although a major goal in the revision was to maintain some continuity between the revised form and the original MMPI (at least with respect to the traditional validity and clinical scales), a number of changes were required. The initial step in the revision process involved redeveloping the item pool to make it more effective and readable. Some of the original items were rewritten because of awkward wording or outmoded expressions. In addition, the original test booklet contained a number of objectionable or irrelevant (unused) items that detracted from the utility of the instrument. Most of these items were deleted to eliminate objectionable content and to make room in the instrument for new items.

2. *Expansion of the scope of the original item pool.* The original MMPI was frequently used to assess people who were experiencing central problems for which the MMPI contained limited item content. For example, although suicide assessment was commonly undertaken, the original item pool actually contained no explicit suicide item content. The item pool for the MMPI-2 was expanded to include more items that addressed a broader range of clinical symptoms and problems in areas including suicide, drug and alcohol abuse, relationship problems, and treatment compliance.

3. *Development of a nationally representative normative sample.* An important goal of the MMPI-2 Restandardization Committee was to obtain a broad representative sample for the norms. A total of 2,600 normal men and women from five regions of the United States (1,138 men and 1,462 women) were included in the normative sample for the MMPI-2. These individuals were recruited through procedures that ensured a random sample from across the United States. Efforts were made to balance the normative sample in terms of ethnicity to provide an unbiased general norm set. For example, people were sampled in areas with large minority populations, including Hispanic (Southern California), African American (urban Philadelphia and North Carolina), and American Indians (an Indian reservation in Washington state).

4. *Development of validational studies of diverse patient and nonpatient groups.* In addition to the normative data collection, a number of other studies were conducted during the MMPI restandardization research. Several clinical samples were collected, including inpatient psychiatric cases, chronic pain medical patients, alcohol and drug abusers, married couples in counseling, women judged as being at risk for child abuse, and prison inmates. Furthermore, several "normal range" groups, such as airline pilot applicants, military personnel, undergraduate college students, and older men were tested to evaluate the new norms with additional samples.

5. *Development of several new personality and symptom scales.* During the MMPI restandardization program, a number of new measures were developed to broaden the range of applications of the inventory. Several new validity scales, the Infrequency-Back Scale [F(B)], Variable Response Inconsistency Scale (*VRIN*), True Response Inconsistency Scale (*TRIN*), and the Superlative Self-Presentation Scale (*S*; described in chapter 2), were constructed to provide a more complete assessment of invalidating conditions. A number of content-based scales (the MMPI-2 content scales) were developed to appraise the major content dimensions in the inventory (Butcher, Graham, Williams, & Ben-Porath, 1990). *Content scales* contain a number of similar items that address a unitary personality characteristic. For example, the Depression Content Scale includes a number of items that center on the theme of depressed affect. Finally, several supplementary scales were developed to assess specific problem areas, such as substance use and abuse problems (Addiction Potential Scale [*APS*] and the Addiction Acknowledgment Scale [*AAS*]), and to examine relationship problems (the Marital Distress Scale [*MDS*]).

The Purposes of the MMPI-2

How is the MMPI-2 used in contemporary psychology? The original MMPI was developed as an aid in psychiatric screening programs in mental health settings in general medical practices. Over the early decades of its use, the instrument was used and researched in a variety of mental health and medical settings and a number of nonmental health contexts, such as correctional facilities, personnel screening programs, alcohol and drug abuse programs, and research. It is not possible to describe all of the current settings and populations for which the MMPI-2 is used, but a few relatively common applications are noted below for purposes of illustration.

- Evaluation of patients in mental health settings to aid in the clarifying of their mental health status
- Symptom appraisal to determine the need for hospitalization
- Assessment of patients in pretreatment planning
- Evaluation of treatment effects
- Epidemiological research using personality-based criteria
- Personality appraisal for public safety positions, such as police, fire, airline pilot, and nuclear power plant personnel
- Psychological research studies in which objective personality appraisals are used as an external criterion to study group differences
- Research into the genetics of personality
- Longitudinal studies of personality processes and change
- Assessments of personality in different cultural contexts to study similarities and differences between different cultures
- Classification of convicted felons at incarceration
- Evaluation of parents in family custody disputes
- Appraisal of personality factors to determine whether a personal injury claimant has the mental health problems he or she claims

Keep in mind that the MMPI-2 is not designed to address all characteristics or behaviors that might be of interest to the clinician. For example, such qualities or conditions as intelligence, the presence of organic brain disorder, or the likelihood of committing a violent act are not addressed by the test.

Things To Know About MMPI-2 Administration

Recognize that there are several different test administration formats for the MMPI-2 available. However, all of the available test versions have the same number of items and an identical item order. The most widely available administration formats are the paper-and-pencil form with a reusable printed booklet (often referred to as the *booklet version*), an audiocassette version for aural administration (currently available in English, Spanish, and Hmong [Laos]), and a computer-administered version. A videotaped (American Sign Language) version of the MMPI-2 is also available for deaf clients. Research shows that the various forms produce equivalent results.

Provide Only the Standard Instructions

In administering the MMPI-2, the test giver must follow the standard instructions and administer the test in a comfortable, private place away from distractions; the test taker should feel that his or her item responses are given in confidence. It makes no difference whether the test is individually or group administered; both conditions are considered appropriate. A proper test-taking atmosphere needs to be created. The MMPI-2 needs to be administered in a controlled context; it is, therefore, not appropriate for people to take the test home or be allowed to take it in an uncontrolled setting, such as a busy cafeteria or noisy waiting room.

Give Clear Instructions

It is also important for the test administrator to acquire the individual's cooperation to ensure a valid test performance. The relative simplicity of MMPI-2 test administration procedures can unfortunately contribute to test administration problems. For example, it may be tempting for the examiner to allow test takers to read the instructions and to figure out the appropriate procedures on their own. It is more appropriate to have a trained person, such as a psychometrician, nurse, or clerical assistant, provide the needed professional atmosphere for the testing and explain the test instructions clearly.

Determine Reading Level and Reading Comprehension

The test giver should ensure that the test taker can read well enough to comprehend the item content. A sixth-grade reading level is required to understand the MMPI-2 items. In situations where potential test takers might have problems reading the items, it might be valuable to use a reading test to determine if the test takers can understand the test content. It may be desirable to use an audiocassette version of the MMPI-2 rather than a printed form, particularly for semiliterate persons—those with marginal reading ability may understand the items better through an oral administration of the test.

Furthermore, in situations where the individual was raised in another language and culture and may not read or understand English, it may be possible to find an appropriate foreign language version to administer. In some situations, other national norms are available for non-English-speaking test takers (Butcher, 1996). Using the English-language version and American norms might be appropriate for test takers from other countries who live and work in English-speaking countries, particularly if they have gone to school in those countries and can read English.

Administer the Full MMPI-2

The MMPI-2 instructions request that all or most of the items be answered. To obtain the maximum information from the MMPI-2, the test giver must make sure the participant answers all 567 test items. Although the traditional validity and clinical scales can be obtained from the administration of only the first 370 items, this abbreviated form does not provide the MMPI-2 content scales or the supplementary scales that are so valuable in test interpretation. Moreover, the abbreviated form of the MMPI-2 does not allow for a thorough assessment of protocol validity (see chapter 2 for a discussion of the validity scales).

Test Scoring

What Is a Scale Score?

There are two types of scores to keep in mind when processing an MMPI-2 protocol: raw scores and *T* scores. Raw scores are obtained by using the scoring keys (either manual or computer based) and adding up the number of "agreements" between the test taker's responses and the scoring key. The *T* scores, on which the profile and code are based, are statistically derived standard-score equivalents for the raw scores for each scale. Two types of standard scores are used in the MMPI-2. Linear *T* scores are used for some scales, such as the validity scales; what has been termed *uniform T scores* are used for most of the symptom-oriented scales. On the MMPI-2, uniform *T* scores are used for clinical scales: Scale 1 Hypochondriasis (*Hs*), Scale 2 Depression (*D*), Scale 3 Hysteria (*Hy*), Scale 4 Psychopathic Deviate (*Pd*), Scale 5 Masculinity–Femininity (*Mf*), Scale 6 Paranoia (*Pa*), Scale 7 Psychasthenia (*Pt*), Scale 8 Schizophrenia (*Sc*), Scale 9 Mania (*Ma*), and Scale 0 Social Introversion–Extraversion (*Si*). In addition, uniform *T* scores are used for the content scales (see chapter 5). Linear *T* scores are used for the Lie Scale (*L*), Infrequency Scale (*F*), Defensiveness Scale (*K*), *Mf* (5), and *Si* (0). The term *uniform T score* is original to the MMPI-2 and is a modification of the linear *T* score that ensures that percentile ranks are equivalent across all the scales. That is, a *T* = 65 would fall roughly at the 92nd percentile for all scales with uniform *T* scores.

The MMPI-2 scale distributions have the following statistics: *M* = 50 and *SD* = 10. Raw scores are converted to *T* scores and plotted on a profile sheet as shown in Figure 1.3, so that scales can be compared in the same metric. A scale elevation, in *T*-score units, is interpreted usually when it is elevated beyond $1\frac{1}{2}$ *SD*s above the mean or when it is greater than *T* = 65. Some of the scales that the reader will encounter later (e.g., the addiction indicators) might be interpreted at *T* = 60 for making some decisions about the significance of a score. Traditionally, MMPI scale score distributions have been developed separately for men and women, that is they are gender-specific norms. Hathaway and McKinley believed that separate gender norms were needed because of observed differences between men and women in their response to items. This tradition has been continued in the MMPI-2. However, in recent times, the suggestion that men and women should be plotted on the same normative distributions has also been studied (Tellegen, Butcher, & Hoeglund, 1993). Gender-neutral norms have been developed for the MMPI-2 on the basis of the MMPI-2 normative sample and are available for some applications. In practice, there are relatively few differences between men and women on the clinical and content scales (most of the item differences appear on the *Mf*). Tellegen et al. believed that either the gender-neutral norms or the traditional "separate" norms could appropriately be used for men or women.

Hand Scoring

Scoring templates are available for manual scoring of the MMPI-2 answer sheets through the test distributor, National Computer Systems.[1] (The scales discussed in this book are listed in Exhibit 1.2). The templates are plastic overlays that contain punched holes that allow the scorer to "see and count" the item responses scored on the answer

---

[1]National Computer Systems, P.O. Box 1416, Minneapolis, MN 55440.

Figure 1.3

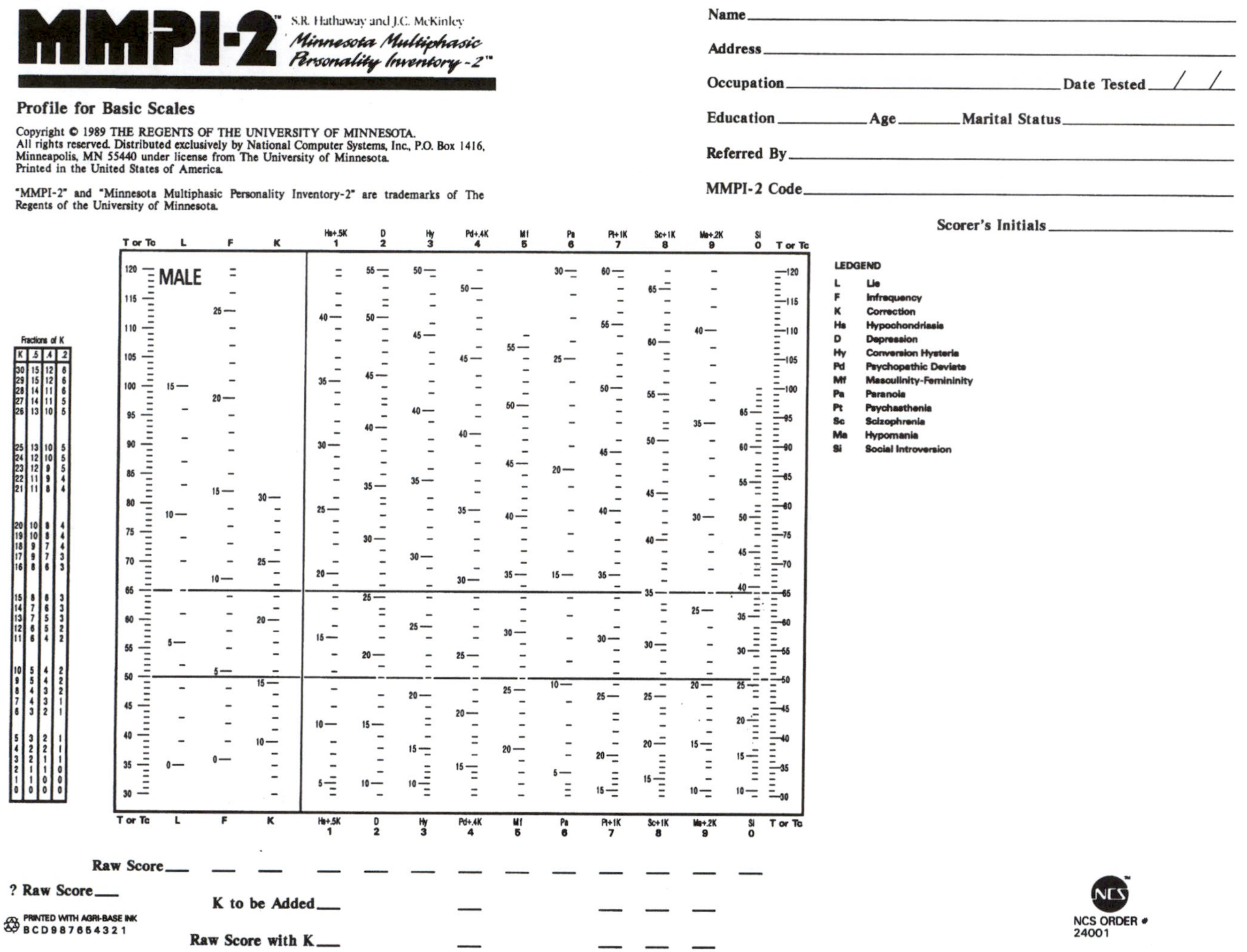

A profile for the basic scales. Copyright © 1989 the Regents of the University of Minnesota. All rights reserved. Distributed exclusively by National Computer Systems, Inc., P.O. Box 1416, Minneapolis, MN 55440, under license from the University of Minnesota.

Exhibit 1.2

Scales of the MMPI-2

Validity Scales (See Chapter 2)

Cannot Say (?)
Variable Response Inconsistency Scale (*VRIN*)
True Response Inconsistency Scale (*TRIN*)
Lie Scale (*L*)
Defensiveness Scale (*K*)
Superlative Self-Presentation Scale (*S*)
Infrequency Scale (*F*)
Infrequency-Back Scale [*F(B)*]
Psychiatric Infrequency Scale [*F(p)*]

Standard Scales (See Chapter 3)

Scale 1 Hypochondriasis (*Hs*)
Scale 2 Depression (*D*)
Scale 3 Hysteria (*Hy*)
Scale 4 Psychopathic Deviate (*Pd*)
Scale 5 Masculinity–Femininity (*Mf*)
Scale 6 Paranoia (*Pa*)
Scale 7 Psychasthenia (*Pt*)
Scale 8 Schizophrenia (*Sc*)
Scale 9 Mania (*Ma*)
Scale 0 Social Introversion–Extraversion (*Si*)

Content Scales (See Chapter 5)

Anxiety Scale (*ANX*)
Fears Scale (*FRS*)
Obsessiveness Scale (*OBS*)
Depression Scale (*DEP*)
Health Concerns Scale (*HEA*)
Bizarre Mentation Scale (*BIZ*)
Anger Scale (*ANG*)
Cynicism Scale (*CYN*)
Antisocial Practices Scale (*ASP*)
Type A Scale (*TPA*)
Low Self-Esteem Scale (*LSE*)
Social Discomfort Scale (*SOD*)
Family Problems Scale (*FAM*)
Work Interference Scale (*WRK*)
Negative Treatment Indicators Scale (*TRT*)

continued

Exhibit 1.2, continued

Supplementary or Special Scales (See Chapter 6)

MacAndrew Addiction Scale–Revised (*MAC-R*)
Addiction Potential Scale (*APS*)
Addiction Acknowledgment Scale (*AAS*)
Marital Distress Scale (*MDS*)
Hostility Scale (*Ho*)
Post-Traumatic Stress Disorder Scale–Keane (*Pk*)

---

sheet. Raw scores for each scale are entered in the appropriate lines on the bottom of the profile sheet. The test scorer should make sure that the correct side of the profile sheet is used for plotting the profile—one side is for men and the other for women. Once the raw scores are entered, it is then necessary to apply the *K* correction to some scales to complete. The correction factor (explained in more detail in chapter 2) is an empirical correction for test defensiveness. To apply this correction, one simply refers to the *K* correction values box printed on the profile sheet (see Figure 1.3) to obtain the exact amount of the *K* score to add to the raw score before plotting the profile. The *K* correction is applied to the five clinical scale scores: *Hs* (0.5*K*), *Pd* (0.4*K*), *Pt* (1.0*K*), *Sc* (1.0*K*), and *Ma* (0.2*K*). The scorer then writes the proper value of the *K* correction for these five scales in the designated blanks at the bottom of the profile sheet and adds the scores to obtain the value, referred to as *Raw* + *K*. Now the scorer is ready to plot the profile.

There are two additional steps in drawing the profile. First, the scorer locates the raw score for each of the person's scales on the profile sheet and makes a dot on the profile sheet corresponding to the raw score for each scale. Once the dots are in the appropriate places, the scorer connects them. It is customary to connect the dots separately for the validity scales and for the clinical scales. Unless the scorer wants to appear as an amateur one, he or she should not connect the lines of the validity and clinical scales together. Connecting the validity and clinical scale lines is a sure tip-off that you have not read this chapter thoroughly.

If a scorer wants to incorporate all the available MMPI-2 scales described in this volume, hand scoring can be time consuming and a bit overwhelming. Thus, test scorers who rely on manual scoring tend to be those who have a reliable clerical assistant with lots of spare time. (More than one clerical assistant has threatened to quit or worse if all the available scales for all patients need to be hand scored.) More frequently, practitioners who use the hand-scoring option tend to limit themselves to fewer scales, for example, just the validity and traditional validity scales, not to the large number of additional scales available.

Machine Processing

Many practitioners process MMPI-2s by computer to avail themselves of the broad number of measures on the inventory. In addition, evidence shows that computer scoring is more reliable than hand scoring (Allard, Butler, Faust, & Shea, 1995). The following computer-scoring options are available to the test scorer.

1. The individual can respond to the items in the traditional paper-and-pencil format, and the responses can be processed by machine in several possible ways:
   - The answer sheet can be scanned by an optical reader and read into the computer for processing.
   - The items can be keyed into the computer by a clerical person.
   - The completed answer sheet can be mailed to National Computer Systems for scoring and processing. The completed results are either mailed or faxed back to the test scorer.
2. Clients can enter their responses directly into the computer in response to the items presented on the computer screen.

Summary

In this chapter, I explored a number of basic elements central to MMPI-2 interpretation. By now, readers have probably gained some initial sense of the empirical approach to clinical assessment and can infer how the objective perspective adds to a practitioner's confidence in the psychological assessment. I now take a closer look at the scales designed to provide an evaluation of the patient's attitudes toward the testing and whether they have responded in a sufficiently cooperative manner, as to provide a valid self-report. Some would consider the assessment of protocol validity the single most important task the MMPI-2 interpreter undertakes.

To Believe or Not To Believe, That Is the Question: Assessing MMPI-2 Test Result Validity

With all of those necessary preliminary details that were piled up in the first chapter, you have probably begun to wonder why so many people use this test anyway. I now turn to a discussion of one of the most fascinating aspects of MMPI-2 interpretation: determining what patients are saying about themselves in the test and whether an examiner can place any credence in the protocol.

It has probably occurred to you that not everyone who takes a self-report questionnaire such as the MMPI-2 will respond to the items in a cooperative, honest manner; this is very true. In fact, some people—particularly those who have clear motivations to appear different than they actually are—respond in a deceptive way to avoid disclosing information about themselves; some people actually provide false clues to the true nature of their problems in an effort to evade self-disclosure. This chapter is devoted to the important task of detecting any invalidating response conditions that a test taker might engage in as a means of deflecting the appraisal away from his or her true personality.

The original MMPI developers, Hathaway and McKinley (1940), were well aware of the problems that invalidating response styles can cause the practitioner and developed measures to assess the credibility of the test taker's performance. They developed one measure to assess "lying" (L) or the tendency to present an overly favorable view of one's personality and problems. They also devised a scale to detect "faking bad" or symptom claiming (F). Later, during the 1940s, Meehl and Hathaway (1946) developed an additional measure of test defensiveness (K), which could also be used to correct scores of people who were defensive, that is, were reluctant to disclose personal information on the test.

These response attitude measures on the MMPI provided, for many years, an effective means of detecting protocol invalidity. Some other psychologists—particularly Cronbach (1942), Edwards (1957), and Jackson and Messick (1962)—postulated invalidating the conditions of social desirability and acquiesence (yeasaying and naysaying) that they thought blocked psychologists' efforts to obtain credible personality descriptions from questionnaires. Although these conditions operate in self-report-based psychological assessment, they are by no means the only invalidating conditions to watch out for or are they sufficient to account for all or even the majority of test administrations. Social desirability and acquiescence are limited explanatory variables. The majority of people assessed in clinical situations respond in a manner to provide useful personality and symptomatic information. Block's (1965) monograph, *The Challenge of Response Sets,* was among the answers to the response set interpretation that still provides a valuable perspective on the issue. Block showed that personality scales based on MMPI items could take these response sets into account and provide valid personality predictions.

Conditions That Tend To Generate Deviant Patterns of Self-Report

Some situations are more likely than others to generate invalid or non-credible patterns of self-report. A person applying for a highly desirable job would likely minimize problems and endorse items that he or she believes makes him or her "look good." Similarly, an individual on trial for a capital crime, who is administered the MMPI-2 as part of a psychological evaluation, might try to show that he or she could not be guilty of the crime because he or she is insane. In this case, the test taker is likely to be motivated to appear psychologically disturbed and to endorse the items in a way to claim many problems.

In any self-report assessment, it is important for the practitioner to have a means of appraising the client's test-taking attitudes and to ensure that the test protocol can be interpreted as a credible self-report. I now describe several known strategies that clients use to deceive, avoid, or deflect assessment through self-report and examine how these invalidating strategies can be detected with the MMPI-2.

Test-Taking Strategies That Invalidate the MMPI-2

People assessed in mental health contexts are usually honest and open when describing their problems and do not simply answer in a socially desirable way nor acquiesce to the items in a yes-or-no manner. Research shows that even in a prison setting, most convicted felons taking the MMPI-2 answer in a credible manner (Gallagher, Ben-Porath, & Briggs, 1997). However, it is important for the practitioner to evaluate test protocols for the possibility of an invalidating response pattern before the clinical profile can be interpreted with confidence. In the initial publication of the MMPI, Hathaway and McKinley were concerned that potentially invalidating conditions could occur if the participants were motivated to distort their true picture in their assessment. Several sources of information developed for detecting invalidating conditions that some test takers use in an effort to avoid honest self-disclosure are described below. All of these potentially invalidating conditions can be detected by MMPI-2 indexes.

Excessive Item Omissions

The instructions to the MMPI-2 encourage the test taker to respond to all of the items. The great majority of the items in the inventory are written in such a way that either a true or false response to the item would be appropriate and relevant to anyone. When items are not endorsed (or both true and false are marked), particularly a large number of them, the scores on the test will likely be attenuated and result in an inadequate assessment. The extent to which the test taker may have failed to comply with the instructions to complete all the questions needs to be evaluated. Incomplete records and a high number of item omissions can make a protocol uninterpretable.

How many omitted items produce an invalid record? Even a few items, if they are saturated by a particular theme or content area, can affect interpretation of a test. For example, a person might leave out 12 items, all in the area of family problems. This might be a very informative clinical finding, but the unanswered items might serve to attenuate some scales, such as Psychopathic Deviate (*Pd*) and Family Problems (*FAM*), whose interpretation will be affected. The content of omitted items can often provide important clues to motivational sets that could underlie the invalidating conditions.

The number of items considered to invalidate a protocol is 30 or more, although recent research (Berry et al., 1997) shows that scales and code types might be negatively affected with lower levels of the Cannot Say score. Rather than simply using a 30-item cut-off score to invalidate a protocol, the interpreter might actually calculate (computer-scoring services do) the exact impact that Cannot Say scores have on each scale. The response percentage is then computed for each scale. Even some records with a large number of omitted items might actually have scales in which all of the items have been endorsed.

Unusual Pattern Responding

Some test takers who are insufficiently motivated to be evaluated may simply answer the items without attending to the content by simply marking answers in a particular pattern. For example, one test taker marked the items on his answer sheet in the shape of his initials, CRL. It is usually a good idea to examine the answer sheet before it is processed to determine if any unusual responses have been recorded. Sometimes patients draw pictures or write messages on the answer sheets. These pieces of information, although extraneous to the resulting MMPI-2 profile, can nevertheless be helpful in understanding the patient. For example, one psychiatric inpatient wrote an obscene poem on the margins of his answer sheet; another patient drew cartoon figures along the border of the answer sheet; and another patient decorated the reusable soft cover booklet with flags, moustaches, and decorative numbers.

An All True or All False Pattern

This response pattern is often produced by test takers who do not wish to comply with the instructions to respond to the content of the items but instead seem to want to appear to have completed the inventory. Two patterns that have been found are the mostly true or mostly false response patterns. Some test takers who want to comply partially with the test will endorse a few items—for example, the first one in each column—in one direction, for example, true—and the remainder in the false direction. A simple visual inspection of the answer sheet can often reveal these uncooperative response patterns. The items are written in such a manner as to draw an equal percentage of both true and false responses. In general, answer sheets that have a preponderance of either true or false responses are usually invalid protocols. Thus, if 20% or less of the items are endorsed in the true or false direction, the protocol is likely to be invalid.

Inconsistent Response Patterns

The best way to obtain an appraisal of inconsistent responding is to determine whether the test taker has endorsed similar items in a consistent manner. Inconsistent responding to personality questionnaire items is relatively easy to detect if the inventory is long enough and has enough items of similar or opposite meaning. The MMPI-2 provides two scales for detecting inconsistent responding to the items.

The Variable Response Inconsistency Scale (*VRIN*) is a good measure of random responding on the MMPI-2. *VRIN* is made up of 67 pairs of items for which one or two out of four possible configurations (true–false, false–true, true–true, and false–false) represents inconsistent responses. For example, answering *true* to "I wake up fresh and rested most mornings" and *true* to "My sleep is fitful and disturbed" represents semantically inconsistent responding. The *VRIN* is scored by obtaining the total number of inconsistent responses.

The True Response Inconsistency Scale (*TRIN*) was developed to appraise the tendency that some people have to respond in an inconsistent manner to items that should be endorsed, to be consistent, in a particular way. *TRIN* is made up of 23 pairs of items to which the same response is semantically inconsistent. For example, answering the items "Most of the time I feel blue" and "I am happy most of the time" both *true* or both *false* is inconsistent. Fourteen of the twenty-three item pairs are scored as inconsistent only if the client responds true to both items. Nine of the item pairs are scored as inconsistent if the client responds false to both items. Three additional pairs are scored inconsistent if the client responds either both true or both false.

High scores on *TRIN* need to be evaluated in terms of whether the direction of inconsistency is toward the true or false direction. A *TRIN* T score in the elevated direction (usually $T > 80$) suggests that the test taker has endorsed several of the items inconsistently in the true direction. *TRIN F* can likewise provide the test interpreter with a picture of inconsistent true responding in which the person is inconsistent in answering items in the false direction.

Fake Good—Highly Virtuous Self-Presentation

Some people have difficulty disclosing personal information and tend to present themselves in an overly favorable light on personality scales. This test-taking strategy is more common in some situations, such as in personnel or forensic settings, in which the client has a need to appear well adjusted to gain some benefit or service. For example, applicants for desirable positions tend to present themselves on self-report instruments in a highly favorable and virtuous manner. The MMPI-2 contains a measure, *L*, designed to detect this invalidating pattern in cases where clients tend to exaggerate their virtues and lay claim to unrealistically higher moral standards than other people. *L*, developed by Hathaway and McKinley (1943) in the original MMPI to evaluate this tendency, has been found to be very effective at appraising this tendency to claim extreme virtue. High elevations on *L* reflect the following possible interpretations: conscious distortion of the items, high need to see oneself as extremely virtuous, rigid personality adjustment, or a tendency to use denial and repression to an extreme degree. People who are extremely religious might obtain some elevation on this scale because they actually possess such qualities. However, extreme elevations ($T > 65$) are unlikely, even for highly religious people.

L has been widely researched and explored in a variety of clinical contexts. When L is elevated above $T = 65$, the client is likely presenting a noncredible and highly virtuous pattern of responses to avoid disclosing problems.

Test Defensiveness or Problem Denial

Another, somewhat related aspect of presenting a good front on personality inventory items involves problem denial. In this response pattern, the test taker simply checked positive adjustment options and denied his or her problems. The test taker does not exaggerate virtues, as described above, but only denies his or her problems.

The Defensiveness Scale (*K*)

The K on the original MMPI was developed by Meehl and Hathaway (1946) for two purposes: to assess test defensiveness and to use this information to correct for defensiveness by adding points to certain scales to make these items more sensitive to detecting problems. The scale was developed by studying a sample of psychiatric patients who produced a normal range profile (i.e., they were assumed to be defensive). *K* is comprised of 30 items that center on the denial of problems and presentation of positive attributes. In developing this measure, the authors had two goals in mind. First, they wanted to develop a scale that was sensitive to defensive responding not assessed by the more blatant content on *L*. Second, they wanted to use measured defensiveness as a means of statistically correcting for cases in which the test taker was defensive and not reporting symptoms as requested in the test instructions.

K works very well as a means of detecting defensiveness (Graham, in press). But does it work well as a correction factor? You have already encountered the *K* correction in chapter 1 when you learned about plotting a profile. The *K* weights used in the *K* correction were derived empirically to improve the discrimination of cases in a psychiatric setting. As noted in the last chapter, five scales were thought to be improved by adding a portion of *K*: Hypochondriasis, *Pd*, Psychoasthenia, Schizophrenia, and Mania. In practice, *K* does not really improve empirical discrimination very much. Even though *K* does not perform as the original authors intended as a correction factor to improve discrimination, the practice of correcting for *K* still continues in MMPI-2 because much of the empirical research supporting test interpretation of the clinical scales involves *K* corrected scores.

The Superlative Self-Presentation Scale (S)

The *S* was developed by Butcher and Han (1995) to improve on *K* as a measure of defensiveness. The authors used the responses of a sample of highly defensive job applicants contrasted with the MMPI-2 normative sample to develop this 50-item defensiveness scale. *S* assesses the tendency of some test takers in personnel screenings to claim positive attributes, high moral values, and high responsibility and to deny having adjustment problems. People who score high on *S* endorse few minor faults and problems—considerably fewer than those who took the test in the MMPI-2 Restandardization Study. *S* has been found to be associated with lower levels of symptoms and the admission of fewer negative personality characteristics than even the normative sample report. High scores are also associated with extreme endorsement of "self-control" in test takers by people who know them. High *S* responders are viewed by their spouses as emotionally well controlled and generally free of pathological behavioral features.

One important way in which *S* is thought to improve on *K* as a measure of test defensiveness is that this scale possesses a greater number of items (50), which allows for a breakdown of items into subscales with a homogeneous content. *S* is comprised of five types of items that make up its subscales.

These homogeneous item component scales focus the interpreter's attention on which of the items in *S* the test taker has endorsed. For example, the test taker may have endorsed (as many parents in custody evaluations do) relatively more items dealing with "Denial of moral flaws" or "Denial of irritability" than with other items on *S*. *S* allows the interpreter to examine five content areas that constitute the items on *S*. These subscale groupings are as follows, along with sample items from each component scale:

- *Beliefs in human goodness:* Most people will use somewhat unfair means to get ahead in life (F); Most people are honest chiefly because they are afraid of being caught (F).
- *Serenity:* My hardest battles are with myself (F); I frequently find myself worrying about something (F).
- *Contentment with life:* If I could live my life over again, I would not change much (T); I am satisfied with the amount of money I make (T).
- *Patience and denial of irritability and anger:* I get mad easily and then get over it soon (F); I easily become inpatient with people (F).
- *Denial of moral flaws:* I have enjoyed using marijuana (F); I have used alcohol excessively (F).

Exaggerated Symptom Endorsement

Some people approach the test content with a motivation to present their problems in an exaggerated manner. This invalidating condition has been referred to in several ways in the literature on deviant response approaches, for example, *faking, exaggerating, plus getting, malingering,* or *infrequent responding.* This response pattern is commonly found in situations in which the test taker feels it is to his or her advantage to appear psychologically disturbed on the test and approaches the test with an effort designed to claim a lot of symptoms. For example, some people in disability determination evaluations endorse many extreme items to ensure that the extent of their problems are "recognizable." This invalidating response condition has been more widely studied than any of the other deviant response attitudes (see Berry, Baer, & Harris, 1991; and Schretlen, 1988).

The Faking or Infrequency Scale (F)

Hathaway and McKinley (1943) developed the F to detect exaggerated responding. This index was new in the original MMPI and has been proven so valuable in psychological assessment that newer personality tests often emulate it. The rationale behind this scale is very simple: People who attempt to present a more disturbed psychological adjustment than they actually are experiencing tend to claim an excessive number of symptoms. Hathaway and McKinley developed F by determining the frequency of response to the MMPI items by the normative sample and chose items that had frequency of response in the keyed direction of less than 10%. Test takers who exaggerate their complaint pattern tend to respond to too many of these extreme items in a pathological direction. Examples of infrequently endorsed items are "I believe in law enforcement" (false) and "I see things or animals or people around me that others do not see" (true).

In addition to being elevated in cases of symptom exaggeration, F is also sensitive to non-content-oriented responding, such as answering in a careless manner without attending to the test item content, for example, by simply endorsing items in a random manner. Random protocols can also be found in situations where the test taker gets mixed up in the items or is unable to read and comprehend the items. The random or mixed-up response pattern to MMPI-2 items can be detected by the infrequency scales, F and Infrequency-Back Scale [F(B)]. In F, which contains 60 items, random performances would produce extremely elevated F scores—about 30 items would be endorsed. That is, with a 60-item scale and a two-choice format, chances are that the person would endorse about 30 true and 30 false.

Extremely high F scores are typically found in protocols of test takers who malinger psychiatric symptoms. Scores greater than $T = 110$ are usually found associated with individuals falsely claiming mental health symptoms.

The Infrequency-Back Scale [F(B)]

All of the items on the traditional *F* appear in the early part of the item pool—within the first 370 items. However, in a test as long as the MMPI-2, it is important to have a measure of symptom exaggeration in the latter part of the test as well. *F(B)* was developed for this purpose. This scale operates much like the original *F* and is usually evaluated in tandem with the original *F*. Elevations on this scale are interpreted similarly, as reflecting exaggerated or dissimulated responding in the items toward the end of the MMPI-2.

The Psychiatric Infrequency Scale [F(p)]

More recently, Arbisi and Ben-Porath (1995, 1997) developed another type of infrequency scale for the MMPI-2 that addresses possible malingering of psychological symptoms in a mental health treatment context. The *F(p)* provides an estimate of symptom exaggeration that is based on a psychiatric data set rather than the normative sample, as is the original *F*. This measure assesses the extent to which the test taker has responded in a manner that is more extreme than would patients in a psychiatric setting. The *F(p)* provides an important new way of focusing on exaggerated responding. High scores on this scale indicate that the person claims more psychiatric symptoms than inpatients who are currently hospitalized for psychiatric disorders. Thus, they are very unlikely scores. It is quite possible that this scale will take on more importance as research accumulates.

Why do psychologists need three different infrequency scales? They all serve a different purpose, and each is useful in providing a picture of exaggerated responding. The traditional *F* provides a good indication of exaggerated responding to the traditional clinical scales, the *F(B)* assesses extreme responding to items in the later part of the MMPI-2, and the *F(p)* provides an indication of extreme endorsement of symptoms as compared with patients with severe disturbances.

The Unlikely Clinical Picture

One value of having a substantial research base on a personality measure such as the MMPI-2 is that the psychologist has a well-explored range of "typical" performances on the scale to guide usage. Groups of test takers, such as patients with depression, police applicants, or alcoholics, tend to respond more like their own group than not. This, of course, is the underlying basis of MMPI interpretation: People showing various circumstances (e.g., depression) possess many common personality features. That is, the scales have established "correlates" for various homogeneous populations. A corollary to this general rule is that if a test taker from a known, well-established population performs in a manner that is extremely different from the expectation, then further evaluation of this protocol is needed. One hypothesis is that the test taker does not possess the characteristics associated with that prototypal group. Another possibility for interpretation is that the deviant pattern is the result of an unusual motivational set.

A very substantial literature has grown up around the important task of assessing protocol validity. Any personality scale that is going to be used for making clinical decisions must have a comprehensive set of validity indexes. However, some test publishers are still producing new personality measures that do not contain a means of assessing protocol validity. It is important for the practitioner or personality researcher to ensure that this critical aspect of self-report is appropriately addressed in the assessment instruments used. Three case examples follow to illustrate the MMPI-2 validity indexes.

Cases Illustrating Invalidating Conditions

The Case of John V.: Malingering of Symptoms?

Description

John V., age 23, was evaluated as part of a pretrial psychological evaluation. He was charged with murdering two night clerks in a bungled robbery of a convenience store. He had pleaded not guilty by reason of insanity, claiming that he did not remember being at the crime scene.

Comment

The extreme elevations on MMPI-2 validity indicators F, $F(B)$, and $F(p)$ (see Figure 2.1) suggest that the defendant attempted to present a picture of someone who is "insane." Unfortunately, the pattern is an extreme and highly unlikely clinical one. His validity profile indicates that his protocol is likely invalid. His high degree of symptom claiming oc-

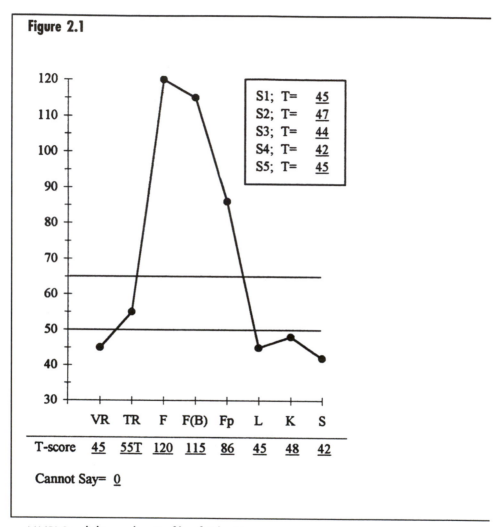

Figure 2.1

	S1; T=	45
	S2; T=	47
	S3; T=	44
	S4; T=	42
	S5; T=	45

	VR	TR	F	F(B)	Fp	L	K	S
T-score	45	55T	120	115	86	45	48	42

Cannot Say= 0

MMPI-2 validity scales: Profile of John V.

curred in the context of a highly consistent manner, as reflected by the low scores on *VRIN*. He was very consistent with his extreme symptom checking.

The Case of Edward B.: Saint or Sinner?

Description

Edward B. was a 48-year-old man who was being evaluated in a drug and alcohol treatment program at the insistence of his wife and employer. He had been experiencing a number of alcohol-related work and family problems; however, he did not consider his problems the result of his drinking. He resented being pressured into having a substance abuse evaluation.

Comment

Edward's extreme elevation on *L* (see Figure 2.2) suggests that he has presented himself in an unrealistic virtuous manner, denying any faults or psychological adjustment problems.

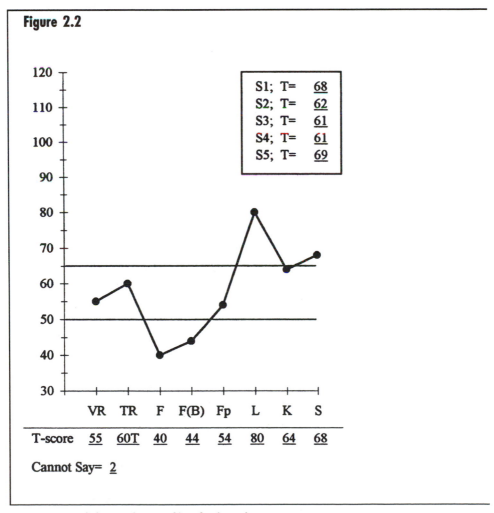

Figure 2.2

	T=	
S1;	T=	68
S2;	T=	62
S3;	T=	61
S4;	T=	61
S5;	T=	69

	VR	TR	F	F(B)	Fp	L	K	S
T-score	55	60T	40	44	54	80	64	68

Cannot Say= 2

MMPI-2 validity scales: Profile of Edward B.

The Case of Susan S.: Questions About Sincerity

Description

Susan was evaluated in a family court setting as part of a court-ordered evaluation to determine whether she should be allowed to regain custody of her two children. Her former husband had been awarded custody of the children following their divorce. She was very reluctant to cooperate in the psychological evaluation and failed to show up for the assessment the first time it was scheduled.

Comment

Her performance on the MMPI-2 validity scales (see Figure 2.3) suggests that she had not cooperated sufficiently with the evaluation to provide

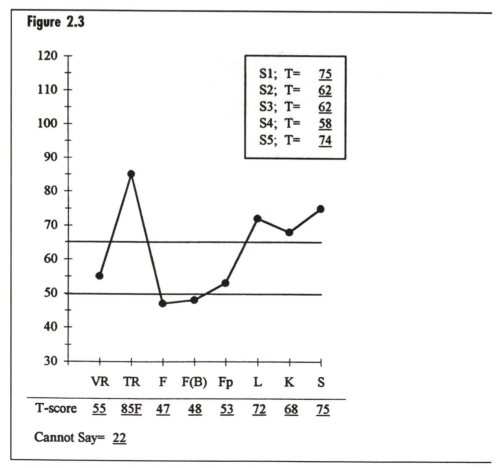

Figure 2.3

	S1; T=	75
	S2; T=	62
	S3; T=	62
	S4; T=	58
	S5; T=	74

	VR	TR	F	F(B)	Fp	L	K	S
T-score	55	85F	47	48	53	72	68	75

Cannot Say= 22

MMPI-2 validity scales: Profile of Susan S.

an interpretable MMPI-2 clinical profile. She did not answer many items on the test (22 items), indicating a reticence to comply with the testing. In addition, she produced a *TRIN* score in the highly inconsistent range (*TRIN* False+ 85*T*), indicating that when she did answer, she tended to be inconsistent, indiscriminately endorsing *false* when a consistent response to an item would call for answering it *true*. In addition, her extreme scores on *L, K,* and *S* indicate a highly defensive response to items when she did answer them.

Summary

Now that I have a good idea as to whether the MMPI-2 profile is valid and interpretable, I can move on to the next phase in the assessment and evaluate the test taker's pattern of clinical symptoms using the MMPI-2 clinical scales.

A Bond With the Past: The MMPI-2 Basic Clinical Scales

The heart of the MMPI for nearly 60 years has been the 10 empirical scales that are displayed on the standard profile sheet shown in Figure 1.3. These scales, which are based on years of accumulated research, serve as the empirical foundation for assessment with the MMPI-2. One guiding philosophy of the MMPI-2 Restandardization Committee during their project was that these classic measures should remain as close to the original scales as possible in terms of item make-up to preserve the experience base of the MMPI. Thus, the MMPI-2 versions of the scales are essentially the same as in the original MMPI. Among the 10 scales making up the *standard profile* (traditional clinical scales), the only scales that lost items were Hypochondriasis (*Hs*; lost 1 item), Depression (*D*; lost 3 items), Masculinity–Femininity (*Mf*; lost 4 items), and Social Introversion–Extraversion (*Si*; lost 1 item). These items were deleted because they contained objectionable content. The psychometric or statistical properties, such as reliability and validity, of the traditional scales are essentially identical to the MMPI versions, with the exception of some rewritten or slightly edited items. There were a number of new items added to the MMPI-2; however, these play no part in the traditional clinical scales and are only included in the newer scales, which are discussed later in this book.

Guidelines for Interpreting the Clinical Scales

Before I launch into a description of the clinical scales, I need to discuss several factors pertinent to appraising the clinical scales.

1. The clinical scales are groups of items that have been developed according to empirical validation; items comprising the scale significantly discriminate a criterion group, usually patients, from a normal reference sample. A given empirical scale is interpreted by reference to empirical correlates established through validity research.

2. A general practice among MMPI users is to cite the scale number when referring to a clinical scale rather than the name it was originally given by the test's authors (see Exhibit 3.1).

3. Scale elevations are interpreted in terms of T-score distances from the mean of the normative sample ($T = 50$). In the range of $T = 60$ ($1SD$) to 64, the personality correlates are considered to apply to the individual. When $T \geq 65$, all of the correlates should be applied to the scale as indicated. The higher a scale score, the more like the criterion group the patient is assumed to be.

4. All of the clinical (and content scales), except Mf and Si, have T-score distributions equal and comparable in terms of uniform T scores.

5. Keep in mind the percentage of cases that tend to obtain scores at the T-score level obtained by the client; the percentile values for various T-score levels are slightly different for men and women (see Exhibit 3.2).

6. When interpreting an MMPI-2 profile, the examiner should take into consideration the scale definition of the profile, that is, the

---

Exhibit 3.1

The Basic Scales of the Minnesota Multiphasic Personality Inventory

Scale 1	Hypochondriasis (Hs)
Scale 2	Depression (D)
Scale 3	Hysteria (Hy)
Scale 4	Psychopathic Deviate (Pd)
Scale 5	Masculinity–Femininity (Mf)
Scale 6	Paranoia (Pa)
Scale 7	Psychasthenia (Pt)
Scale 8	Schizophrenia (Sc)
Scale 9	Mania (Ma)
Scale 0	Social Introversion–Extraversion (Si)

Exhibit 3.2

Values for Various *T*-Score Levels: Men Versus Women

T	Men	Women
60	84.4 percentile	84.9 percentile
65	92.4 percentile	91.7 percentile
70	96.2 percentile	95.8 percentile
75	98.2 percentile	98.0 percentile
80	99.2 percentile	99.3 percentile
85	99.7 percentile	99.8 percentile

extent to which a high point score is elevated above the next scale in the profile. *Profile definition* involves how elevated the interpreted clinical scales (e.g., the high point or high point code) are above the next highest scales in the profile. For example, if the highest two scales are 10 or more *T* points above the third ranked scale in the profile, the profile code is well defined or has a very high-profile definition; if a profile code is 5–9 *T* points higher than the next score, it has a high-profile definition. Those profiles with $T \le 4$ separating the code from the next score have a low-profile definition. Research shows that profiles with a high- or very high-profile definition tend to be stable at retest (Graham, Smith, & Schwartz, 1986). Moreover, MMPI-2 profiles with very high- or high-profile definition are likely to be similar if they were scored on the original MMPI norms (Graham, Timbrook, Ben-Porath, & Butcher, 1991). When profiles are high or very high in profile definition, one can be confident that profiles are interpretable according to the accumulated database on the original MMPI.

7. The interpretation of a given scale is also determined, in part, by other scales that are elevated in the critical range. This issue is discussed further in chapter 4.

8. Typically, low scores on a clinical scale cannot be interpreted. There are some exceptions; for example, the *Mf* and *Si* are "dimensional" personality measures that have meaning as low and high points on the scale. Some of the clinical scales, for example, the *Ma*, have had meaningful correlates reported.

The Basic Clinical Scales

Scale 1 (Hypochondriasis)

The *Hs* was developed as a means of providing an assessment of the tendency for many patients in mental health settings to present with somatic problems. The patients in the criterion group to define this MMPI scale were diagnosed with problems psychologists would consider today under the rubric of *somatoform disorders* (a psychologically based disorder manifested through physical symptoms). These patients tend to develop psychologically based physical complaints, commonly referred to as *hypochondrical* complaints.

Individuals who score high on *Hs* tend to report excessive bodily concern in their initial symptom description. They have a broad variety of somatic symptoms that tend to be vague and undefined, for example, epigastric complaints, fatigue, chronic pain, and muscle weakness. In addition to the physical complaints, individuals who score high on *Hs* tend to show little manifest anxiety compared with other psychotherapy patients. They are also reported as selfish, self-centered, and narcissistic. Research shows that they often have personality characteristics such as pessimism, defeatism, dissatisfaction with others, and generally unhappiness. They are reported to have a cynical outlook on life.

Interpersonally, people with high *Hs* tend to be difficult to get along with and make others feel miserable with their chronic complaining. They tend to whine and complain a great deal and are thought to be demanding and critical of others. They express hostility indirectly. They rarely act out and are seen by others as dull, unenthusiastic, and unambitious. They are typically viewed as ineffective in oral expression. Individuals with this high point score on Scale 1 tend to function at a reduced level of efficiency without any major incapacity. They are not very responsive in therapy and tend to terminate therapy if their therapist is seen as not giving them enough attention and support. They tend to seek medical solutions to their problems.

The Case of Evelyn M.: A Chronic Pain Patient

Description

The profile shown in Figure 3.1 reflects a pattern of excessive physical complaints that is commonly found among some medical and psychiatric patients who present with excessive physical complaints but do not

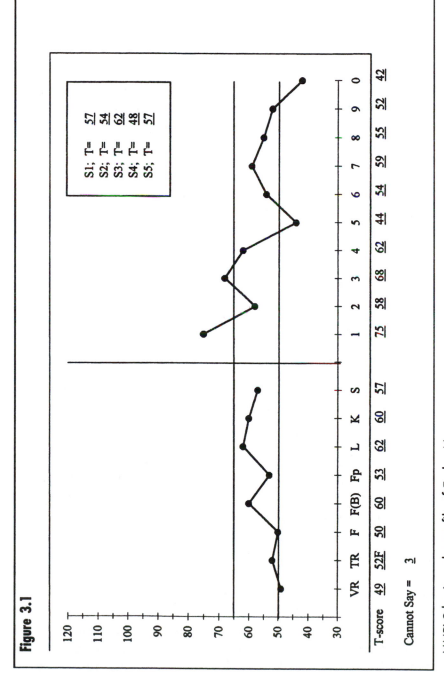

Figure 3.1

MMPI-2 basic scales profile of Evelyn M.

have a detectable organic basis to their symptoms. Evelyn M. was a 47-year-old medical patient who was referred to a chronic pain treatment program for unremitting pain following an alleged injury to her back at work 2 years earlier. She had been on disability from work since shortly after the incident. She reported a pattern of pain that was unlikely to occur in the areas in which she reported them. On the basis of several examinations, physicians had been unable to determine the organic factors that would account for her persistent pain. Her pain apparently became more severe during times of emotional conflict—a situation she had been experiencing a great deal as a result of both work and marital problems. The clinical diagnosis provided for her pattern of symptoms was psychogenic pain disorder.

Comment

Ms. M.'s MMPI-2 pattern is consistent with that of a person who presents a vague pattern of somatic complaints in a framework of excessive symptom claiming. Her MMPI-2 validity pattern is valid and indicates that the clinical profile is probably a good indication of her current personality functioning. She claims an extreme degree of physical complaints that are unlikely to be based on actual organic problems, as shown by her extremely high evaluations on the *Hs*.

Scale 2 (Depression)

Scale 2 of the MMPI was developed as a means of assessing depressed mood or clinical depression. Most of the patients included in the criterion group for this scale were diagnosed as having either a depressive disorder or manic depression. Individuals who score high on this scale report feeling depressed and unhappy. They indicate that they are dysphoric and pessimistic about the future. They typically are self-deprecating and feel guilty, often without reasons. They feel that their health is failing; they are sluggish, feel weak, and tired. Many also report feeling tense and agitated; they often refer to feeling high strung and irritable over minor events.

Individuals with this high point profile freely report feeling useless and unable to function and often report being a failure at school or work. High Scale 2 scorers tend to be nonaggressive, shy, and lacking in self-confidence and are prone to worry over small things. Social withdrawal is not uncommon, and they tend to be somewhat aloof and maintain a psychological distance from others, often avoiding personal involvement. Many individuals with this clinical pattern tend to show a pattern of ruminative behavior and indecisiveness or have difficulty in making decisions. High D score patients are usually receptive to therapy.

The Case of Charles C.: Depressed Mood

Description

Charles, a 47-year-old accountant, was hospitalized following a suicide attempt by carbon monoxide. His wife discovered him one evening when she came home from work; he was in the garage, unconscious in his automobile with the engine running. Charles had been despondent for the past 6 months but was reluctant to seek psychological treatment when his wife and family physician had urged him to do so because he felt that he was "already condemned." Charles had been unhappy with his life for a number of years. He was very dissatisfied with his job, feeling that he was in a dead end. His wife reported that Charles has always been a shy, introverted person but that in recent months, his social aversion has intensified. He actively avoided other people and spent a great deal of time alone. Following his suicide attempt, he was admitted into an inpatient unit for further psychological evaluation. After the initial intake interview, Charles was diagnosed as having a major depressive disorder. His doctor prescribed an antidepressant medication.

Comment

Charles's MMPI-2 pattern reflects a severe mood disorder. His high score on the D (Scale 2) suggests that he endorsed numerous symptoms of affective disorder. In addition, Charles appears to be a very shy, unhappy person who has a great deal of difficulty in social relationships. Note the extreme elevation on the Social Introversion Scale (Scale 0; see Figure 3.2). This scale is often elevated for individuals who have mood disorders and probably reflects long-term personality maladjustment problems.

Scale 3 (Hysteria)

Patients who have Scale 3 as their highest profile peak tend to report vague physical symptoms, such as headaches, chest pains, muscle weakness, irregular heart beat, or other vague physical states in the absence of clear medical findings. Elevations on Scale 3 can best be understood in terms of a presentation of somatic symptoms in the context of personality features that reflect an inability to deal effectively with life stress-

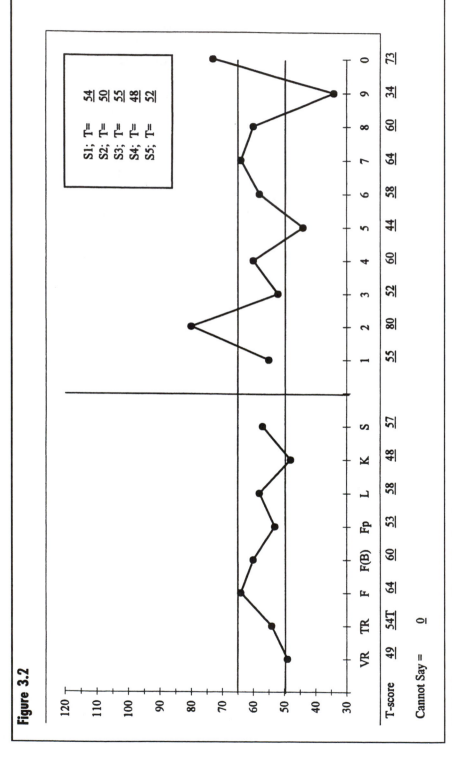

Figure 3.2

MMPI-2 basic scales profile of Charles C.

ors. Those with this profile deny and repress conflict to such an extent that they often fail to manage life problems well. They usually show a lack of insight about causes of their symptoms; they also show low insight into their own motives and feelings.

High *Hy* scorers rarely report having delusions, hallucinations, or suspiciousness and usually experience little anxiety, tension, or depression. In cases where they do have anxiety attacks, the symptoms may appear and disappear suddenly in reaction to stress. The high scorer also tends to be viewed as psychologically immature, childish, and infantile and to be self-centered, narcissistic, and egocentric. High scorers tend to expect a great deal of attention and affection from others.

People who score high on Scale 3 tend not to express anger or resentment openly but are somewhat indirect interpersonally. Moreover, they are viewed as manipulative to gain attention, and they show interest in others for selfish reasons. They are socially involved but in a superficial manner and can be friendly, talkative, and enthusiastic in social situations. They might act out in an inappropriate manner and show little apparent insight.

Patients with this clinical pattern tend to be somewhat difficult to engage in therapy as a result of their excessive denial and tendency to see themselves in an overly positive light. Although they may be initially enthusiastic about treatment, they tend not to respond well to insight-oriented treatment because of their resistance to psychological interpretations. These patients are usually slow to gain insight into the causes of their own behavior. Many high *Hy* patients respond best to direct advice or suggestion rather than to insight-oriented therapy.

The Case of Andrew W.: A Stressed-Out Airline Captain

Description

Andrew W., age 44, was referred for psychological evaluation by his physician after the medical examination the physician was conducting proved to find no organic basis for Andrew's recent problems. Andrew had experienced two recent blackouts when he was flying as the pilot in command of a commercial airline flight. His copilot reported the incidents to the chief pilot, who grounded Andrew contingent on the results of a medical evaluation. The neurological and other medical tests proved negative. Following the medical evaluation, he was referred for a psychological evaluation for possible stress factors. The psychological evaluation found extensive evidence of recent stressors in his life that were likely to be instrumental in producing his symptoms.

Andrew was recently served with divorce papers that ended a 20-year marriage. Three months earlier his teenage daughter was raped and became pregnant; Andrew felt the need to counsel her to get an abortion (which was against his religion). He recently discovered that he had lost over $100,000 in a failed business venture. In addition, his brother, a likely paranoid personality, wrote a critical letter to Andrew's employer accusing Andrew of immoral behavior because Andrew had become less active in his church. This letter proved an embarrassment for Andrew. The amount of life stress he had experienced would have created a great deal of concern in most people; however, the patient tended to rely on denial and repression to deal with such conflict and did not acknowledge feeling particularly troubled by the events.

Comment

Andrew's MMPI-2 profile (see Figure 3.3) reflects a personality pattern of excessive denial, repression, and tendencies to ignore or gloss over conflicts that might occur. This interpretation is reflected in his elevated validity configuration. His clinical profile, particularly the extreme elevation on the *Hy* (Scale 3), suggests a tendency to develop physical symptoms under conditions of stress.

Scale 4 (Psychopathic Deviate)

People who score high on Scale 4 endorse characteristics of antisocial behavior, including rebellious actions toward authority figures, stormy family relationships, and acting-out behavior, without considering the consequences of their actions. High-scoring individuals tend to blame other people for their problems, which may be reflected in a history of underachievement in school, poor work history, or marital or other relationship problems. Problems with the law are common.

High *Pd* scorers are reported as impulsive in their actions and tend to have a low frustration tolerance; they often strive for immediate gratification of their impulses. They do not plan well, and they show poor judgment and take risks that other people would not. They do not seem to profit from experience and tend to repeat negative behavior, even though they may receive censure or punishment for it. They are viewed by others as immature, childish, narcissistic, self-centered, and selfish. They are hedonistic, ostentatious, exhibitionistic, and insensitive to the needs of others. They are viewed by others as manipulative and tend to

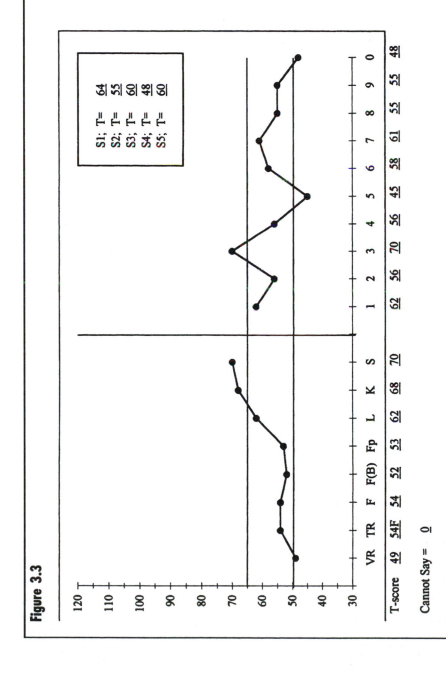

Figure 3.3

MMPI-2 basic scales profile of Andrew W.

develop interpersonal relationships that they can use for their own gains. Although they are often likeable and may create a good first impression, their relationships tend to be shallow and superficial. They appear unable to form warm attachments.

Individuals who score high on *Pd* are socially extroverted and usually are seen as outgoing, talkative, hyperactive, and spontaneous in groups. They are often seen as intelligent and self-confident; however, they typically lack definite goals. Their relationships are characterized as hostile, aggressive, sarcastic, cynical, resentful, and rebellious. They may act in aggressive outbursts and may engage in assaultive behavior. They tend to show little guilt over their negative behavior. The high *Pd* scoring person is typically free from disabling anxiety, depression, and psychotic symptoms. High scorers are most likely diagnosed as having a personality disorder, such as antisocial or passive–aggressive personality.

Patients in a mental health setting who obtain this MMPI-2 high point score are considered to have a poor treatment prognosis because they show little insight into their behavior and low amenability to change in therapy. One problem is that they tend to blame others for their problems and intellectualize rather than face responsibility. They are likely to terminate treatment before changes are made.

The Case of Conway F.: An Incarcerated African American Felon

Description

Conway, age 23, was the oldest of seven children who lived in a four-room urban tenement house in South Chicago. His mother, a single parent, worked as a hotel maid, often leaving her two oldest children (Conway and his sister) in charge of the younger children for several days at a time. This task created resentment in Conway, and he mistreated the younger children on occasion. When he was 14 years of age, he became involved in a youth gang; with increasing drug use, he became less involved with his family. At age 15, he left home and took up residence in the "Rat Palace," an old house in an adjacent neighborhood that served as a gang hangout and crack house. He was arrested the first time at age 16 for possession and sale of cocaine and for possession of a handgun. He was sentenced to 18 months in a juvenile detention program. When he was released from the program to the custody of his mother (he was not yet 18), he remained at her home on and off for 2 years before moving back into the Rat Palace. At age

20, he shot and killed a woman during a robbery attempt. At the trial, he was sentenced to 20 years on a second degree murder charge.

During his 2nd year in prison, he was charged with another murder; this time a fellow inmate at the correctional facility was the victim. The correctional staff considered Conway a very "hard case" criminal, although he was seemingly friendly, spontaneous, and always joking around. He was manipulative and usually conned others into doing things for him. Prison staff have suspected him of being the center of a drug-smuggling ring in prison, but thus far he has avoided discovery. He was considered a troublemaker—typically in conflict with the guard staff and frequently in solitary for fighting with other inmates. A psychological evaluation was conducted in preparation for his upcoming trial on the second murder charge.

Comment

Conway's MMPI-2 profile is shown in Figure 3.4 and is valid and interpretable. The inmate approached the testing in a cooperative manner. His clinical pattern is highly consistent with those of individuals who are incarcerated. The *Pd* is typically the most frequent and highly elevated scale in convicted felons. Conway appeared to fit a pattern of severe antisocial disorder on the MMPI-2, which was validated by his behavioral identity. He was likely a highly irresponsible, impulsive, and aggressive individual who was extremely self-oriented at the expense of others.

Scale 5 (Masculinity–Femininity)

Scale 5 is not really a psychopathology measure; it does not assess clinical problems, as do the majority of other MMPI-2 scales. Scale 5 addresses issues related to gender role. This scale is essentially an interest scale that focuses on appraising traditional masculine and feminine roles, and some would question its use in assessing patients in mental health settings. The scale was developed for men, and the scoring of the scale is simply reversed for women. In this book, I focus particularly on the application of this scale in the assessment of patients in treatment planning because Scale 5 does address an individual's attitudes toward interpersonal relationships—an important variable in psychological treatment planning.

Men

T > 80. Men who score extremely high on Scale 5 tend to show conflicts in the area of sexual identity and insecurity in masculine roles.

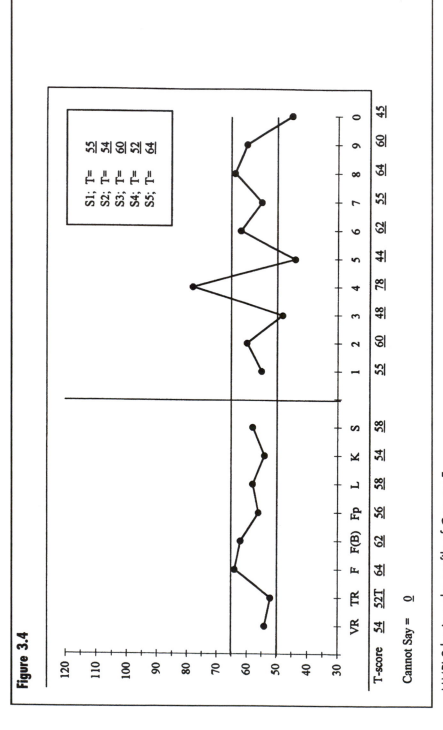

Figure 3.4

MMPI-2 basic scales profile of Conway F.

They may be effeminate and have greater involvement with aesthetic and artistic interests than most men do. Research shows them to be intelligent and capable and to value cognitive pursuits. They are variously reported as ambitious, competitive, persevering, clever, clear thinking, and organized and show good judgment. They are often considered to be curious, creative, and imaginative in their interests. They tend to be sociable, sensitive to others, tolerant, and capable of expressing warm feelings toward others. Others may find them passive, dependent, and submissive as well as nonaggressive in orientation. They tend to makes concessions in situations of interpersonal conflict to avoid confrontations. Men with higher levels of education tend to score higher on the *Mf* than men with lower education levels.

T = 70–79. High Scale 5 scorers in this range are viewed as sensitive, insightful, tolerant, and somewhat effeminate. They tend to have broad cultural interests and may be somewhat submissive and passive in relationships. In clinical settings, the patient might show sex-role confusion or heterosexual adjustment problems.

T < 35. Men who have low scores on *Mf* tend to have a "macho" self image and need to view themselves as extremely masculine. They tend to overemphasize strength and physical prowess and tend to be aggressive. They may show a pattern of thrill-seeking and adventurous behavior and may be coarse, crude, and vulgar in interpersonal contexts. They may actually harbor doubts about their own masculinity and feel the need to "prove" themselves in this area. Men with low *Mf* scores are noted to have limited intellectual and cultural interests and to have inflexible and unoriginal approaches to problems. They tend to be more oriented toward practical and nontheoretical activities. Low-scoring men tend to prefer action to thought and tend not to like discussing interpersonal relationships; thus, they are typically resistant to psychological treatment. They tend to be unaware of their own social stimulus value and lack insight into their own motives.

The Case of Warren G.: A Mental Health Outpatient With Low Treatment Potential

Description

Warren was referred to an outpatient mental health center for treatment for his persistently low mood problems and an inability to function in daily life. He reportedly had been depressed for the past 6 months and had been slow to follow his wife's suggestions to obtain psychological treatment. His family doctor prescribed an antidepressant medication; however, the medication has not provided much relief. At his wife's insistence and because the medication was slow to improve his mood, he also entered psychotherapy. His participation in treatment sessions was minimal at best. He felt extremely uncomfortable in the therapy sessions and was reticent about discussing problems with his therapist. After two sessions, he decided not to return to therapy because the sessions and the discussion of problems seemed to make him "feel worse" and as though he was a failure in not being able to handle his own problems.

Comment

Warren's MMPI-2 pattern (see Figure 3.5) is interpretable. However, he endorsed the items in such a way as to present himself in a good light. He attempted to project a good social image. He clearly shows a pattern of mental health symptoms, including depressed mood and feelings of alienation from others. Notably, his MMPI-2 *Mf* score appears to be in a range that suggests that he was overly concerned about being able to handle his own problems and not wishing to discuss problems he might have with others. He felt very uncomfortable in disclosing personal information, even to his therapist. The MMPI-2 *K* elevation, suggesting defensiveness, and the low score on *Mf* and the high score on *Si* indicate that he would likely have difficulty becoming engaged in psychotherapy.

Women

T > 70. Women with high scores on *Mf* tend to reject traditional female roles and activities and are more interested in traditionally masculine pursuits in the areas of work, sports, and hobbies; they tend to be active and competitive. These individuals are typically more aggressive and dominating than most women are; they may be coarse, rough, and tough in their manner. They are often outgoing, uninhibited, and self-confident. They may be easy going but also unemotional and somewhat unfriendly.

T ≤ 35. Women who score extremely low on *Mf* tend to describe themselves in terms of stereotyped female roles. They report being ultrafeminine, passive, submissive, and yielding in relationships. They tend to defer to men in decision making. Research shows that the standard interpretations for low Scale 5 women do not apply for women who have higher degrees of education.

Figure 3.5

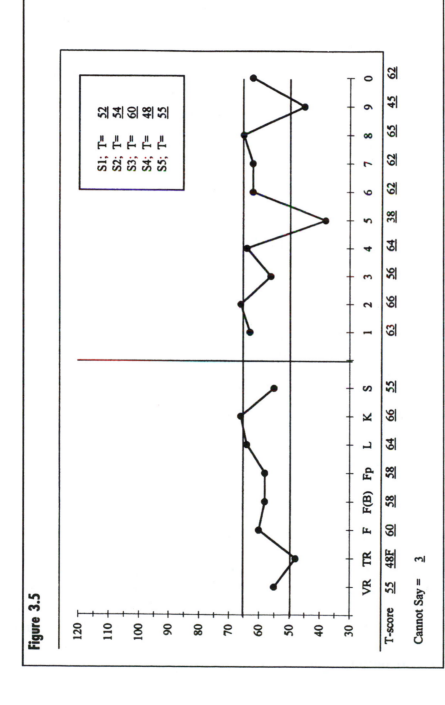

MMPI-2 basic scales profile of Warren G.

Scale 6 (Paranoia)

The *Pa* scale was developed in the original MMPI to appraise symptoms and personality characteristics of individuals experiencing paranoid disorders. The *Pa* scale measures suspicion and mistrust, along with personality features of interpersonal hypersensitivity. The correlates for *Pa* are, in part, dependent on the level of elevation of the scale score.

Patients with extremely high elevations ($T > 80$) on Scale 6 typically and frankly show psychotic behavior, disturbed thinking, delusions of persecution or grandeur (or both), and delusional beliefs such as ideas of reference. They typically feel that other people are mistreating them, working against them, and picking on them. They are usually viewed as angry and resentful. They often harbor grudges because of perceived wrongs that others have committed against them. High *Pa* patients typically use projection as a defense mechanism. They are most frequently diagnosed as having schizophrenia or a paranoid state.

Patients with moderate elevations on *Pa* ($T = 65-79$) show a paranoid predisposition if not actually open symptoms of delusional disorder. They are overly sensitive, vigilant, and responsive to the reactions of others. They appear to feel that they get a raw deal from life. These patients tend to rationalize their frailties and blame others for their own problems. They are found to be suspicious and guarded, and they may react to others in a hostile, resentful, and argumentative manner. They show a pattern of moralistic and rigid behavior. Patients with high elevations on *Pa* tend to have a poor prognosis for therapy because they do not like to discuss their own problems and failings openly. They also seem to have difficulty establishing a treatment relationship with their therapist.

The Case of Susan S.: The Suspicious Computer Programmer

Description

Susan, a 37-year-old, was referred for a psychological evaluation by her supervisor following two incidents in which she appeared to those around her as having delusionally based emotional problems. On her job, she began to have feelings that other employees were talking about her and laughing at her behind her back. She would see people across a large room talking and laughing and assumed that they were talking about her. One day, she went to her supervisor and asked the supervisor to build a cage around her area because someone was messing around her desk and putting "bugs" in her programs. In her interview with the psychologist, she appeared hypersensitive to other people's views, suspicious about the motivations of others, and tense about issues in her marriage (she felt that her husband was not being sympathetic to her present problems). She was referred to another psychologist (one not associated with her company) for psychological treatment.

Comment

Susan's MMPI-2 validity pattern is valid and interpretable (see Figure 3.6). Despite the fact that she was referred by her employer to an employee assistance program psychologist, she was open and cooperative with the evaluation. Her *L, K,* and *S* scores were well within the normal range. Her MMPI-2 profile shows a pattern of suspicion, mistrust, and paranoid ideation, with Scale 6 elevated at $T = 70$. This high scale *Pa* score suggests that she had a problem in the area of trusting others. Her interpersonal problems at work may have been due in large part to her tendency to misinterpret how others react to her.

Scale 7 (Psychasthenia)

Scale 7 of the MMPI-2 can best be viewed as a measure of anxiety and general maladjustment. Patients who score high on this measure report being anxious, tense, and uncomfortable. They tend to worry a great deal and are apprehensive over even minor situations. They often report feeling agitated and jumpy and have difficulties in concentrating. Others tend to view them as high-strung individuals who are introspective, ruminative, obsessive, and compulsive at times. Their presenting symptoms often take the form of physical complaints, particularly heart-related concerns. Patients with this high point score often mistake symptoms of anxiety with having a heart attack.

High-scoring Scale 7 patients usually possess personality characteristics that make them vulnerable to pathological self-criticism: They are shy and do not interact well socially, feel very insecure and inferior, lack self-confidence, and are plagued with self-doubts. They are quick to criticize themselves and are very self-conscious. Usually rigid in their approach to interpersonal relationships, they are often moralistic and guilt ridden. People tend to see them as overly perfectionistic and conscientious. They impress others as being too organized and meticulous to the point of rigidness. Their rigidity manifests itself in persistence (to the point of preservation), uncompromising, and inflexible in interpersonal settings. They often have difficulty making decisions because they "see too many possibilities" in the situations they face.

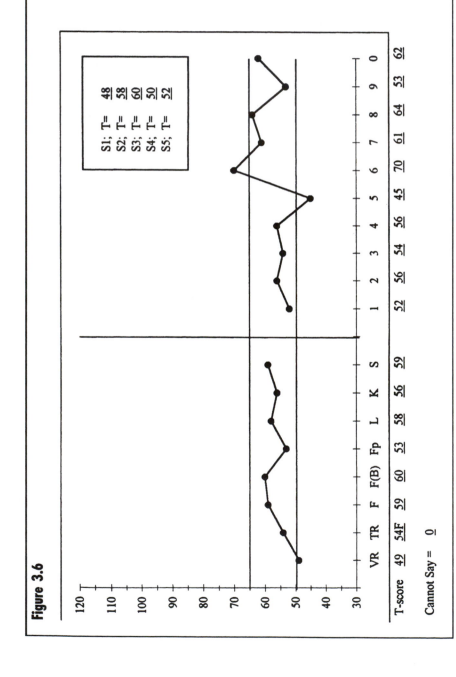

MMPI-2 basic scales profile of Susan S.

Patients who score high on Scale 7 tend to be motivated for psychological treatment because they feel very uncomfortable with their life circumstances. They tend to remain in therapy longer than most patients but also make slow but steady progress. These patients tend to be very ruminative but usually show some insight into their problems. They are prone, however, to unproductive intellectualization and rationalization. They may be somewhat resistant to interpretations in therapy as a result of their rigidity. They may also express open and over-determined hostility in therapy. Periods of symptom intensity can occur in therapy as a result of these patients' "catastrophising." They typically distort the importance of problems and overreact to minor situations as if they were major disasters.

The Case of John B.: A "False Alarm" Heart Attack Victim

Description

John B., a 39-year-old medical patient, was recommended for a psychological evaluation following an incident in which he appeared at an emergency room with symptoms of a heart attack that proved not to have an organic basis. The emergency room physician recognized the symptoms as anxiety based rather than the result of a coronary event. In the psychological evaluation, John appeared as a very tense and anxious person in describing his "scary" hospital visit. He talked freely about his problems, including his many fears over failing in his job, concerns that his wife was going to leave him, fears of dying early, and so forth. John reported a number of related problems, such as an inability to fall asleep, pains in the area of his chest, a fullness in his throat much of the time, and a constant worry over what was going to happen to him. John was provided a prescription for antianxiety medication and was recommended for psychological treatment. He eagerly accepted a treatment referral because he "needed help fast."

Comment

John's MMPI-2 validity pattern suggests a valid protocol (see Figure 3.7). Although he reported a number of symptoms, reflected in his *F* and *F(B)* scores, his profile probably reflects his high state of distress rather than a conscious distortion of symptoms. His MMPI-2 clinical pattern reflects a high degree of tension and anxiety. His prominent score on *Pt* indicates that he was tense, anxious, and ruminative. He was likely to have a great deal of difficulty making decisions and managing daily

Figure 3.7

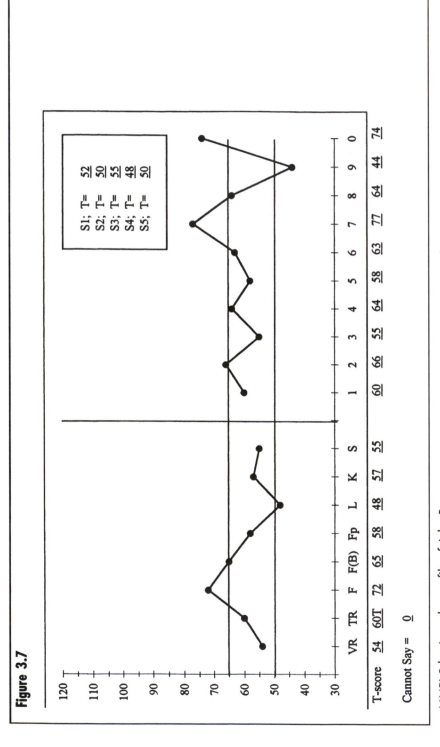

MMPI-2 basic scales profile of John B.

affairs. He also showed a pattern of somatic distress that centered on likely coronary symptoms.

Scale 8 (Schizophrenia)

Because of its relative complexity, interpretation of Scale 8 requires some initial considerations. First, note that not everyone obtaining some elevation on this scale is schizophrenic; some elevation can occur with people who are antisocial or countercultural in their life style. Second, levels of elevation tend to be associated with more severe psychological disorders; however, moderate elevation ranges can occur among some individuals who are not experiencing a thinking disorder but are alienated and disorganized in their approach to life.

T = 80–90
These individuals are usually associated with blatantly psychotic behavior. Individuals with this pattern appear to be confused, disorganized, and disoriented. They have unusual thoughts or attitudes and delusional beliefs, and they may experience hallucinations. Poor judgment and a disorganized pattern of behavior are also characteristic of these people.

T = 65–79
This score level suggests a schizoid life style. These individuals feel alienated from their social environment. They usually feel isolated and misunderstood by others. They are withdrawn and reclusive people who seem inaccessible in interpersonal relations. They avoid dealing with people and are seen by others as odd, shy, aloof, and uninvolved. High-scoring *Sc* patients typically experience generalized anxiety and depression and tend to react to stress by withdrawing into fantasy and daydreaming. They are often seen as hostile and aggressive and may act out their impulses in inappropriate ways.

These *Sc* patients typically show a long-standing pattern of maladjustment, including nonconforming behavior, unusual attitudes, and unconventional behavior. They show strong feelings of inferiority, dissatisfaction with life, sex-role confusion, and sexual preoccupation. Others tend to see the high-scoring *Sc* patient as eccentric, stubborn, moody, immature, and impulsive.

Psychological treatment with Scale 8 patients can be challenging for a number of reasons. They are usually considered to have a poor prognosis for insight-oriented therapy, in part because of the difficulty they have relating to a therapist. Short-term therapy tends to be ineffective because of the extent of their problems. Longer term therapy can be effective if a therapist provides an accepting context in which Scale 8 patients may eventually come to trust him or her. Treatment needs to be extended over a long time in most cases. Patients with this personality pattern appear to lack basic information for problem solving and might benefit from directive guidance at times.

The Case of Alan W.: Disorganized Behavior at Hospital Intake

Description

Alan W., age 27, was committed to an inpatient mental hospital by his parents because he was a danger to himself as reflected in two serious suicide attempts in 2 days. Alan had a long history of psychological problems, dating from adolescence. His first psychiatric hospitalization occurred at age 16 when he was in high school. He was unable to finish high school and has never held a job. When he was not in a psychiatric hospital, he lived with his parents. He had no friends and tended to spend much of his time at home in his room. According to his mother's description, he had been having hallucinations for about 6 months since he quit taking his medication.

Comment

Alan's MMPI-2 profile, administered 1 week postadmission to the hospital, shows a moderate pattern of symptoms checking on the validity scales (see Figure 3.8). Both the F and $F(B)$ are elevated at $T = 65$. These elevations do not produce an invalid report. He appears to have presented a number of symptoms of severe mental disorder. This is reflected in his high score on the Sc, indicating an extreme pattern of bizarre symptoms including likely hallucinations and delusions.

Scale 9 (Mania)

This scale is best viewed as a measure of manic or hypomanic behavior—a group of affective disorders that involve the experience of pathologically elevated mood. The Ma assesses "lower" levels of manic behavior (pure, extreme manic disorders are often untestable). Three levels of Ma are described as follows.

T > 80

These individuals show a pattern of disruptive behavior, including overactive and scattered behavior and accelerated speech—verbosity to the

Figure 3.8

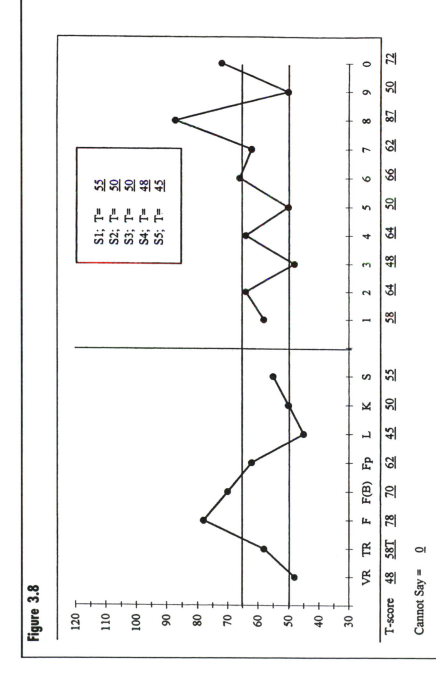

T-score	VR	TR	F	F(B)	Fp	L	K	S	1	2	3	4	5	6	7	8	9	0
	48	58T	78	70	62	45	50	55	58	64	48	64	50	66	62	87	50	72

S1; T= 55
S2; T= 50
S3; T= 50
S4; T= 48
S5; T= 45

Cannot Say = 0

MMPI-2 basic scales profile of Alan W.

point of having an incoherent "flight of ideas." These people may experience hallucinations or delusions of grandeur. These individuals appear very energetic and interested in a wide range of activities. They show a pattern of disturbed sleep and tend not to use energy wisely. They may have numerous goals and projects but do not see them through to completion. They may, on first impression, appear bright, creative, enterprising, and very warm and friendly.

These high-scoring *Ma* individuals tend to have difficulty following a routine and attending to detail. They show unrealistic ideas reflecting an unqualified optimism and at times grandiose aspirations. They characteristically fail to see their own limitations. They often show an exaggerated sense of self-worth and self-importance. They readily become bored and restless and get frustrated easily. High Scale 9 individuals often have problems with other people or legal difficulties because they do not inhibit their free expression of impulses and may engage in irresponsible and immoral behavior in an ostentatious manner. They experience episodes of irritability, hostility, and aggressive outbursts.

In terms of personality features, high Scale 9 patients tend to be outgoing, sociable, and gregarious; they like to be around other people. They exude self-confidence, are usually very warm and friendly toward others, and tend to create a good first impression on people. They often talk to everyone in a pleasant, enthusiastic, and seemingly incessant manner. In general, however, their relationships are superficial, and the Spike 9s (a *spike* is a single-elevated scale score) tend to manipulate others for their own ends. They can be deceptive and unreliable and tend to stretch the truth considerably when they are talking. Many of these individuals have periodic episodes of depression.

Treatment for high Scale 9 patients typically involves medication for their mood disorder. Psychological treatment, if conducted, is often taken up by the management of their negative environmental circumstances, for example, legal problems or school or work difficulties. Individuals with elevated *Ma* scores tend to repeat problems in a stereotypical manner. In addition, they tend to be highly resistant to interpretations in therapy when they do attend sessions. Many do not attend therapy regularly because they have other activities that have caught their attention. Many high Scale 9 people terminate therapy prematurely or become hostile and aggressive toward their therapist.

65 < T ≥ 79

The interpretation of moderately elevated scores requires more caution because some individuals who are "normal," that is, do not have apparent affective disorder problems, obtain scores in this range. Scorers in this range tend to be viewed as overactive, energetic, and talkative. They tend to show a wide range of interests and have an exaggerated sense of self-worth. These high-scoring people tend to get themselves overextended on projects or activities and cannot see projects through to completion. They are often seen as enterprising and ingenious but tend to get themselves "in over their head" because of their overinflated sense of worth and a lack of recognition of their own limitations. Their impulsive behavior and grandiose aspirations cause them to take on things they cannot complete. They tend to lack interest in routine matters, so they often fail to complete tasks or fulfill promises. They tend to become bored and restless easily. Individuals who have a high score on *Ma* tend to have a low frustration tolerance and may show unexplained episodes of irritability, hostility, and aggressive outbursts.

In interpersonal contexts, they appear outgoing, sociable, and gregarious. They seem to enjoy being around other people and are typically friendly, pleasant, and enthusiastic in a superficial way. They tend to be manipulative, deceptive, and unreliable at times. Individuals who score high on *Ma* in this range are usually not interested in psychological treatment because they profess to "feel great." They tend to be resistant to interpretations and tend to miss therapy sessions frequently. Additionally, they tend to terminate therapy prematurely.

T < 35

These individuals' scores may reflect problems as well. Patients with low scores tend to be viewed as having low energy level, low activity level, and a lack of interest in life. They are considered lethargic, listless, apathetic, and difficult to motivate in treatment.

The Case of June C.: A Manic Postal Clerk

Description

June C. was referred to a mental health center by her employer when she began behaving in a very disruptive manner on the job—throwing mail around the room, laughing in an uncontrolled manner, and making lewd comments to fellow employees. June had also received three recent speeding tickets, the last one of which resulted in a loss of her driving privileges for 6 months. She was clocked at 90 miles an hour in a 35-mile zone on a city street. In the psychological evaluation, June was hyperactive in her mannerisms and paced around the room as she answered the questions. She laughed inappropriately at times and made numerous references to extraneous events. June related during the interview that she had experienced similar episodes in the past. She also reported that she often gets so depressed that she is unable to go to work. June was referred to a psychiatrist for possible medical treatment of her likely bipolar disorder.

Comment

June's MMPI-2 validity pattern (see Figure 3.9) indicates that she presented herself in a very favorable manner. Although her profile is valid and interpretable, she nevertheless presented herself in somewhat of an overly positive manner, with both *K* and *S* slightly elevated. Additionally, she endorsed some symptoms on the *F* but not in an exaggerated manner. Her clinical profile shows a high score on *Ma* and a subclinical elevation on *Pd* (it is common to find these two scales elevated among individuals with features of personality disorder). Her expansive mood is shown in her high-point *Ma* score. She appeared hyperactive and showed disorganized behavior. She was likely manifesting symptoms of a manic episode, such as accelerated speech, thought incoherence, and feelings of grandiosity, as well as disturbed sleep and behavioral excesses and had difficulty managing routine details and recognizing her own limitations.

Scale 0 (Social Introversion)

The *Si* was developed to assess the personality characteristics of introversion–extraversion. This scale is a dimensional personality measure and can be interpreted throughout the range of scores. That is, the dimension is marked by introversion in the high range and extraversion in the low range. Individuals who score high on this scale (*T* > 65) report being extremely shy and socially introverted. They report that they are more comfortable when they are alone or with a few close friends than in groups. They typically feel uncomfortable around members of the opposite sex and are hard to get to know. They are usually oversensitive to what others think of them. Individuals who score high on the *Si* are overcontrolled and inhibited and tend to be submissive and compliant in relationships. High-scoring individuals tend to be very serious, conventional, and overly accepting of authority.

Some of the other personality features that characterize these high-scoring patients include the following: They are thought to be slow in personal tempo and cautious and unoriginal in their approach to prob-

Figure 3.9

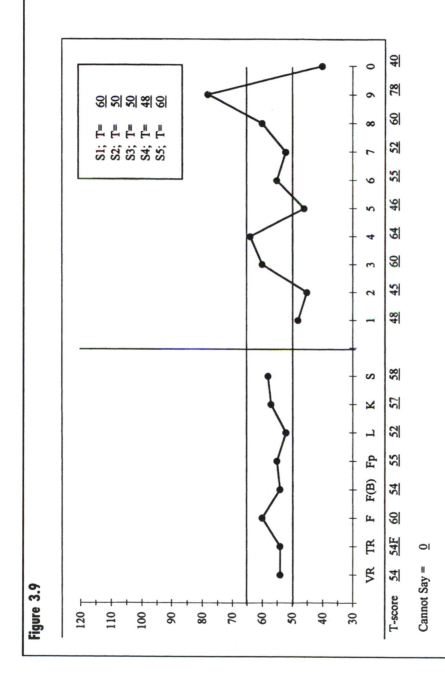

MMPI-2 basic scales profile of June C.

lems. They reportedly have difficulty making even minor decisions and tend to worry a great deal. They are also prone to moodiness and have episodes of depression and anxiety. A set of *Si* subscales have been developed to aid in the interpretation of elevated *Si* subscales (see Exhibit 3.3).

Psychological treatment for high *Si* patients is often very difficult. These individuals are not likely to express their feelings openly, making participation in social groups and in psychological therapy very strained. Moreover, they tend to be very rigid and inflexible in their thinking and attitudes, making these individuals resistant to change.

Low scores on the *Si* scale, *T* < 45, are also interpretable. People who score low on *Si* tend to be very sociable and extroverted. They are viewed by others as outgoing, gregarious, friendly, and talkative. They seem to have a strong need to be around other people and get along well in group situations. They are spontaneous and expressive and appear to seek out competitive situations. Some very low *Si* scorers tend to be immature, impulsive, and self-indulgent.

The Case of Bill C.: A Socially Introverted Computer Engineer

Description

Bill, age 31, was referred to a psychologist for assertiveness training by a family practice physician. Bill, an only child, lived alone and reportedly had no family or friends. His mother and father were deceased, and it had always been very difficult for Bill to make friends, so he would spend much of his time by himself. He was employed in a job that tends to promote "aloneness." He worked in an office that was distant from other people, and most of his communication was by electronic mail. He could go an entire day on the job without human contact. In the initial assessment interview with the psychologist, Bill appeared to be an extremely shy man, who had difficulty maintaining eye contact. Most of the session, he looked at the wall or down at his shoes, avoiding eye contact with the therapist. He found it very difficult to describe himself or his problems. The session was replete with long silences—interrupted only by questions from the therapist. Bill mostly responded with *yes* or did not respond at all. The psychologist found it difficult to construct a family history because of Bill's intense inhibition.

Comment

Bill's MMPI-2 profile is valid and likely to be a good indication of his personality functioning. All of his validity indicators are within the nor-

Exhibit 3.3

Harris–Lingoes and *Si* Subscales for the MMPI-2

Scale and level	No. of items	Symptoms
Scale 1 Hypochondriasis	(none)	
Scale 2 Depression		
D1 Subjective Depression	32	Depression, unhappiness, nervousness, concentration problems, feelings of inferiority, shyness, and low self-confidence
D2 Psychomotor Retardation	14	Lethargy, low energy, immobilized, and withdrawn; avoids people
D3 Physical Malfunctioning	11	Preoccupation with physical functioning, denial of good health, a wide variety of somatic complaints
D4 Mental Dullness	10	Lack of energy; feelings of tension, problems in attention, lacks self-confidence, and feels that life is not interesting nor worthwhile
D5 Brooding	10	Broods, ruminates, lacks energy, feels inferior, is easily hurt by criticisms, and feels like one is losing control of one's thought processes
Scale 3 Hysteria		
Hy2 Denial of Social Anxiety	6	Socially extroverted and comfortable, is not easily influenced by social standards and customs
Hy2 Need for Affection	12	Strong needs for attention and affection, sensitive to others, optimistic, and trusting; avoids confrontations; denies negative feelings toward others
Hy3 Lassitude–Malaise	15	Uncomfortable and not in good health; tired, weak, and easily fatigued; problems in concentration; poor appetite; sleep disturbance; unhappy
Hy4 Somatic Complaints	17	Multiple somatic complaints, uses repression and conversion of affect, little or no hostility is expressed
Hy5 Inhibition of Aggression	7	Denial of hostile and aggressive impulses, sensitive about response of others, decisive
Scale 4 Psychopathic Deviate		
Pd1 Familial Discord	11	Views home situation as unpleasant and lacking in love, support, and understanding; feels that one's family is critical and controlling

continued

Exhibit 3.3, continued

Harris–Lingoes and *Si* Subscales for the MMPI-2

Scale and level	No. of items	Symptoms
Pd2 Authority Problems	10	Resents authority; has trouble in school and with the law, possesses definite opinions about right and wrong, stands up for one's beliefs
Pd3 Social Imperturbability	12	Social comfort, self-confident, tendencies toward exhibitionistic behavior, defends opinions strongly
Pd4 Social Alienation	18	Misunderstood, alienated, isolated, estranged, lonely, unhappy, uninvolved, blames others, self-centered, insensitive, inconsiderate, manipulative
Pd5 Self-Alienation	15	Discomfort with self, unhappy, has problems with concentrating, sees life as not interesting or rewarding, is hard to settle down, excessively uses alcohol
Scale 6 (Paranoia)		
Pa1 Persecutory Ideas	17	Views the world as threatening; feels misunderstood and unfairly blamed or punished; acknowledges suspicions and is untrusting; blames others; sometimes has delusions of persecution
Pa2 Poignancy	9	Feels high strung and hypersensitive, more intensely than others, and lonely and misunderstood; looks for risk and excitement
Pa3 Naivete	9	Has extremely naïve and optimistic attitudes toward others, is trusting, has high moral standards, denies hostility
Scale 7 Psychasthenia	(none)	
Scale 8 Schizophrenia		
Sc1 Social Alienation	21	Misunderstood and mistreated; reports that one's family situation lacks love and support, feels lonely and empty, expresses hostility and hatred toward one's family, never experienced a love relationship
Sc2 Emotional Alienation	11	Depression and feelings of despair, wishes he or she were dead, feels frightened and apathetic

continued

Exhibit 3.3, continued

Harris–Lingoes and *Si* Subscales for the MMPI-2

Scale and level	No. of items	Symptoms
Sc3 Lack of Ego Mastery, Cognitive	10	Fears losing one's mind, has strange thought processes, has feelings of unreality, has problems with concentration and attention
Sc4 Lack of Ego Mastery, Conative	14	Life is a strain, feels desperate and worries, has problems coping with everyday problems, life is not interesting nor rewarding, seem to have given up hope, wish one were dead
Sc5 Lack of Ego Mastery, Defective Inhibition	11	Out of control of emotions and impulses; feels restless, hyperactive, and irritable; has laughing or crying episodes; may not remember previously performed activities
Sc6 Bizarre Sensory Experiences	20	Body is changing in unusual ways; has hallucinations, unusual thoughts, external reference; experiences skin sensitivity, weakness, ringing in ears, and so forth
Scale 9 Mania		
Ma1 Amorality	6	See others as selfish and dishonest, feels justified in being the way one is; derives vicarious satisfaction from manipulative exploits of others
Ma2 Psychomotor Acceleration	11	Has accelerated speech, thought processes, and motor activity; is tense and restless; feels excited and is elated without cause; is easily bored; seeks out excitement; has impulses to do harmful or shocking things
Ma3 Imperturbability	8	Denies social anxiety, is not especially sensitive about what others think, is impatient and irritable toward others
Ma4 Ego Inflation	9	Does unrealistic self-appraisal, resents demands made by others

Note. *Si* subscales (Ben-Porath, Hostetler, et al., 1995): Si1 = Shyness, Si2 = Social Avoidance, and Si3 = Self–Other Alienation.

mal range. His MMPI-2 clinical profile shows a clinical pattern of depression and alienation from others in the elevations of *D* and *Pa* (see Figure 3.10). His ultra high elevation on *Si* indicates that he was extremely introverted and socially distant from others. He reported feeling more comfortable when he was alone or with a few close friends rather than in a group. He reported feeling uncomfortable with women. He appeared oversensitive to what others thought of him and never could think of anything to say when he was in the presence of women. He was likely overcontrolled and inhibited and had a tendency to be very submissive and compliant in social contexts. He readily became nervous when he was around other people.

The Use of Homogeneous Content Subscales To Refine Interpretation of the Clinical Scales

In this chapter, I provided a description of the meanings and correlates that can be applied to patients with elevations on the traditional MMPI-2 clinical scales. The behavioral correlates for the scales are empirically determined factors, evolving out of research on the scales. The scales are not interpreted according to the content of the items comprising the scales because in many cases these scales are heterogeneous in make up and do not reflect a single problem theme. The *empirical test interpretation strategy* for describing a personality based on elevations on MMPI-2 scales involves essentially listing the empirical relationships for the most elevated scale. For example, if the client obtains a high elevation on *Pd,* then the interpreter would simply list the established correlates for *Pd.* As an illustration, the scale descriptors (also referred to as *empirical correlates*) as measured by Scale 4 are in Exhibit 3.4.

However, not all of the correlates of *Pd* would apply in each and every case. A valuable method of refining empirical interpretation is available through the use of content themes to focus the interpretation more specifically on the individual case. This approach is referred to as *content subscale interpretation*. The content subscale approach evolved to "subdivide" the heterogeneous items by grouping them according to similar content themes. For example, the items on Scale 2 were rationally grouped into five content groupings by Harris and Lingoes (1955/1968): Family Discord, Authority Problems, Social Imperturbability, Social Alienation, and Self-Alienation. These rational item groupings were

Figure 3.10

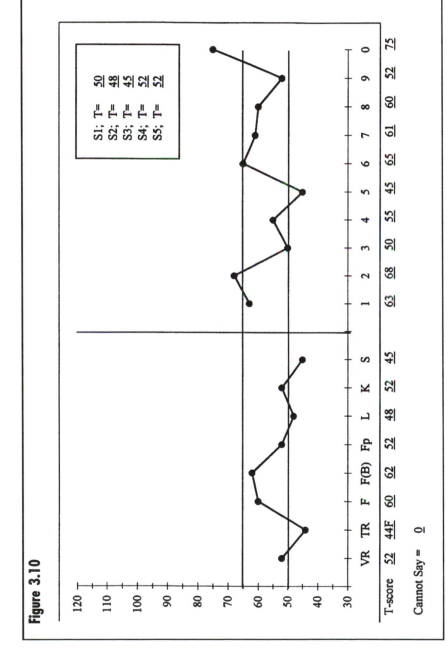

MMPI-2 basic scales profile of Bill C.

Exhibit 3.4

Descriptors for Scale 4

1. Have difficulty incorporating the values and standards of society.
2. May engage in asocial and antisocial acts, including lying, cheating, stealing, sexual acting out, and excessive use of alcohol and/or other drugs.
3. Are rebellious toward authority figures.
4. Have stormy relationships with family.
5. Blame family members for difficulties.
6. Have histories of underachievement.
7. Tend to have marital problems.
8. Are impulsive and strive for immediate gratification of impulses.
9. Do not plan their behavior well.
10. Tend to act without considering the consequences of their actions.
11. Are impatient and have limited frustration tolerance.
12. Show poor judgment and take risks.
13. Tend not to profit from experiences.
14. Are seen by others as immature and childish.
15. Are narcissistic, self-centered, selfish, and egocentric.
16. Are ostentatious and exhibitionistic.
17. Are insensitive to the needs and feelings of others.
18. Are interested in others in terms of how they can be used.
19. Are likable and create good first impressions.
20. Have shallow, superficial relationships.
21. Seem unable to form warm attachments with others.
22. Are extroverted and outgoing.
23. Are talkative, active, adventurous, energetic, and spontaneous.
24. Are judged by others to be intelligent and self-confident.
25. Have a wide range of interests but behavior lacks clear direction.
26. Tend to be hostile, resentful, rebellious, antagonistic, and refractory.
27. Have sarcastic, cynical, and suspicious attitudes.
28. May act in aggressive ways, although women may do so in less direct ways.
29. May feign guilt and remorse when in trouble.
30. Are not seen as overwhelmed by emotional turmoil.
31. May admit feeling sad, fearful, and worried about the future.
32. Experience absence of deep emotional response.
33. May feel empty, bored, and depressed.
34. In clinical settings are likely to receive diagnoses of antisocial or passive–aggressive personality disorder.
35. May agree to treatment to avoid something more unpleasant.
36. Have poor prognosis for psychotherapy or counseling.
37. Tend to terminate treatment prematurely.
38. In treatment they tend to intellectualize excessively and to blame others for their own difficulties.

Adapted from Graham (in press).

developed for six of the clinical scales in the profile that were most heterogeneous in content (see Exhibit 3.4 for descriptions).

This interpretive approach works as follows. When Scale 4 is elevated above $T = 65$ and particularly if it is the peak score on the clinical profile, then the empirical correlates from this list would apply to the patient. These correlates would serve as the basic "raw material" for the patient's MMPI-2 interpretation. Do all of the correlates apply to all clients? Does each of the 38 external behaviors apply with equal strength? If not, which are given priority in the development of a personality description for a patient?

The MMPI-2 interpreter can also use the Harris–Lingoes homogeneous content groupings to determine what problems are more likely to be "driving" the elevation of the peak score, that is, are likely to be the most salient problems. If one or two of the Harris–Lingoes subscales (see Exhibit 3.4) are more prominent (e.g., elevated at $T \geq 65$), the correlates that correspond to the content of the external behaviors would be given prominence in the clinical report. As an illustration of this clinical interpretation strategy, the following clinical profile to interpret is shown in Figure 3.11, and the Harris–Lingoes subscales for the only elevated clinical scale (*Pd*) in this clinical pattern are in Exhibit 3.5.

The Case of Doris E. in a Family Custody Dispute

Description

Doris was administered the MMPI-2 as part of a clinical evaluation to determine custody. The clinical profile of the MMPI-2 suggests that she probably shows features of an antisocial personality disordered individual because of her high elevation on *Pd*.

Comment

The item contents that are most salient from the *Pd* descriptors are as follows:

- Have stormy relationships with family
- Blame family members for difficulties
- Tend to have marital problems
- Are seen by others as immature and childish
- Have shallow, superficial relationships
- Seem unable to form warm attachments with others
- Are insensitive to the needs and feelings of others.

Figure 3.11

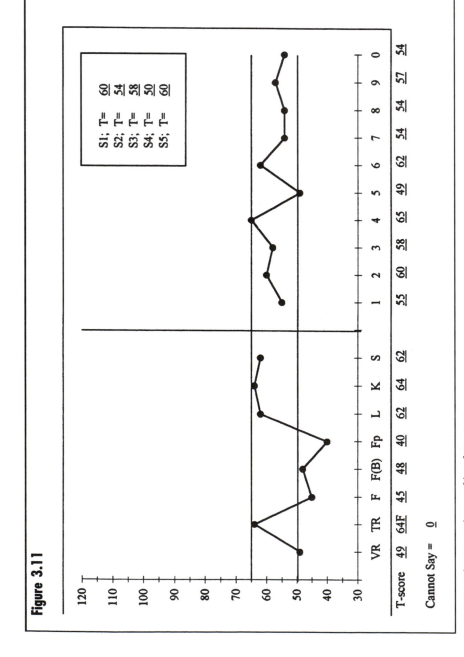

MMPI-2 basic scales profile of Doris E.

Exhibit 3.5

Harris–Lingoes Subscale Profile for Doris E.

Pd level	Subscale	T
1	Familial Discord	68
2	Authority Problems	62
3	Social Imperturbability	52
4	Social Alienation	58
5	Self-Alienation	56

In formulating the report on this patient, one should focus initially on the most prominent content—a good starting point. However, the other correlates could also be considered appropriate and could become a part of the evaluation. Keep in mind the following points when using the Harris–Lingoes subscales in interpretation. The Harris–Lingoes subscales should not be considered as psychometric scales for use in the prediction of external behaviors, as are the parent scales but should be interpreted as follows:

- These subscales provide the practitioner with an appraisal of the extent to which a patient has endorsed particular contents that served to elevate the scale in question. They should not be interpreted in isolation from the parent scale.
- They should only be interpreted as an adjunct to the parent scale to provide clues as to which of the scale correlates for the parent scale are most salient. For example, they can help the practitioner determine which correlates are most salient among the external correlates of a scale.
- Harris–Lingoes subscale scores below $T = 60$ are probably not very useful in the interpretive process.

Summary

In this section, I used homogeneous content themes comprising the MMPI-2 clinical scales to refine the examiner's understanding of the high elevation on the scale. A particular response to some of the item themes can provide important clues as to which of the MMPI-2 clinical scale correlates should be emphasized in an evaluation. This approach to test interpretation is a scale development and interpretation method that evolved considerably over the past 3 decades and has gained an important place in empirically based personality assessment. I explore a more extensive treatment of content interpretation in chapter 5.

Next, I turn to an important issue that occurs in the real world and sometimes gives MMPI-2 interpreters pause as to what to conclude. How do you interpret a clinical profile that has more than one clinical scale elevated in the interpretable range? Which scores should receive prominence in the interpretation?

The Analysis of Complex Cases: Code-Type Interpretation

In this chapter, the use of MMPI-2 profile types, often referred to as code types, are described and illustrated. *Code types* are MMPI-2 clinical scale summary indexes that include the most elevated scale scores of the basic MMPI-2 patterns. Code-type interpretation for the MMPI-2 was developed early in MMPI history when it was recognized that for some patients, more than one clinical scale might be elevated. It is interesting to note that MMPI interpreters observed that some scale score combinations occurred with greater frequency in some settings, so the interpreters developed empirical descriptions of individuals who matched these MMPI patterns. Research on these patterns draws a valuable picture of the various profile code types and their utility in describing a patient's behavior. In this chapter, I focus on the factors considered important to understand and use the MMPI-2 code types. Well-established behavioral correlates for several of the most frequent MMPI-2 profile codes are illustrated next.

Before I describe and illustrate code-type interpretation, I first need to show how profiles are coded—a practice that ensures that everyone working in the area is using the same profile classification rules to summarize cases.

Coding an MMPI-2 Profile Using Results From the Basic Clinical Scales

The profile coding in wide use today is a modification of the procedure developed by Welsh (1951). The MMPI-2 scale scores to code are displayed in the profile of Figure 4.1.

Figure 4.1

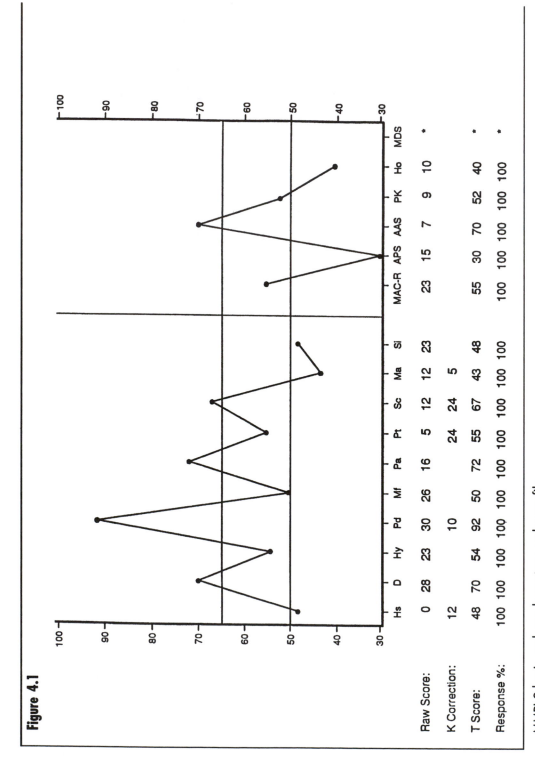

	Hs	D	Hy	Pd	Mf	Pa	Pt	Sc	Ma	Si	MAC-R	APS	AAS	PK	Ho	MDS
Raw Score:	0	28	23	30	26	16	5	12	12	23	23	15	7	9	10	*
K Correction:	12			10			24	24	5							
T Score:	48	70	54	92	50	72	55	67	43	48	55	30	70	52	40	*
Response %:	100	100	100	100	100	100	100	100	100	100	100	100	100	100	100	*

MMPI-2 basic and supplementary scales profile.

Step 1. First, write down the numbers of the scales in descending order based on the *T*-score elevation. For the profile in Figure 4.1, the highest scale is *Pd* with *T* = 92, so 4 (as in Scale 4) is the first number in the code. The next highest scale score is *Pa*, or Scale 6, at 72; so now the code is 46. The third highest is *D*, so the code becomes 462. This ranking procedure is followed until all the scales are listed by number from highest to lowest score. The digit sequence for the example is 4628735109. To check for accuracy, the interpreter should read through the completed sequence to determine if any scale has been omitted or repeated.

Step 2. The second step involves entering the appropriate symbols to denote scale elevation. Scales with *T* ≥ 90 are followed by an asterisk (*), 80–89 by a double quotation mark ("), 70–79 by a single quotation mark ('), 60–69 by a minus sign (−), 50–59 by a slash (/), 40–49 by a colon (:), and 30–39 by a pound or number symbol (#). In addition, in MMPI-2 a plus symbol (+) is used to denote the *T* = 65 score range. When two or more scales fall in the same range of 10 *T*-score points, the elevation symbol follows the digit for the lowest scale. These symbols (used on typewriter keyboards) were selected because they are familiar to most people.

In Figure 4.1, the highest elevation is 92 on the *Pd*, indicating the scale digit 4 should be followed by an *. However, there are no scales elevated at the 80–89 range, so a " symbol is also included. *Pa* and *D* follow at *T* = 72 and 70, respectively, so the ' symbol is inserted after Scales 6 and 2. Next, comes the *Sc* at 67, which is followed by the + symbol. Likewise, because there are no scale scores between 60 and 64, the − symbol is also inserted after Scale 8. The *Pt*, *Hy*, and *Mf* fall in the same elevation range, between *T* = 50 and 55. Therefore 7, 3, and 5 scores are followed by the / symbol. The final three scales *Hs*, *Si*, and *Ma* are within the *T* = 40–49 range. Thus, the numbers 1, 0, and 9 are followed by the : symbol and the # symbol. At this point, the code is 4*"62'8+−735/109:#.

Step 3. Next, the traditional validity scales are coded separately and placed to the right of the clinical scale code. The scores on the validity scales for the sample MMPI-2 profile are as follows:

Scale	L	F	K
T score	61	64	68

The full code is now 4*''62'8+735/109:# *K+FL−*.

It should be noted that only the original MMPI validity scales are traditionally coded. The Cannot Say, *VRIN, TRIN, S, F(B)* and *F(p)* scores are not included in the coding on MMPI-2 in this book.

Step 4. Some researchers begin and end each code with an elevation symbol; although the beginning and ending symbols are redundant, their use allows the practitioner to locate cases by the highest (or lowest) score. Because no elevations fall in the 100+ ranges and if I were using this refinement, my sample code would begin with **, as follows: The complete code for this MMPI-2 profile would now be **4*''62'8+−735/109:#*K+FL−*.

Step 5. When two or more scales are within 1 *T* point of each other, it is customary to underline both code digits. In the example, *Pt* = 55 and *Hy* = 54; therefore, in the code, the digits would appear as <u>73</u>. When two or more scales have the same *T* score, they are placed in the usual ordinal sequence and underlined: For example, if *Pd* and *Pt* both = 65, then the code would be <u>47</u>+. If the scales fall into two different ranges but are still within 1 *T* point, they and the elevation symbol are all underlined: *D* = 70 and *Pt* = 69 would be <u>2'7</u>. The final code in the example is now **4*''62'8+−<u>735</u>/<u>1</u>09:#*K+FL−*.

Step 6. Other elevation symbols are sometimes used to denote very high scores. *T* scores from 110 to 119 are denoted by the ! symbol and if *T* ≥ 120, it is denoted by !!. This practice may be useful if a large number of cases have extreme elevations, for example, in an inpatient facility. Some profile codes contain gaps because no scale falls in some elevation ranges. The appropriate elevation symbol for the missing range must be included. For example, if a 20-point range is skipped, all the symbols marking that range should be included, even though the middle symbol is actually redundant.

Empirical Correlates Applicable to Profile Types

What Is an MMPI-2 Code Type?

A code type is made up of the highest elevated scale or scales in the clinical profile based on their rank order and profile elevation. Early empirical research on MMPI code types included only the eight clinical scales—*Hs, D, Hy, Pd, Pa, Pt, Sc,* and *Ma.* However, more recent research on special populations, such as college students, includes other scales, such as *Mf* and *Si* (Graham, Ben-Porath, & McNulty, in press; Kelly & King, 1978). Research on MMPI code types can be confidently applied to individuals whose profile matches the code type.

Why Code Profiles?

One reason is that the profile code provides a shorthand that enables accurate communication of the "type" of patient one is assessing. A profile configuration summarizes a great deal of information about a given client. For example, MMPI-2 users can convey by a simple numerical combination of scores (e.g., 2-7) a great deal of information about a patient in a symbolic form. It is customary to denote the code type by the high point scores; for example, the Depression Scale (2) and Psychastenia Scale (7) would have a 2-7 code. It is frequently written as a 2-7/7-2 because the correlates apply whether the 2 or 7 is highest in the code. Another reason for using code types in research is that coding allows similar profiles to be readily grouped from a list of patient codes. For example, if a number of profiles have been coded and filed in sequence, it is possible to locate quickly all the cases that begin with a particular sequence.

A number of code types have been well researched in the empirical literature. Of course, you have already become familiar with single point codes or *profile spikes*—when a single clinical scale is elevated in the critical range in the profile. The *two-point code type* is also a very widely researched profile code. The two-point code occurs when two clinical scales, such as *D* and *Pd,* are elevated in the critical range (i.e., $T > 65$). This code type would be defined as a two-point code of 2-4/4-2. Also a number of *three-point codes* have been identified and researched. This profile occurs when three clinical scales are elevated in the profile. For example, clinical elevations on scales *D, Pd,* and *Sc* produce a three-point code of 2-4-8—a profile type often found in individuals with severe personality disorder. The *four-point code* is somewhat rare, although some are well researched (e.g., the 1-2-3-4 code type is often found in medical settings). There are no research studies defining five or more point codes.

Four Examples of MMPI-2 Code-Type Interpretation

In this section, I describe and illustrate four MMPI-2 code types: the 1-3/3-1, 2-7/7-2, 4-9/9-4, and 6-8/8-6. Readers can find a more complete listing of profile code correlates in Appendix A. In this section, the empirical correlates are summarized and each profile code is illustrated with a clinical case.

The 1-3/3-1 Profile Code

This profile code typically describes patients diagnosed as psychophysiologic or neurotic (hysterical, hypochondriacal) disorders. The syndrome, referred to as *classic conversion,* may be present. Severe anxiety and depression are usually absent. This type of person functions at a reduced level of efficiency and develops physical symptoms under stress that may disappear when the stress subsides. In terms of their basic personality characteristics, patients with this profile pattern tend to be overly optimistic and superficial in social situations. They tend to be immature, egocentric, and selfish. They feel insecure and have strong needs for attention and affection. They frequently tend to seek sympathy from others. In addition, they often show a pattern of dependency.

High 1-3/3-1 patients are usually found to be outgoing and socially extraverted, but their interpersonal relationships are superficial. They tend to lack genuine involvement with people and may be exploitive in social relationships. They are reportedly naïve and lacking in skills to deal with the opposite sex. Many patients with this code type appear low in sexual drive but may be flirtatious. They seek attention and may show resentment and hostility toward those who do not offer enough attention and support to them. They are overcontrolled and passive–aggressive and have occasional angry outbursts. They are mostly conventional and conforming in attitudes and beliefs.

These patients are usually not motivated for psychotherapy, and when there they expect definite answers and solutions to their problems. They may terminate their therapy prematurely if their therapist fails to respond to their demands. Individuals who fall into this code-type group tend to prefer medical explanations for their symptoms and to resist psychological interpretations for their problems. They tend to deny and rationalize their behavior and to be uninsightful. They may see themselves as normal, responsible, and without fault. They tend to be "Pollyanna-ish" about their symptoms and lack appropriate concern, even though their symptoms and problems, if genuine, are extremely disabling.

The Case of Ellen B.: A Question of Chronic Fatigue Syndrome

Description

For many years, this patient had made frequent visits to her family physician and other medical specialists across a broad range of fields for medical complaints of a vague nature and which were typically unsupported by medical findings. Most recently, Ellen requested that her family practice physician refer her to a new program, which she had seen described on television, that specialized in chronic fatigue syndrome. Her MMPI-2 profile (see Figure 4.2) was from a series of testing that she underwent (prior to entering a chronic pain treatment program that she did not complete) 3 months earlier.

Comment

Ellen's MMPI-2 pattern is within interpretable limits. Although she tended to respond to the items in a favorable manner, her profile is valid. Her MMPI-2 profile clearly meets criteria of the 1-3/3-1 profile type. Both *Hs* and *Hy* T scores are elevated above 65 and substantially above the next highest scale. This client was functioning at a reduced psychological efficiency—she was defensive and managed stress by developing physical symptoms. Such symptoms may disappear when stress subsides. She was likely to show histrionic personality characteristics. She was also likely to be outgoing, superficial, and immature in social relationships. People with this pattern tend also to be egocentric and selfish. There may have been an element of attention seeking in Ellen's clinical picture, and she may have sought a great deal of sympathy from others. There may have been as well an element of secondary gain in her symptom pattern; that is, she may have gotten social reinforcement in the form of attention for her symptoms.

Figure 4.2

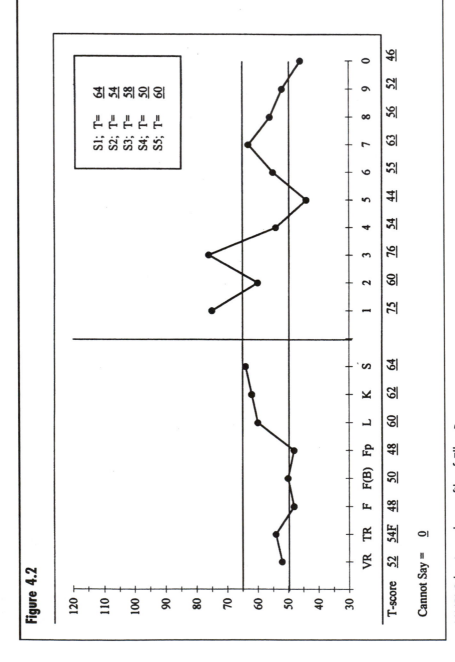

MMPI-2 basic scales profile of Ellen B.

The 2-7/7-2 Profile Code

People with this profile type typically present with mood symptoms, such as depression, anxiety, and tension. They reportedly feel nervous a great deal of the time and worry to excess. They tend to be vulnerable to real and imagined threats and tend to anticipate problems before they occur. They reportedly overreact to minor stress with feelings of "catastrophic doom." Symptomatically, they report a variety of physical problems, centering on fatigue and feeling exhausted. They usually report that they feel unhappy and sad. They often acknowledge that they feel sluggish in their actions and speech and may display a slowness of their thought processes. In conversations, they are usually very pessimistic about being able to overcome their problems. They usually report that their daily activities are filled with dull and uninteresting activities. Others typically view them as brooding, moody, and ruminative.

People with the 2-7/7-2 code type tend to be overly conscientious and reportedly have a strong need to do what is right. They may have high and unrealistic expectations of themselves. They often report feeling guilty at times without having done anything wrong. Clinically, they report being indecisive and feeling inadequate, insecure, and inferior to others. They are viewed as intropunitive and rigid in their thinking and problem-solving styles. In addition, they are often meticulous, perfectionistic, and somewhat compulsive. Many with this pattern are excessively religious and extremely moralistic. They tend to be docile, passive, and dependent in relationships. They have difficulty asserting themselves in social situations. They show a high capacity for forming deep, emotional ties and actively tend to seek nurturance and reassurance from others. They usually are highly motivated for psychotherapy and tend to remain in therapy for a long time. Individuals with this pattern tend to show considerable improvement in therapy. They are variously diagnosed as depressive, obsessive–compulsive, or having anxiety disorder.

The Case of Carol V: A Life of Despair in a Land of Plenty

Description

Carol V. was the 44-year-old divorced daughter of a wealthy real estate developer. Carol, who had never worked, was left a substantial inheritance when her father recently died. Carol had married at age 18, but the marriage only lasted for 6 months. She had no children and lived with her mother and an aunt on the family estate. Carol had been hospitalized on two prior occasions for depression. In both instances, she was hospitalized until her depressed mood was altered—the first time through antidepressant medication and the second time through unilateral electroshock. Carol was evaluated at her third hospital admission.

Comment

Carol's MMPI-2 profile is clearly within interpretable limits (see Figure 4.3). Her test performance is likely to be a good indication of her present personality functioning. The patient appeared to be experiencing extreme mood symptoms, including both depression and anxiety. She was likely to report feeling tense and nervous. She was also likely to worry so much about the future that she felt threatened easily. It is likely that she ruminated a great deal and anticipated that problems were going to happen. The patient was likely to feel as though the world was coming to an end, even though, objectively, things might not be all that bad. The patient also reported a lot of physical complaints, particularly of being fatigued and unhappy about her life situation. She was likely to feel lethargic and lacking in energy. She tended to be somewhat shy and was quite pessimistic about being able to overcome her problems. The patient was quite indecisive and felt inadequate, insecure, and inferior to others.

The 4-9/9-4 Profile Type

Individuals with this profile type tend to show marked disregard for social standards and values. They are usually viewed as antisocial; they appear to have a poorly developed conscience, easy morals, and fluctuating ethical values. It is not unusual to find that they have legal difficulties or work problems. They tend to have a wide array of problem behaviors, such as alcoholism, fighting, and sexual acting out.

In terms of personality features, the 4-9/9-4 patient is likely to be narcissistic, selfish, self-indulgent, and impulsive. These individuals tend to be viewed as irresponsible. They cannot delay gratification of impulses and show poor judgment. They also reportedly act out, without considering the consequences of their behavior. People with this pattern tend to fail to learn from punishing experiences. When in trouble, they rationalize their shortcomings and failures, blame their difficulties on others, and lie to avoid responsibility. They reportedly have a low frustration tolerance and are seen as moody, irritable, and having a

Figure 4.3

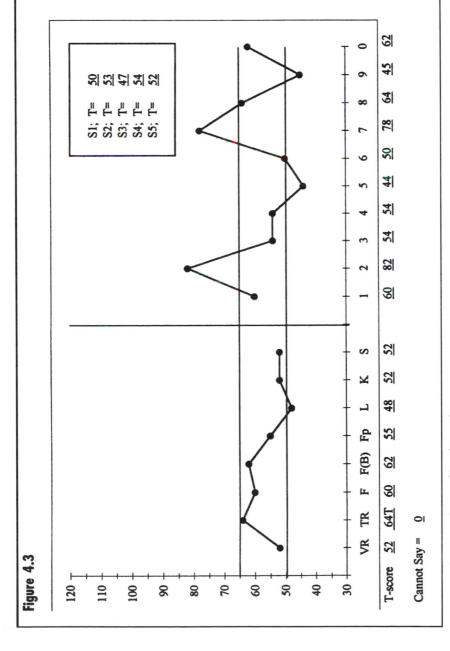

MMPI-2 basic scales profile of Carol V.

caustic manner. They are often angry and hostile and may have occasional emotional outbursts.

These patients are also energetic, restless, and overactive. They tend to seek out emotional stimulation and excitement. They are uninhibited, extraverted, and talkative in social situations. They often create a good first impression because they are glib and spontaneous; however, their relationships are usually superficial. They appear to avoid deep emotional ties. They are considered "loners" who keep others at an emotional distance. They usually present as self-confident and secure but are quite immature. The usual diagnosis for this profile type is antisocial personality.

The Case of the High-Flying Flight Attendant

Description
Carla T., age 37, had been a flight attendant for 15 years when she was suspended from her job and was required to take a leave of absence to obtain treatment for her substance abuse problem before returning to flying. Her use of alcohol and cocaine had been interfering with her job performance over the past year. She had missed two of her scheduled trips and, on one occasion, showed up for a trip drunk. A psychological evaluation was conducted as part of her substance abuse evaluation.

Comment
The MMPI-2 profile that Carla produced, although revealing some defensiveness, is interpretable (see Figure 4.4). She attempted to present her psychological adjustment as good and her problems as minimal. Her MMPI-2 pattern involves a well-defined 4-9 profile code, suggesting that she was likely to show a pattern of antisocial behavior, including irresponsible and immature behavior, acting out, lack of regard for authority, and relationship problems. Carla's pattern of behavior was likely a long-standing problem rather than the result of situational factors. Individuals with Carla's profile pattern, the 4-9 code type, often have problems with substance abuse. The likelihood of an addictive disorder should be evaluated further. (See the discussion of the MMPI-2 substance abuse indicators in chapter 6.)

The 6-8/8-6 Profile Type

Patients with this profile type usually experience severe mental disorder and are diagnosed as having schizophrenia, paranoid type. They man-

Figure 4.4

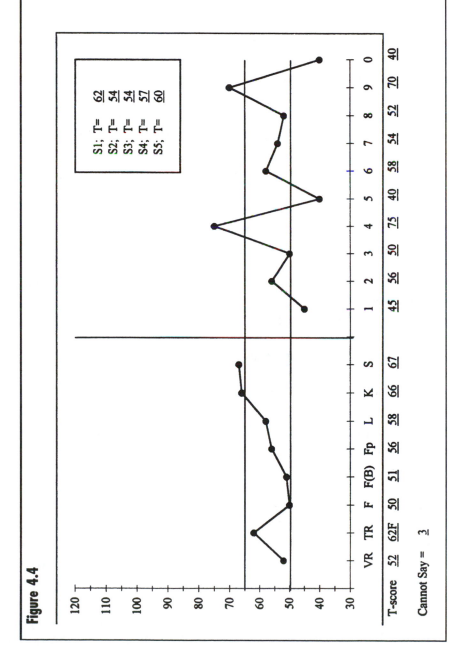

MMPI-2 basic scales profile of Carla T.

ifest clearly psychotic behavior; their thinking is autistic, fragmented, tangential, and circumstantial. They usually experience bizarre thought content and have difficulties in concentrating, attention, and memory. They usually have poor judgment, delusions of persecution or grandeur, and feelings of unreality. They typically show a preoccupation with unusual, abstract thoughts. Delusions and blunted affect are often present. These individuals may have rapid and incoherent speech. They tend to lack effective defense mechanisms and show extreme anxiety at times. They are likely to react to stress and pressure by withdrawing into fantasy and daydreaming. They tend to have difficulty in differentiating between fantasy and reality.

Feelings of inferiority and insecurity are common in this type of patient, as is a lack of self-confidence and self-esteem. People with this pattern often feel guilty about perceived failures. Social withdrawal from activity and emotional apathy are likely to be prominent in their clinical pattern. These patients are usually not involved with other people and are suspicious and distrustful, usually avoiding deep emotional ties. Their poor social skills are likely to limit efforts at rehabilitation. They are most comfortable when they are alone. They resent interpersonal demands placed on them, and they become moody, irritable, unfriendly, and negative. They tend to have a long-term pattern of maladjustment and usually a schizoid life style. They are typically treated with phenothyzianes to control their psychotic thought patterns and behaviors.

The Case of John Z.: A Homeless Mentally Ill Person

Description

John Z., age 31, had been hospitalized in a state mental institution for 2 years (his third hospitalization since he was age 16) but was discharged into a board and care facility because the institution was in the process of reducing the number of inpatient beds. John's behavior was judged as sufficiently stabilized by psychotropic medications, so he was considered capable of handling the supervised living setting of the facility. He remained in the group living home only a few days, when he decided that people did not like him, so he left. He lived on the streets for about 2 months, eating some meals at a church-sponsored homeless shelter. However, living on the streets became more and more difficult as the winter set in. At one point, after a freezing night, he had to be taken to an emergency room for frostbite after a particularly cold spell. While treating him for frostbite, the staff at the emergency room noted his incoherent speech, disordered thinking, and delusional behavior, so they sent him to the psychiatry unit of the hospital for an evaluation.

Comment

John's MMPI-2 pattern is valid but shows some extreme symptoms on F (see Figure 4.5). The profile he produced is likely to provide useful information about his symptom pattern. His type of MMPI-2 profile code is usually associated with patients having a severe mental disorder. It further shows a pattern of thinking disturbance, delusions, and likely hallucinations. He showed a pattern of disturbed interpersonal relationships and poor social skills, which were likely to prove detrimental to his efforts at adjusting to complex life situations.

Points To Consider When Using Code Types

When is a code type used rather than a simple scale-by-scale interpretation? MMPI-2 interpreters are often faced with the question of which test prototype, either in terms of a single scale elevation or code type, should be used to obtain the empirical descriptors. Here are a few guidelines to consider when deciding on the most appropriate patient descriptors to use:

- Interpreting a 1-point code involves referring to the established descriptors for the highest score.
- Complex code types (two-, three-, or four-point codes) should be used when two or more scales reach interpretive significance, and empirically derived descriptors are available for them.
- The profile should be clearly defined to ensure that the correlates for the particular code are applied.
- The appropriate behavioral descriptions for the code should be applied (some code types, e.g., the 2-6-9 code type, may not have sufficient empirical descriptors to provide much information about the client). In such cases, the most appropriate two-point code should be used or if no two point applies, a scale-by-scale interpretation strategy should be followed.
- As with the clinical scales, information from the code-type literature can be organized (in terms of likely importance) by using the Harris–Lingoes subscale elevations of the pertinent scales in the code.

Figure 4.5

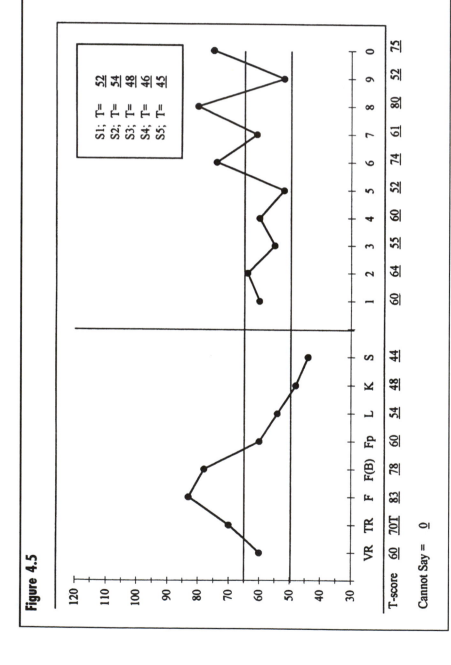

MMPI-2 basic scales profile of John Z.

Summary

In this chapter, I examined empirical interpretation of profiles—the use of empirically derived behavioral correlates for MMPI-2 code types and the combined scale indexes that were statistically related to a broad range of external behavior. In the next chapter, I shift gears dramatically and examine MMPI-2 test responses as direct communications between the patient and the clinician—an approach to test interpretation that was not a part of the original MMPI developmental strategy. However, as seen later, this approach to test interpretation has a great deal to contribute to the task of understanding the client's problem situation and personality.

The Content Scales: An Assessment of Client Content Themes

When mental health patients are asked to complete an MMPI-2 as part of their initial psychological assessment, most of them willingly take the test as a means of sharing their personal problems and concerns with the practitioner who they hope will help them with their problems. Most clients are motivated to describe their problems in ways that will provide the clinician with accurate and appropriate information. Their responses to test items are then viewed as direct communications between the patient and clinician and can be treated as open self-disclosures. This approach to MMPI-2 items requires that the practitioner "listen" to the problems as they are "described" by the patient.

You can see that content interpretation is based on different assumptions than traditional empirical interpretation of MMPI scale elevations and code-type analyses. You already saw in chapter 3 how the content of an individual's responses can refine the interpretation of the MMPI-2 clinical scales by arranging correlates in a meaningful order. In this chapter, I describe the value of content interpretation and the more formal scales for summarizing the client's content themes in a sound psychometric way.

The primary hypothesis underlying content interpretation is that the participant wishes to reveal his or her ideas, attitudes, beliefs, and problems and to cooperate with the clinician through the testing, so that his or her problems can be understood. Most people who take the MMPI in clinical settings do provide accurate personality information. They want to assist the clinician in understanding their problem situation. Of course, people taking the MMPI under extraneous pressure, such as by court order or employment selection situations, may not cooperate fully with the evaluation. In these cases, the content scales are likely to be low in terms of elevation (with most T scores below 50) because the person wishes to present a benign and problem-free persona.

There are several ways in which the content of client responses is used in interpretation. You have already encountered one way, the Harris–Lingoes subscales. Next, I look at two additional ways in this chapter: the MMPI-2 content scales and "critical item responses."

The MMPI-2 Content Scales

Jerry Wiggins pioneered MMPI interpretation using content themes as the primary source of information during the 1960s. Wiggins held the view that the content of a client's item responses could provide important clues to his or her personality if the psychologist had a means of accurately measuring his or her "themes." Wiggins (1966, 1969), using the original MMPI items, developed a number of content clusters or content scales and showed that these measures have strong psychometric properties, for example, high scale reliability in assessing important problem areas. The Wiggins content scales have become widely used as a valid and useful "alternative" way of approaching patient problems. However, with the revision of the MMPI item pool, which included dropping some out-of-date items and incorporating a number of new items into the inventory, it was considered necessary to develop new MMPI-2 content scales that represented the full MMPI-2 item pool (Butcher, Graham, Williams, & Ben-Porath, 1990). The MMPI-2 content scales were constructed following the procedures outlined in Exhibit 5.1. In the section that follows, I describe these scales.

The Anxiety Content Scale (ANX)

This scale is comprised of items that center on feelings of tension and anxiety. High scorers on this general anxiety scale ($T > 65$) acknowledge that they experience symptoms of anxiety, including tension, somatic problems (i.e., heart pounding and a shortness of breath), sleep difficulties, worries, and poor concentration. High-scoring patients report a fear of losing their mind and having difficulties making decisions. They acknowledge that life is very difficult for them, and they find life a

---

Exhibit 5.1

MMPI-2 Content Scale Development: An Approach Based on Acknowledging Problem Themes

- Items were initially selected for each scale on the basis of their rationally judged relationship to a clinical construct (e.g., low self-esteem).
- Each scale is statistically refined using a coefficient α to ensure scale homogeneity.
- Item clusters or content scales also are required to possess scale validity for detecting the problem behaviors they are thought to possess.
- In the MMPI-2 revision, the scales were normed on a nationally representative sample of normal individuals (1,138 men and 1,462 women).
- Scales are interpreted as measures of the extent to which the client has endorsed the characteristics and problems summarized by the content scale.
- Scales are also interpreted on the basis of their empirical relationships or personality correlates.
- A high score on a particular scale indicates the likelihood that the individual possesses the characteristics known to be associated with that scale.

---

strain. They seem to have insight into their problems; they are aware of the symptoms and problems they are experiencing and are willing to discuss them with others.

The Fears Scale (*FRS*)

This scale contains items that focus on specific fears. A high score on *FRS* is obtained when the patient acknowledges many specific fears. These specific fears can include such diverse themes as blood, high places, money, snakes, mice, spiders, leaving home, fire, storms and natural disasters, water, the dark, being indoors, and dirt. A high score reflects an unrealistic number of fears or phobias.

The Obsessiveness Scale (*OBS*)

This scale contains items that deal with indecisiveness and a preoccupation with obsessive thoughts. Patients who score high on the *OBS* have great difficulty making decisions. They are likely to ruminate excessively about unimportant things. They also are impatient with others. They have difficulty making changes in their behavior. They also acknowledge having some compulsive behaviors, such as counting or saving unimportant things. They tend to worry excessively to the point of feeling overwhelmed by their own thoughts.

The Depression Scale (*DEP*)

This scale is comprised of item content reflecting depressed mood and suicidal ideation. Patients who score high on *DEP* are characterized by significant depressive thoughts, hopelessness, and suicidal thinking. They report feeling uncertain about their future and are uninterested in their lives. They are likely to brood, be unhappy, cry easily, and feel hopeless and empty. Very high scorers acknowledge suicide or wish that they were dead. They acknowledge that they feel as though they are condemned or may have committed unpardonable sins. They tend to feel that other people do not provide them with enough emotional support.

The Health Concerns Scale (*HEA*)

The *HEA* contains items that deal with somatic complaints and health concerns. Individuals with high scores on the *HEA* scale acknowledge many physical symptoms concerning several bodily systems, including gastro-intestinal symptoms (e.g., constipation, nausea and vomiting, stomach trouble), neurological problems (e.g., convulsions, dizziness and fainting spells, paralysis), sensory problems (e.g., poor hearing or eyesight), cardiovascular symptoms (e.g., heart or chest pains), skin problems, pain (e.g., headaches, neck pains), and respiratory troubles (e.g., coughs, hay fever or asthma). Patients who score high on *HEA* worry about their health and indicate that they feel sick a lot.

The Bizarre Mentation Scale (*BIZ*)

The item content on this scale involves extreme psychotic symptoms. All of the items are symptoms of severe mental disorder. Psychotic thinking characterizes people who score high on this scale. These items suggest auditory, visual, or olfactory hallucinations. People who score high on this scale appear to be aware that their thoughts are strange and peculiar. Paranoid ideation (e.g., the belief that they are being plotted against or that someone is trying to poison them) is reported. People who score high on this set of items appear to feel that they have a special mission or power in life.

The Anger Scale (*ANG*)

This scale contains items that reflect anger control problems. They center on loss of emotional control and hotheadedness. People who score high on this scale acknowledge anger control problems. They report being irritable, grouchy, impatient, hotheaded, annoyed, and stubborn; they acknowledge that they sometimes feel like swearing or smashing things. They tend to lose self-control and report personal incidences of physical abuse toward other people and objects.

The Cynicism Scale (CYN)

The items on the *CYN* scale involve cynical beliefs and attitudes toward other people. People who score high on this scale endorse misanthropic beliefs about other people. They seem to expect that other people have hidden, negative motives behind what they do (e.g., they believe that most people are honest simply through fear of being caught). They think other people should not be trusted. They hold the view that other people use each other and are only friendly for selfish reasons. High scorers hold negative attitudes about people who are close to them, including fellow workers, family, and friends.

The Antisocial Practices Scale (ASP)

The items on this scale are blatant antisocial attitudes and behaviors. High scorers on this scale hold similar misanthropic attitudes as high scorers on *CYN*, but, in addition, they acknowledge problem behaviors during their school years and other antisocial practices, such as being in trouble with the law, stealing, or shoplifting. High scorers indicate that they sometimes enjoy the antics of criminals and like to see "clever crooks" get away with crimes. They tend to believe that it is appropriate to get around the law as long as it is not broken.

The Type A Scale (TPA)

This scale is comprised of items to assess the pattern of behavior that includes hostility, driven behavior, and compulsive schedule orientation. People who score high on this scale tend to be hard-driving, fast-moving, and work-oriented individuals, who frequently become impatient, irritable, and annoyed. It bothers them to have to wait or be interrupted at a task. There is never enough time in a day for them to complete the tasks they have planned. They tend to be very direct in interpersonal situations and are likely to be overbearing in their relationships with others.

The Low Self-Esteem Scale (*LSE*)

This scale is made up of items that reflect negative self-views and strong feelings of inadequacy. People who score high on *LSE* present themselves as having low opinions of themselves. They are not well liked by others and feel unimportant. They hold many negative attitudes about themselves, including perceptions that they are unattractive, awkward, clumsy, and useless. They often feel as though they are a burden to others and lack self-confidence. They find it hard to accept compliments from others and, at times, feel overwhelmed by all the faults they see in themselves.

The Social Discomfort Scale (*SOD*)

This scale was designed to assess personality characteristics related to the experience of social discomfort and distress. People who score high on this scale are very uneasy around others. They prefer to be by themselves; when they are in social situations, they are likely to sit alone and avoid joining in a group. They tend to see themselves as shy and dislike parties and social events.

The Family Problems Scale (*FAM*)

The items on this scale focus on family and relationship problems. Those who score high on this scale report substantial family discord. Their families are described as lacking in love, quarrelsome, and unpleasant to be around. Some items on this scale reflect hatred for other family members. High scorers on *FAM* tend to portray their childhood as having been abusive and their marriages as being unhappy and lacking in affection.

The Work Interference Scale (*WRK*)

The items on this scale focus on negative attitudes toward being able to work effectively. Those scoring high on the *WRK* endorse behaviors or attitudes that are likely to contribute to poor work performance. Some of the problems relate to low self-confidence, concentration difficulties, obsessiveness, tension and pressure, and decision-making problems. Others suggest lack of family support for their career choice, personal questioning of their career choice, and negative attitudes toward coworkers.

The Negative Treatment Indicators Scale (*TRT*)

The items on the *TRT* are focused on negative views toward being able to change one's behavior and attitudes toward mental health treatment. Persons who score high on *TRT* have negative attitudes toward doctors and mental health treatment. They tend to believe that no one can understand their problems or help them; they have problems that they are not comfortable discussing with anyone. They may not want to change anything in their lives, nor do they feel that change is even possible. They acknowledge that they would rather give up than face a crisis or difficulty.

Two cases illustrating the use of the MMPI-2 content scales are provided below. See the content scale profiles illustrated in Figures 5.1 and 5.2.

The Case of Alleged Child Abuse

Description

Robert C., age 51, a seasonal construction worker, was charged with having physically abused his 13-year-old son. In addition, he had been arrested on two occasions for violence against his wife and his sister-in-law. The incidents of abuse were alleged to have occurred when his estranged wife (separated for 2 years) refused to reconcile. The MMPI-2 was administered as part of a court-ordered evaluation.

Comment

The MMPI-2 profile that Robert provided was valid and interpretable (see Figure 5.1). His clinical code type (4-9/9-4) elevated above $T = 64$ suggests the probability of a severe personality disorder. (His profile code was $4''\underline{97}'5+8\underline{-263}/1{:}0\#FK/L{:}$.) Robert's performance on the MMPI-2 content scales shows a pattern of negative and cynical attitudes toward others. He endorsed a number of family relationship problems. His most prominent content theme centers on anger control problems, indicating that he acknowledged problems involving a loss of control when he was angry. He also acknowledged being anxious, perhaps related to his current legal circumstances.

The Case of an Angry Police Officer

Description

Mr. T., age 38, was employed as a police officer for a small town police force. Although he was thought of as an outstanding officer, he was

Figure 5.1

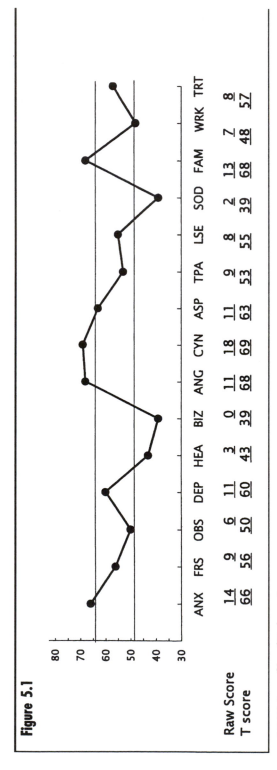

	ANX	FRS	OBS	DEP	HEA	BIZ	ANG	CYN	ASP	TPA	LSE	SOD	FAM	WRK	TRT
Raw Score	14	9	6	11	3	0	11	18	11	9	8	2	13	7	8
T score	66	56	50	60	43	39	68	69	63	53	55	39	68	48	57

MMPI-2 profile of Robert C.

Figure 5.2

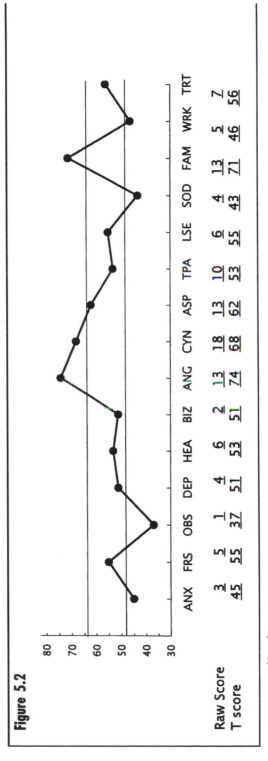

	ANX	FRS	OBS	DEP	HEA	BIZ	ANG	CYN	ASP	TPA	LSE	SOD	FAM	WRK	TRT
Raw Score	3	5	1	4	6	2	13	18	13	10	6	4	13	5	7
T score	45	55	37	51	53	51	74	68	62	53	55	43	71	46	56

MMPI-2 profile of Mr. T.

removed from duty and required to seek psychological attention for his anger control problems, following an incident in which he lost his temper and got into an argument with another officer in a public facility. He was placed on suspension from the force, contingent on his receiving treatment for his anger problems. The current testing was conducted in the context of a "fitness for duty" assessment after Mr. T. had completed 10 sessions of anger management therapy.

Mr. T. had a history of aggressive behavior that was thought to be relevant to his current problems. He had been divorced by his wife of 2 years about 5 years earlier because he had physically abused her following an argument. Reportedly, his current live-in partner had left the home on two occasions following arguments with Mr. T. His aggressive behavior could be found in other earlier situations as well. A few years earlier, he shot his dog in a "fit of temper" because the dog seemingly refused to be housebroken.

Comment

Mr. T.'s MMPI-2 validity configuration suggests that he was somewhat defensive on the testing (as sometimes occurs among individuals assessed in an employment-related evaluation); however, his clinical profile is within an interpretable range. His high elevation on the clinical scale *Pd* (profile code: 4+653918/72:0#*K*+*L*/*F*:) suggests that he was likely to be an immature, rebellious, and impulsive individual, who had difficulty with interpersonal relationships. He tended to be somewhat of a high risk taker and acted at times without concern over the consequences. Mr. T.'s performance on the MMPI-2 content scales is shown in Figure 5.2. Although he attempted to show a pattern of good adjustment, as reflected in the high *K* score, he did show some symptoms of problems in the area of anger control (*ANG*), cynical attitudes (*CYN*), and family problems (*FAM*).

A Cautionary Note About Content-Based Measures

Test defensiveness is the primary limiting consideration in content interpretation. Because content measures have face validity (i.e., they are comprised of fairly obvious items), they are vulnerable to conscious distortion. People taking the test can choose not to endorse items that they do not wish the psychologist–evaluator to know about. Clients can attempt to create a particular impression in the testing by endorsing or not endorsing certain problem areas. Test defensiveness, therefore, tends to lower the elevation of content scales. The higher the *K* elevation, the more likely the person has failed to endorse problem areas on the MMPI-2 content scales. In most clinical situations, however, test defensiveness does not serve to reduce the problem presentation of the client. In clinical settings, most patients are cooperative with the assessment and tend to present honestly, so that their problem situations can be understood by the psychologist. In cases of defensive records, however, it is not uncommon to find the content scale profiles attenuated ($T < 50$).

Critical Item Analysis

Thus far in this volume, I examined two approaches to using item content in profile interpretation. In chapter 3, I used item content through the Harris–Lingoes subscales to aid in determining how to interpret elevations on the MMPI-2 clinical scales. Earlier in this chapter, the MMPI-2 content scales were described and illustrated. There is one additional set of content-based indicators that clinicians can use to provide clues as to the client's behavior and problems. This approach involves the use of the client's responses to specific items as cues to the client's important problem areas.

The first efforts to incorporate individual item data into MMPI interpretation involved the "critical item" set developed by Grayson (1951). These items were derived through rational item selection procedures; that is, the psychologists who developed this item list simply read through the items and selected those that were believed to reflect important problem areas. No efforts were undertaken to validate externally the Grayson critical items. Two empirically based item sets were published in the 1970s by Koss and Butcher (1973) and by Lachar and Wrobel (1979). See Exhibit 5.2 for a listing of the Koss–Butcher and Lachar–Wrobel empirically based critical item sets. These items were found to assess the problem behaviors validly of patients in mental health crises.

Koss–Butcher and Lachar–Wrobel Critical Items

How are critical items used in test interpretation? Critical items are used to gain an impression of possible problems that the patient is experiencing. The clinician does not use these items as predictors but simply as starting points in the clinical interview to follow up, as illustrated in the case discussed below.

Exhibit 5.2

Koss–Butcher Critical Items Revised

Acute Anxiety State

2. I have a good appetite. (F)
3. I wake up fresh and rested most mornings. (F)
5. I am easily awakened by noise. (T)
10. I am about as able to work as I ever was. (F)
15. I work under a great deal of tension. (T)
28. I am bothered by an upset stomach several times a week. (T)
39. My sleep is fitful and disturbed. (T)
59. I am troubled by discomfort in the pit of my stomach every few days or oftener. (T)
140. Most nights I go to sleep without thoughts or ideas bothering me. (F)
172. I frequently notice my hand shakes when I try to do something. (T)
208. I hardly ever notice my heart pounding and I am seldom short of breath. (F)
218. I have periods of such great restlessness that I cannot sit long in a chair. (T)
223. I believe I am no more nervous than most others. (F)
301. I feel anxiety about something or someone almost all the time. (T)
444. I am a high-strung person. (T)
463. Several times a week I feel as if something dreadful is about to happen. (T)
469. I sometimes feel that I am about to go to pieces. (T)

Depressed Suicidal Ideation

9. My daily life is full of things that keep me interested. (F)
38. I have had periods of days, weeks, or months when I couldn't take care of things because I couldn't "get going." (T)
65. Most of the time I feel blue. (T)
71. These days I find it hard not to give up hope of amounting to something. (T)
75. I usually feel that life is worthwhile. (F)
92. I don't seem to care what happens to me. (T)
95. I am happy most of the time. (F)
130. I certainly feel useless at times. (T)
146. I cry easily. (T)
215. I brood a great deal. (T)
233. I have difficulty in starting to do things. (T)
273. Life is a strain for me much of the time. (T)
303. Most of the time I wish I were dead. (T)
306. No one cares much what happens to you. (T)

continued

Exhibit 5.2, continued

Depressed Suicidal Ideation (continued)

388. I very seldom have spells of the blues. (F)
411. At times I think I am no good at all. (T)
454. The future seems hopeless to me. (T)
485. I often feel that I'm not as good as other people. (T)
506. I have recently considered killing myself. (T)
518. I have made lots of bad mistakes in my life. (T)
520. Lately I have thought a lot about killing myself. (T)
524. No one knows it but I have tried to kill myself. (T)

Threatened Assault

 37. At times I feel like smashing things. (T)
 85. At times I have a strong urge to do something harmful or shocking. (T)
134. At times I feel like picking a fist fight with someone. (T)
213. I get mad easily and then get over it soon. (T)
389. I am often said to be hotheaded. (T)

Situational Stress Due to Alcoholism

125. I believe that my home life is as pleasant as that of most people I know. (F)
264. I have used alcohol excessively. (T)
487. I have enjoyed using marijuana. (T)
489. I have a drug or alcohol problem. (T)
502. I have some habits that are really harmful. (T)

Mental Confusion

 24. Evil spirits possess me at times. (T)
 31. I find it hard to keep my mind on a task or a job. (T)
 32. I have had very peculiar and strange experiences. (T)
 72. My soul sometimes leaves my body. (T)
 96. I see things or animals or people around me that others do not see. (T)
180. There is something wrong with my mind. (T)
198. I often hear voices without knowing where they come from. (T)
299. I cannot keep my mind on one thing. (T)
311. I often feel as if things are not real. (T)
316. I have strange and peculiar thoughts. (T)
325. I have more trouble concentrating than others seem to have. (T)

continued

Exhibit 5.2, continued

Persecutory Ideas

17. I am sure I get a raw deal from life. (T)
42. If people had not had it in for me, I would have been much more successful. (T)
99. Someone has it in for me. (T)
124. I often wonder what hidden reason another person may have for doing something nice for me. (T)
138. I believe I am being plotted against. (T)
144. I believe I am being followed. (T)
145. I feel that I have often been punished without cause. (T)
162. Someone has been trying to poison me. (T)
228. There are persons who are trying to steal my thoughts and ideas. (T)
241. It is safer to trust nobody. (T)
251. I have often felt that strangers were looking at me critically. (T)
259. I am sure I am being talked about. (T)
314. I have no enemies who really wish to harm me. (F)
333. People say insulting and vulgar things about me. (T)
361. Someone has been trying to influence my mind.

Note. From Koss and Butcher (1973). T = true; F = false.

A Case of Social Isolation

Description

Elizabeth D., a 48-year-old widow, was referred for a psychological evaluation by her physician, who was concerned about her apparent low mood and social isolation. Elizabeth had gone to see her doctor to request a prescription for sleeping medication. She reportedly had had severe bouts of insomnia for several months. She found it difficult to fall asleep and usually awoke at 2:00 or 3:00 a.m. and could not fall back to sleep. Elizabeth had lived alone since her husband died about 10 years earlier. A trucking firm presently employed her as a traffic clerk. Her job involved handling paperwork and tracking shipments. She had little social contact with people on the job and had no family or close friends outside of work with whom she spent time. She also spent most of her evenings alone watching television. Elizabeth's physician requested a psychological evaluation to assess her current mood and to determine if a psychological treatment referral would be appropriate.

Comment

Elizabeth's test performance resulted in valid and interpretable MMPI-2 profiles (see Figures 5.3 and 5.4). She was open and honest in her self-presentation. Her clinical scale elevation shows her to be extremely isolated and socially introverted. She also appeared moderately depressed on Scale 2 of the MMPI-2. Her performance on the Depression Content Scale (*DEP*) is more prominent, in part, resulting from the scale's greater focus on subjective depression and suicidal ideation. Her response to several critical items are important to consider in further clinical interviews. She appeared to have strong feelings of hopelessness and suicidal thoughts that require further assessment and that provided an important focus for psychological intervention. She endorsed most of the critical item content in the Koss–Butcher critical item list of "Depressed–Suicidal" (see Exhibits 5.3 and 5.4).

Limitations to the Critical Item Analysis Approach

One should exercise caution when using critical items in interpretation. Single-item responses cannot be relied on as scale data can to predict or describe behavior. Clients may mismark questions or answer *true* when they meant to respond *false*. Critical items are only used to provide "clinical hypotheses," which can be followed up in further evaluations and interviews. They should not be used as predictor variables because of their limited reliability.

Summary

This chapter was devoted to a type of test interpretation—content analysis—that is very different from traditional ways of analyzing MMPI profiles by empirical scales. Content interpretation assumes that in responding to test items, a client was capable of providing symptomatic and behavioral information about himself or herself and was motivated to share this information in the test situation. Two approaches to content interpretation were discussed in this chapter: (a) A set of 15 MMPI-2 content scales was developed to summarize important personality dimensions or symptom themes in the MMPI-2 item pool. The MMPI-2 content scales tell how people view their problems. Yet the content

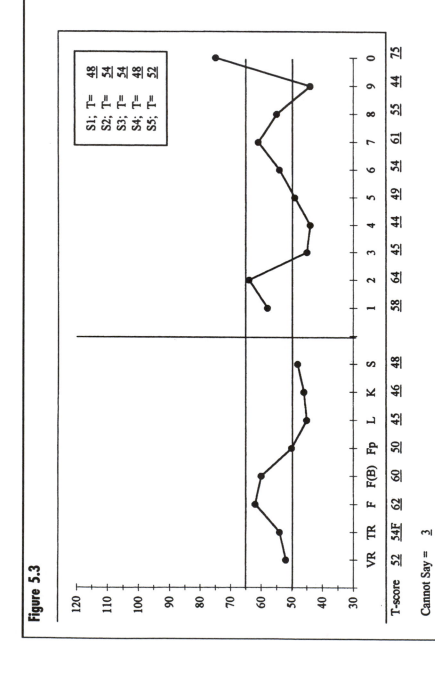

Figure 5.3

	VR	TR	F	F(B)	Fp	L	K	S	1	2	3	4	5	6	7	8	9	0
T-score	52	54F	62	60	50	45	46	48	58	64	45	44	49	54	61	55	44	75

S1; T= 48
S2; T= 54
S3; T= 54
S4; T= 48
S5; T= 52

Cannot Say = 3

MMPI-2 basic scales profile of Elizabeth D.

Figure 5.4

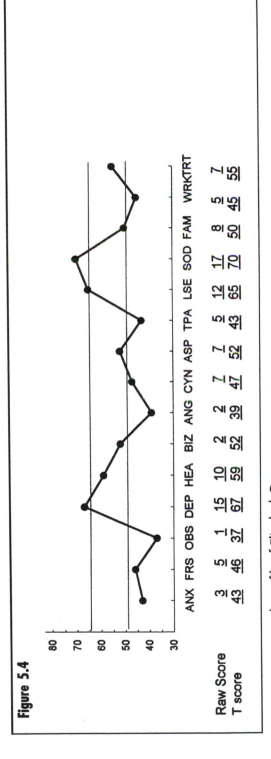

	ANX	FRS	OBS	DEP	HEA	BIZ	ANG	CYN	ASP	TPA	LSE	SOD	FAM	WRKTRT
Raw Score	3	5	1	15	10	2	2	7	7	5	12	17	8	5	7
T score	43	46	37	67	59	52	39	47	52	43	65	70	50	45	55

MMPI-2 content scale profile of Elizabeth D.

Exhibit 5.3

Lachar–Wrobel Critical Items Endorsed by Elizabeth D.

Characterological Adjustment (Antisocial Attitude)

27. When people do me a wrong, I feel I should pay them back if I can, just for the principle of the thing. (T)
35. Sometimes when I was young I stole things. (T)
84. I was suspended from school one or more times for bad behavior. (T)
105. In school I was sometimes sent to the principal for bad behavior. (T)
227. I don't blame people for trying to grab everything they can get in this world. (T)
240. At times it has been impossible for me to keep from stealing or shoplifting something. (T)
254. Most people make friends because friends are likely to be useful to them. (T)
266. I have never been in trouble with the law. (F)
324. I can easily make other people afraid of me, and sometimes do for the fun of it. (T)

Characterological Adjustment (Family Conflict)

21. At times I have very much wanted to leave home. (T)
83. I have very few quarrels with members of my family. (F)
125. I believe that my home life is as pleasant as that of most people I know. (F)
288. My parents and family find more fault with me than they should. (T)

Somatic Symptoms

18. I am troubled by attacks of nausea and vomiting. (T)
28. I am bothered by an upset stomach several times a week. (T)
33. I seldom worry about my health. (F)
40. Much of the time my head seems to hurt all over. (T)
44. Once a week or oftener I feel suddenly hot all over for no real reason. (T)
47. I am almost never bothered by pains over the heart or in my chest. (F)
53. Parts of my body often have feelings like burning, tingling, crawling, or "going to sleep." (T)
57. I hardly ever feel pain in the back of my neck. (F)
59. I am troubled by discomfort in the pit of my stomach every few days or oftener. (T)
101. Often I feel as if there is a tight band around my head. (T)
111. I have a great deal of stomach trouble. (T)
142. I have never had a fit or convulsion. (F)
159. I have never had a fainting spell. (F)
164. I seldom or never have dizzy spells. (F)

continued

Exhibit 5.3, continued

Somatic Symptoms (continued)

175. I feel weak all over much of the time. (T)
176. I have very few headaches. (F)
182. I have had attacks in which I could not control my movements or speech but in which I knew what was going on around me. (T)
224. I have few or no pains. (F)
229. I have had blank spells in which my activities were interrupted and I did not know what was going on around me. (T)
247. I have numbness in one or more places on my skin. (T)
255. I do not often notice my ears ringing or buzzing. (F)
295. I have never been paralyzed or had any unusual weakness of any of my muscles. (F)
464. I feel tired a good deal of the time. (T)

Sexual Concern and Deviation

12. My sex life is satisfactory. (F)
34. I have never been in trouble because of my sex behavior. (F)
62. I have often wished I were a girl. (Or if you are a girl) I have never been sorry that I am a girl. (T for males, F for females)
121. I have never indulged in any unusual sex practices. (F)
166. I am worried about sex. (F)
268. I wish I were not bothered by thoughts about sex. (T)

Note. From Lachar and Wrobel (1979). T = true; F = false.

scales have strong psychometric properties (reliability and validity) and predict behavior, as do the clinical scales. (b) A second approach to analyzing a client's item response content—the use of MMPI-2 critical items—was discussed and illustrated. Interpretation strategies for incorporating item content into the clinical evaluation were discussed, and the limitations of content interpretation in assessment were noted.

Exhibit 5.4

A Listing of Critical Item Content Endorsed by Elizabeth D.

9. My daily life is full of things that keep me interested. (F)
38. I have had periods of days, weeks, or months when I couldn't take care of things because I couldn't "get going." (T)
65. Most of the time I feel blue. (T)

continued

Exhibit 5.4, continued

A Listing of Critical Item Content Endorsed by Elizabeth D. (continued)

75. I usually feel that life is worthwhile. (F)
95. I am happy most of the time. (F)
130. I certainly feel useless at times. (T)
146. I cry easily. (T)
215. I brood a great deal. (T)
233. I have difficulty in starting to do things. (T)
273. Life is a strain for me much of the time. (T)
303. Most of the time I wish I were dead. (T)
306. No one cares much what happens to you. (T)
388. I very seldom have spells of the blues. (F)
411. At times I think I am no good at all. (T)
454. The future seems hopeless to me. (T)
485. I often feel that I'm not as good as other people. (T)
506. I have recently considered killing myself. (T)
520. Lately I have thought a lot about killing myself. (T)
524. No one knows it but I have tried to kill myself. (T)

Note. The above responses are predicted for a profile of Depressed Suicidal. T = true; F = false.

The MMPI-2 Supplemental Scales: An Appraisal of Special Problems

So far, I covered a lot of scales—the clinical, validity, and content scales. What is left? Several specific problem areas are not addressed by the aforementioned scales that have become the focus of researchers and practitioners. The additional scales developed for the MMPI-2 are referred to as *special problem* or *supplemental scales*. The MMPI-2 item pool covers a broad range of problems and symptomatic behaviors and, therefore, lends itself well to assessing a great number of clinical problems that were not the focus of the original scale development. Consequently, a number of specific scales have been developed for special purposes.

In this chapter, I look at six scales that have become widely used in clinical assessment: The three scales used to assess drug and alcohol problems are the MacAndrew Alcoholism Scale–Revised (*MAC-R*), the Addiction Proneness Scale (*APS*), and the Addiction Acknowledgment Scale (*AAS*). The Marital Distress Scale (*MDS*) is used for assessing relationship problems, the Post-Traumatic Stress Disorder Scale–Keane (*PTSD-Pk*) is used for assessing posttraumatic symptoms, and the Cook–Medley Hostility Scale (*Ho*) is widely used in health care settings to assess a pattern of behavior, namely, hostility, that is found to have interesting associations with coronary disease.

The Assessment of Alcohol and Drug Abuse Problems: The MacAndrew Alcoholism Scale

The most widely researched and one of the most effective personality scales devised to assess substance abuse potential is the *MAC* on the original MMPI. It was developed with a sample of alcoholic veterans to assess alcohol abuse problems (MacAndrew, 1965). Items on the scale were selected *empirically*—items that statistically differentiated patients with alcohol abuse problems from general psychiatric patients who were presenting with non-alcohol-related problems. The initial *MAC* contained 51 items. However, MacAndrew dropped two items from the scale because they contained specific alcohol-related content: "I have used alcohol excessively" and "I have used alcohol moderately or not at all"; he wanted to base the scale on items that were not obviously related to alcohol use. He believed that many alcoholic people do not admit to abusing alcohol and that the presence of these items in the scale would weaken the scale's validity. Past research supports the use of the *MAC* score for detecting potential substance abuse problems. High scores are associated with addiction problems, such as drug abuse and pathological gambling (Graham & Strenger, 1988). The scale is not specific to the abuse of a particular substance, however, and *base rates* (the percentage of cases in a particular population) need to be considered for interpreting the scale (Gottesman & Prescott, 1989).

Although the *MAC* was developed on a sample of male veterans, researchers testing substance abusing women found that the scale works as well with women as with men, except that a slightly different cut-off score is recommended. In general, women tend to obtain scores that are roughly 2 points lower than men. Thus, a lower raw score for women tends to be associated with substance abuse problems. The interpretation of the *MAC-R* on the MMPI-2 is based on T score cut-off points rather than raw scores, as in the original MMPI. The MMPI-2 Restandardization Committee viewed the *MAC* as an effective clinical assessment instrument and incorporated a revised version of it into the MMPI-2. The primary change in the *MAC* score during the revision involved dropping four items from the original scale because their content was considered objectionable. The MMPI-2 committee replaced these deleted items with four new items on the *MAC-R* that discriminated a group of alcoholic people from a group of psychiatric patients in a manner similar to MacAndrew's (1965) original sample.

High scores ($T > 65$) on the *MAC-R* are interpreted as indicative of a potential for developing a substance abuse problem. In some situations, particularly when the base rates for substance abuse are high, $T = 60$ might be interpreted as being suggestive of a substance abuse problem. The lower cut-off point might be more appropriate in some situations (e.g., $T \geq 60$) if the psychologist is interested in detecting possible substance abusing people at the expense of making some classification errors by misclassifying those without a substance abuse problem. Low scores on the *MAC-R* are usually not interpreted because many reasons can be found for low scores (e.g., omitted items, denial of problems, actually free of substance abuse problems). Some evidence suggests that high scores on *MAC-R* are associated with personality disorder—a situation also generally found among alcoholic and drug-abusing clients.

In the MMPI revision, the item pool was expanded to include a number of potentially useful new items to assess substance use and abuse problems. This enabled the development of two new approaches to assess substance abuse problems, (a) an empirically derived substance abuse potential scale, the Addiction Potential Scale, and (b) a scale designed to assess denial of substance abuse or the admission of alcohol and drug abuse problems, the Addiction Acknowledgments Scale.

Addiction Potential Scale

With a broader range of substance abuse items available in the MMPI-2 item pool, the scale developers were interested in developing an empirical scale to try to improve the detection of substance abuse problems (Weed, Butcher, McKenna, & Ben-Porath, 1992). The *APS* was designed as a measure of the personality factors underlying the development of addictive disorders. As with the *MAC-R*, items that differentiated alcoholic and drug abusing people from psychiatric patients and normals were selected for the *APS*. In the development of the *APS*, larger samples of substance abusing people, psychiatric patients, and normals were tested in a cross-validated design. The *APS* contains a total of 39 items, and only 9 of the items on the scale overlap with the *MAC-R*. A high score on the *APS* is associated with the likely membership in samples of substance abusing patients. Elevations are interpreted as reflecting a great potential for developing substance abuse problems. Low scores on *APS* are not interpreted because no data exist that support the meaning of low scores.

Addiction Acknowledgment Scale

Previous alcohol and drug abuse scales attempted to assess the potential for developing substance abuse problems rather than whether such problems are actually acknowledged by the patient. Weed et al. (1992) took a somewhat different approach in an effort to develop a scale that addressed a patient's willingness—that is, his or her unwillingness—to acknowledge problems of abuse. The *AAS* research was initiated with the hopes of developing a substance abuse problem denial scale.

The *AAS* was developed as a means of assessing a client's willingness to acknowledge problems with alcohol or drugs by providing a psychometric comparison of the client's actual admission of alcohol or drug problems. This 13-item scale was developed by using a combined rational–statistical scale development strategy. Items were initially selected because they contained clear substance abuse problems on the basis of judged content. These 13 items were then item correlated with the remaining MMPI-2 items to determine if additional items were significantly associated with the initial pool. The item set was refined further by examining the α coefficients, keeping only those items that increased the scale's homogeneity.

Interpretation of the *AAS* is relatively straightforward. A high score ($T \geq 60$) indicates that the client has acknowledged a large number of alcohol or drug use problems compared with the normative sample. The higher the score, the more problems the individual endorsed. What does a low score on *AAS* mean? It does not mean, of course, that the individual does not have a substance abuse problem, only that the individual has not admitted to having or has denied having problems. The patient could have very substantial problems but is in denial and not open to acknowledging his or her problems.

In the case examples reported below, all three substance abuse detection scales, the *MAC-R, APS,* and *AAS,* are illustrated together because their conjoint use provides different types of information about a client. The scales measuring potential for developing addictive disorders provide information regarding the individual's lifestyle, and the *AAS* scale provides a clear assessment of whether the client is aware of and willing to acknowledge these problems in the evaluation.

A Case of Substance Abuse Denial

Description

Charles D., a 48-year-old hotel catering manager, was evaluated in the context of a treatment referral. He was pressured into seeking alcohol treatment by his wife, who threatened to leave him if he did not follow through. He agreed to the evaluation; however, he adamantly insisted that he did not have a problem with alcohol, claiming that he only

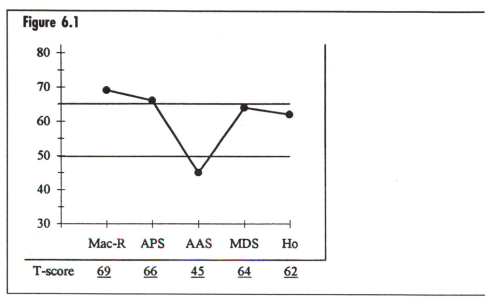

MMPI-2 supplementary scales profile of Charles D.

drank socially and to be friendly with his customers as required by his job.

Comment

Charles's approach to the MMPI-2 suggests that he was likely experiencing a substance use or abuse disorder on the basis of his performance on the *MAC-R* and *APS* (*MAC-R T* = 69; *APS T* = 66; *AAS T* = 45; see Figure 6.1). He responded to both of these scales in a manner similar to an alcoholic person in a substance abuse treatment program. However, his relatively low score on *AAS* indicates that he denied having such problems. His low acknowledgment of substance abuse problems reflected a low potential for success in a treatment program.

A Case Of Substance-Related Homicide

Description

Truman C., age 29, was arrested and charged with murdering a prostitute. He and a friend had been binge drinking and smoking marijuana for 2 days. During this episode, they picked up a streetwalker and took her to a "hideout" that they frequented, underneath a bridge near the downtown area. According to Truman's friend, who was also arrested for the crime, Truman clubbed the prostitute to death after having a

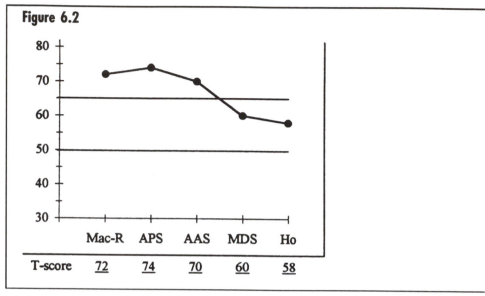

Figure 6.2

MMPI-2 supplementary scales profile of Truman C.

disagreement with her over money. Truman claimed that he had no memory of the incident.

Comment

The pattern of scores suggests that the defendant endorsed the MMPI-2 items in such a way as to indicate that he has had many of the lifestyle characteristics (*MAC-R* and *APS*) associated with those who develop substance abuse problems (*MAC-R* $T = 72$; *APS* $T = 74$; *AAS* $T = 70$; see Figure 6.2). Moreover, his high score on the *AAS* also indicates that he acknowledged his problems with drugs and alcohol, without attempting to cover up or deny such problems.

The Assessment of Marital Distress

Traditionally, the assessment of marital relationship problems using the original MMPI centered on examining the personality profiles of husbands and wives using the traditional clinical scales. Most of the early studies of marital distress found that the *Pd* scale was the most frequently elevated scale among individuals experiencing marital problems (Hjemboe & Butcher, 1991). Of course, scale elevations on the *Pd* are associated with many things, more than just marital problems. Research on couples in marital distress using the MMPI-2 also found *Pd* to be the most prominent scale elevation but one of the new content scales, Family Problems (*FAM*), was also found to be significantly related to marital distress. These scales were not actually developed to assess marital distress directly, and their discriminating power in this situation was the result of their sensitivity to family problems rather than to marital problems (Hjemboe & Butcher, 1991).

Hjemboe, Almagor, and Butcher (1992) developed a special MMPI-2 scale for assessing marital distress. The *MDS*, a 14-item empirically derived scale, was developed by the selection of items that were strongly associated with a measure of marital distress, the Spanier Dyadic Adjustment Scale. This scale contains items with content related to marital problems or relationship difficulties. The *MDS* shows a higher degree of relationship to measured marital distress than either the *Pd* or the *FAM* (Hjemboe et al., 1992).

How is the *MDS* scale used in clinical assessment? In many situations, couples who are having marital problems describe these concerns openly to the clinician in an interview. It is therefore not surprising that they might also have a high *MDS* score. A scale such as the *MDS* can be most helpful when it provides information that the clinician does not know, for example, in a mental health setting in which the primary referral was not for marriage counseling.

The Assessment of Posttraumatic Stress Disorder

The PTSD-*Pk* was developed by Keane, Malloy, and Fairbank (1984) according to an empirical scale construction strategy. In the development of this scale, the authors used a group of 100 male veterans who had been diagnosed with posttraumatic stress disorder (PTSD) in contrast with 100 male veterans having other psychiatric problems. They obtained 49 items that significantly discriminated the PTSD group from the general psychiatric sample. They reported that this scale had an 82% hit rate in the classification of veterans with PTSD. The *Pk* shows a high degree of relationship to other anxiety measures on the MMPI-2 such as the *Pt* and is negatively correlated with the *K*. The *Pk* has been shown to measure psychological distress, although not necessarily acute problems. The scale is also elevated in chronic psychiatric samples.

The Assessment of Hostility

In the 1950s, Cook and Medley (1954) were interested in studying personality characteristics related to a person's ability to relate harmoniously to others, to establish interpersonal rapport, and to maintain morale in a group setting. They developed the *Ho* empirically by contrasting groups of schoolteachers who had been determined to differ with respect to the capability of getting along with their pupils. High *Ho* scorers were judged as difficult to get along with. High scorers were considered hostile and considered their students to be dishonest, insincere, untrustworthy, and lazy.

Subsequent research with the *Ho* expanded its application into an entirely different direction and with a very different population than the developmental sample of schoolteachers. The *Ho* became widely used as a measure of hostility in medical patients with coronary disease (Barefoot, Dahlstrom, & Williams, 1983). It also became a measurement of premorbid personality characteristics considered associated with the development of heart disease. People who have high levels of interpersonal hostility and cynical attitudes tend to have a greater likelihood of developing hypertension than those having nonhostile interpersonal styles.

The *Ho* was retooled somewhat following the publication of the MMPI-2. In the MMPI-2 Restandardization Project, 9 of the 50 items on the scale were slightly reworded to make them more readable and contemporary. Han, Weed, Calhoun, and Butcher (1995) found *Ho* scores highly related to other MMPI-2 scales that measure cynicism and hostility (i.e., *CYN*, *TPA*, and *ASP*). Moreover, they reported that high *Ho* scores were associated with spousal ratings of being hotheaded, bossy, demanding, and argumentative. The interpretation of the *Ho* is relatively straightforward; high scorers on the scale are seen as possessing personality characteristics of cynicism and hostility. Low scores on the *Ho* are not considered meaningful because only high point scores have been validated.

Summary

Several additional or supplemental scales were discussed in this chapter. These scales have been developed as a means of focusing on special problem areas, such as addiction proneness (*MAC-R*, *APS*, and *AAS*).

Other special scales in wide use include *MDS, Ho,* and *Pk.* These scales are valuable in providing specific diagnostic or descriptive information about a client. In the next chapter, I turn my attention to the important tasks of integrating the various kinds of interpretive information available from the MMPI-2 and organizing the inferences and interpretations into integrated, internally consistent themes.

Putting It All Together: How To Interpret a Profile and Organize Test Inferences

Now that you have learned what the different MMPI-2 scales measure and have observed their operation in a number of practical cases, I now turn to a more explicit description of how these diverse measures can operate to provide the practitioner with a picture of the client's symptoms and personality. This chapter is devoted to presenting a general overview of an MMPI-2 interpretation strategy; I suggest a set of specific steps that practitioners might follow in organizing inferences about their client and developing interpretations for MMPI-2 profiles.

Background Considerations

The MMPI-2 scales are somewhat of a "one size fits all" variety of measures, in that the descriptors that define their meaning apply for all adults age 18 and older. However, the interpretations you develop and the reports you generate about clients might vary somewhat, depending on particular situational factors. Several of the most prominent considerations that have been thought to affect or alter the meanings of some scales are summarized in this chapter, and then hypotheses about clients that are based on MMPI-2 measures are described.

In developing test-based hypotheses about your client, you should note any potential influences that you consider relevant to the particular case. You need to approach the task with assurance that the profile to interpret has not been compromised by any of the following circumstances.

Setting Biases

The setting in which the test is administered can influence the profiles obtained. Profile configurations follow common pathways through the external clinical correlates; similar patients, that is, those obtaining a common code type, tend to manifest similar behaviors and symptoms. Research on specific populations shows, for example, that chronic pain patients tend to fall into relatively few types (about four or five similar profiles codes, usually involving different combinations of Scales 1, 2, and 3) that account for the majority of pain patients; and groups of alcoholics tend to be comprised of about four to six profile types (with different combinations of Scales 2, 4, and 7 and sometimes 9). In addition, different settings tend to produce similar scale elevations; for example, family custody cases tend to have relatively high scores on *L* and *K*, and many clients obtain high elevations on the *Pa*. Therefore, with these "situational pulls," it is important for the practitioner to be aware of the types of patients that tend to make up the "case load" for a particular setting. That is, it is important for the practitioner to be aware of the base rates of the population from which the case was obtained and use relative frequencies of profiles from the particular setting in giving weight to particular scale scores. (See the informative article by Finn & Kamphuis, 1995, for a discussion of how to use population base rates in clinical interpretations.)

Response Biases Resulting From the Use of "Nonstandard" Instructions

You may recall from the discussion in chapter 1 that it is very important for the test administrator to follow the standard instructions when administering the test. This becomes critical when you are comparing a client's profile with the MMPI-2 norms because a primary assumption is that the client responded to the items according to the standard instructions. If clients have been "helped" or briefed in developing their strategy for answering the items (e.g., if an attorney has prepped them "not to answer extreme items as *true*") and if the interpreter follows standard interpretive assumptions, then he or she might assess the case incorrectly. However, clients also develop their own response "sets" or strategic approaches to the items, often as a function of the purposes for which the test is given. For example, in a personnel screening, people desiring an attractive job might "define" their situation as needing to respond with a minimal problem presentation. A client seeking social security disability benefits might define the test situation as to appear as sick or disabled as possible on the test. If you ignore these special situational influences, your interpretation may not accurately reflect the individual's personality and symptoms.

Demographic Biases

The five demographic factors that might be suspected to influence psychological test performance and interpretation are age, gender, ethnic, regional, and socioeconomic factors. These factors have been well studied in regards to the MMPI and MMPI-2. As described in chapter 8 of this book, these demographic factors are not generally considered to influence MMPI-2 performance adversely because they have been taken into consideration and "accounted for" in the development of the norms. MMPI-2 scores tend to be robust across cultural groups. These demographic factors have been shown to have relatively little impact on MMPI-2 scores as long as the client is able to read and understand the English language and takes the inventory in a cooperative manner. There might be circumstances in particular cases, however, where these variables might warrant further evaluation to ensure that they have not affected the testing.

Age Differences

As noted earlier, the MMPI-2 norms were developed from samples of men and women who were age 18 and older. There is one general "norm" for men and one for women; scores on MMPI-2 are not age corrected. Some research shows that there might be small (1 or 2 points) differences occurring for some older individuals, but these differences were not considered sufficient to develop statistical corrections for age. The MMPI-2 scales that might be slightly different for some older individuals are *Hs* and *D* with slightly higher scores and *Pd* and *Ma* with lower scores. The MMPI-2 profiles are, however, not interpreted any differently for older clients because these differences are generally within the acceptable limits of the error measurement for the scales.

Socioeconomic and Ethnic Differences

There are no important socioeconomic or ethnic differences on MMPI-2 scores (as noted in chapter 7). However, in testing clients from different ethnic or cultural backgrounds, the practitioner would want to ensure that the particular client's test results were appropriate and that the clients have the requisite reading level to comprehend the questions. (When the client's reading level is marginal, as is the case with some lower socioeconomic people, then it would be better to use the audio form of the test.) A broad range of ethnic and diverse socioeconomic levels was included in the norms, and as seen in chapter 7, the normative samples showed few practical differences on the MMPI-2 variables. There is a slight tendency for lower socioeconomic groups to score slightly lower on the *K*. These differences were not extreme enough to warrant the development of an adjusted normative score.

Gender Differences

There are small gender differences on some scales, such as *ANX*, however, these differences do not amount to a great deal of difference in terms of *T* score on the scales addressing psychopathology. Of course, there are substantial differences between men and women on the *Mf* scale. Keep in mind that the standard MMPI-2 scores are gender specific; consequently, when you are plotting scores, it is necessary to use the appropriate gendered norm.

The practitioner should be aware of the fact that it is possible to plot a client's profile on nongendered norms. *T* scores have been developed with a combined sample of men and women from the normative sample. One might choose to view a client's score on the nongendered norms in cases where, for example, "gender discrimination" might be considered problematic. In general, the *T*-score distributions are separate for men and women, although a given raw score would likely be highly similar regardless of the *T*-score distributions used.

Regional Differences

No regional differences were obtained in the MMPI-2 normative study; consequently, no adjustments need to be made in an interpretation for location.

Unusual Aspects of Test Administration

In developing hypotheses about a client, you need to consider any unusual aspects of the test administration or referral problem. For example, if a client took the MMPI-2 by having the examiner mark the items because he had both arms in casts, the practitioner would want to include this situation in the "Observations" section of the report and incorporate such information when developing the test inferences.

Appraising the Validity Pattern

The first task in appraising the validity pattern of the MMPI-2 is to determine whether the protocol to interpret is a valid and credible self-report. In appraising protocol validity, one can ask oneself a series of questions about the various components making up the validity pattern. Keep in mind also that the most pointed interpretations are those for which one can accurately describe and specify the testing situation. Some questions follow, which I raise about each element in the validity pattern to help in the organization of the hypotheses about a client:

- Has the person complied with the instructions? Did he or she complete all of the items? Were a sufficient number of items answered to produce a valid self-report? If not, were any particular content themes omitted? Can one confidently interpret the scales in a particular protocol with omitted items because particular scales were not affected?

- Were there any unusual patterns of responding noted on the answer sheet? What were the percentages of true and false responses? Is an essentially all true or all false response pattern present?

- Was the test taker consistent with respect to answering similar items? What are the scores on *VRIN* and *TRIN*? If either of them is above $T = 80$, it is likely that the test taker has not attended carefully to the content of the test.

- Was the test taker open and honest in the evaluation? Did he or she attempt to present in unrealistically and incredibly virtuous ways? Most people who want to be viewed correctly in clinical settings answer the MMPI-2 questions honestly. If the L score was greater than $T = 65$, then one needs to evaluate further to determine what "message" the client may be trying to convey. Evaluate other elements in the clinical picture that might shed light on the client's need to present such a highly unrealistic and "phony" view of himself or herself.

- Did the client show any test defensiveness, as measured by the less obvious defensiveness measures K and S? Are K and S elevated above $T = 65$? Does the client tend to present himself or herself in an overly positive manner? Do particular themes appear in this pattern of evasive responding? Which of the S subscales are elevated above $T = 65$? If much of the scale elevation can be accounted for by a single subscale elevation, such as S4

(Denial of Irritability and Anger), then this personality area might have more significance in the case.

- Is there any evidence of exaggerated responding in the client's validity pattern? What are the elevations of *F* and *F(B)*? *T* scores in the 60–80 range on these scales may simply reflect a large number of mental health problems. However, when scales range higher, particularly over *T* = 90, then the symptom exaggeration takes on more meaning and produces more concern as to the veridicality of the symptom pattern seen. Could the individual be malingering mental health symptoms? What is the elevation on *F* and *F(B)*? If it is over 100, one should begin to suspect malingering; when it is elevated beyond 110, then one can be pretty confident that the test taker proclaimed mental health symptoms in an extreme way, possibly to obtain services or financial gain. What is the elevation on *F(p)*? Elevations over *T* = 80 on the *F(p)* mean that this individual has endorsed considerably more mental health symptoms than most psychiatric patients do. Is this scale elevation credible for the type of assessment involved?

Applying Appropriate Clinical Scale Empirical Correlates

After one determines that the MMPI-2 protocol is valid and interpretable, it is now important to decide on the most pertinent clinical prototype to use in the development of the empirical descriptors for the profile. The steps to follow in deciding on the particular scale or profile type to use involve several factors:

- Determine the highest single point elevation or profile configuration in the clinical profile that can serve as the prototype for the report. For example, if only one clinical scale (e.g., the Depression Scale) is elevated in the clinical range, then the prototype would be Scale 2. If both the Depression and Psychopathic Deviate Scales are elevated above *T* = 65, then the 2-4/4-2 two-point code-type descriptors would be considered the appropriate prototype to apply.
- Keep in mind the concept of profile definition. If the scale or code-type prototype scores are elevated at least five points higher than the next scale in the code, then rely on the descriptors for that index. However, if the profile is not well defined, then also

take into consideration the next highest score in the profile code. This secondary score might "move up" in placement in the code at retesting.

- Apply the appropriate empirical descriptors from the literature on the scale score or profile type to serve as the basic structure of the personality description.
- Use the Harris–Lingoes subscales, if they are in the proper range, to help organize the correlates into a likely relevant clinical picture.

Enhancing Personality Descriptions With Content Interpretations

The next step in developing MMPI-2-based hypotheses for a personality assessment involves incorporating any relevant content themes that the patient may have endorsed in the self-report. A suggested approach to incorporating relevant content is as follows:

- Keep in mind that content-based measures tend to be "suppressed" among individuals who are defensive on the testing. To put it another way, the content scales are negatively correlated with the K score. The higher the K score, the lower the elevations on the content scales. When the K is in an appropriate range and the individual is cooperating with the assessment, as is the general rule in clinical settings, then the content scales can be extremely valuable in understanding the client.
- Determine which, if any, content themes are appropriate to incorporate into the evaluation, for example, high point scores, namely those elevated above $T = 65$.
- Incorporate content descriptions into the report by highlighting the main themes or problem areas that the client addressed. It is customary to include a statement informing the reader of the report that the interpretations in this section are based on the content of the individual's responses.
- In the application of the most important content themes, be aware of possibly seeming inconsistencies or contradictions that can come into play in this stage of the evaluation. It is important to eliminate any internal inconsistencies or contradictions that might result from using data from different sources within the MMPI-2. Seeming contradictions can result from drawing infer-

ences from different types of scales. For example, some MMPI-2 scales have similar names—Scale 2 (Depression) and *DEP* both address symptoms of affective disorder. Given the different item focus of the two different scales, it is actually possible for a patient to obtain a high score on Scale 2 and a relatively low score on *DEP*, making the interpretation appear confusing and contradictory. If this scenario occurs, the test interpreter could draw opposite conclusions from the two different scale elevations; for example, "the client is depressed but, on the other hand, the client is not depressed." In such a case, it is important to be aware that both scales may be correct because they are somewhat different in focus. The clinical Depression Scale (Scale 2) is a measure of symptomatic depression but has broad ranging and heterogeneous content, such as Subjective Depression, Alienation, Social Introversion (shyness), and physical problems, whereas the content Depression Scale only focuses on depressed mood and suicidal ideation—a more narrow definition of depression.

The Use of Critical Items in the Development of Personality-Based Hypotheses

In developing hypotheses from the MMPI-2, the practitioner may find that the critical items sometimes provide interesting clues about a client's problems. For example, if the person has scored high on Scale 2 or the content scale *DEP* of the MMPI-2, it would be valuable to examine his or her responses to the Koss–Butcher critical item category "Depressed–Suicidal" or even to examine the responses to the three suicide items in the MMPI-2 to evaluate further the potential of self-harm. The items include the following:

506. I have recently considered killing myself. (T)
520. Lately I have thought a lot about killing myself. (T)
524. No one knows it but I have tried to kill myself. (T)

Critical items can be used to develop hypotheses about possibly significant problem areas that the client might experience. These potential problem areas might be followed up in an interview to determine the extent of the problems. The critical items were developed for use in psychiatric settings; they should not be used in forensic evaluations.

The Incorporation of Hypotheses From Special Scales

Additional potential problem areas might be unveiled through the special problem scales on the MMPI-2. Several questions are pertinent to address in developing a picture of a client's symptoms and behaviors:

- Does the client show a substance abuse potential through the *MAC-R* or *APS*? Has the person endorsed substance use-related problems on the MMPI-2? What is the individual's score on the *AAS*? If the score is elevated higher than $T = 60$, then he or she acknowledged significant substance use. This possibility should be followed up to determine whether there is a significant pattern of current substance abuse or whether the high problem admission results from past abuses not relevant now.
- What is the quality of the individual's intimate, significant relationships? Does he or she report problems in his or her marriage? Is there an elevation of the *MDS*? Does the person have an elevation on the *FAM* content scale?

The Incorporation of Inferences Provided by Computer-Based Test Reports

Many practitioners in clinical and counseling psychology today process their psychological tests by computer because this has been shown to be a fast, reliable, and cost-effective way to obtain MMPI-2-based information about a client's test results (American Psychological Association, 1986). Practitioners use automated MMPI-2 reports in the hypothesis-generating stage of the psychological evaluation to obtain relevant test-based inferences. Computerized MMPI-2 interpretation services are simply electronic textbooks devised to help the practitioner conveniently locate relevant materials for the case. They are not considered completed diagnostic studies.

Electronic test processing has a long history in psychological practice, dating back to test-scoring machines in the 1940s. During the 1950s, large mainframe computers were used to process batches of test data. Several psychological testing services also became available to process individual data in a cost-effective manner. Then in 1961, the first computerized MMPI test interpretation program was developed at the Mayo Clinic in Rochester, Minnesota, by John Pearson and Wendell Swenson (Pearson, Swenson, Rome, Mataya, & Brannick, 1965; Rome et al., 1962). This program, although somewhat rudimentary by today's standards, was novel. In addition to scoring the MMPIs, the computer actually provided interpretive statements, obtained through descriptions pertinent to various scale elevations stored in the computer. This demonstration of the practicality of computer-generated reports stimulated the development of other computer-based MMPI interpretation programs. By the 1970s, there were several computer services for the scoring of the MMPI-2 (see the discussion by Fowler, 1985). Later generation programs, in addition to scoring the test, provided a narrative report that summarized the MMPI-2 correlates and predictions.

The computer-derived MMPI-2 reports (Butcher, 1993, 1995) illustrated in chapter 8 are designed to summarize the personality information obtainable from an MMPI-2 profile in a narrative manner. The information provided by the computer involves interpretations that the practitioner would find if he or she conducted a review of the pertinent literature. Next I examine the benefits and cautions the practitioner needs to consider when using a computer-based personality assessment.

Benefits

- Computer-based assessments provide an objective summary of the MMPI-2 on the basis of the information available in the literature.
- Computer-based narratives provide standard interpretations of MMPI-2 indexes for mental health clients that are based largely on actuarial data, which are automatically applied for well-established test scores (see the research on the MMPI-2 by Archer, Griffin, & Aiduk, 1995; and Graham, Ben-Porath, & McNulty, in press).
- Test scoring by computer is more reliable than when it is manually processed (Allard, Butler, Faust, & Shea, 1995). Moreover, the narrative reports provided by computer programs are completely reliable; they always produce the same report. This is unlike what occurs with clinical interpreters, who are likely to produce somewhat different results on different occasions or different from what two interpreters would obtain if evaluating the same data.
- Computer-derived reports are more comprehensive than those developed by clinicians.
- MMPI-2 reports by computer are generalizable across diverse

populations. Reports developed in the United States are found to be accurate with those of patients in other cultures (Berah et al., 1993; Butcher et al., 1998; Gillet et al., 1996).

- Computer-processed interpretive reports are available to the practitioner much quicker than are manually processed evaluations; such reports can expedite one's clinical assessment by having test information available as soon as the test is completed.
- Computerized MMPI-2 evaluations are more cost effective than are human-processed evaluations. Manual scoring of all of the MMPI-2 indexes needed for an evaluation requires substantial clerical time.

Cautions

- Computer reports should be viewed as consultations provided to other professionals who incorporate the assessment information into an evaluation. They should be used only by practitioners who are familiar with the technical and clinical use of the instrument interpreted.
- Computer-based reports are "generic" personality and symptomatic descriptions based on empirical research from specific settings. It is important for the practitioner to determine whether the available research supports a particular application.
- The practitioner needs to ensure that the protocol interpreted is appropriate and relevant for each client assessed. The report needs to be verified to ensure that it summarizes the answers provided by the client and that the prototype used in the narrative report matches the behavior of the client.
- The availability of computer-based reports can produce a degree of complacency in the practitioner conducting the assessment because such reports appear "complete and polished." Practitioners need to keep in mind that these reports are summaries of likely external correlates that need to be integrated into an evaluation.

Summary

This chapter was devoted to the process of integrating MMPI-2-related information into an interpretation or a discussion of "how to interpret an MMPI-2 profile." Possible external influences on profile interpretation, such as demographic or setting characteristics, were discussed. An outline suggesting a model of structuring the MMPI-2 evaluation was provided. Finally, computer-based test scoring and interpretation (commonly used in clinical assessment today) was also discussed.

In chapter 8, I turn my attention to illustrating the various kinds of interpretive information available from the MMPI-2 and show how the instrument can be of value in the assessment of a wide variety of settings. Some examples of computer-based MMPI-2 interpretations are provided in chapter 8 to illustrate their use. In chapter 9, the final chapter of this book, I describe the process of communicating the results of an MMPI-2 evaluation to others.

Using the MMPI-2 in Clinical Cases From Diverse Settings

Now it is time to put all of the information about the diverse measures included in the MMPI-2 into practice and examine how they operate in some cases. In this chapter, I explore several applications of the MMPI-2 to illustrate how the instrument can provide the practitioner with valuable personality information. I selected the first case to show how test takers in forensic contexts present themselves on the MMPI-2. Next, I explore the use of the MMPI-2 in an assessment of an African American woman being evaluated in a medical clinic. Later in the chapter, I examine the use of the MMPI-2 in an international application, a psychiatric patient being assessed in the United Arab Emirates using the Arabic version of the MMPI-2.

To illustrate these different applications, I take the following approach: Information pertaining to the person's life circumstances is described, next, the person's MMPI-2 profile is given, and finally a computer-based narrative MMPI-2 report (described more fully in chapter 7) is included to illustrate how a computer-derived assessment would describe the case.

The Use in Forensics

The MMPI-2 can be very valuable for assessing clients in court-related evaluations. Many people taking the test in this situation have a motivation to present themselves in particular ways. For example, in cases where financial rewards might come of demonstrated "severe psychological distress," the client might be motivated to endorse an extreme range or excessive number of symptoms or problems. Or in situations where it is important to appear psychologically sound, such as in a child custody dispute, the person may present with an unrealistically favorable view of his or her adjustment. The validity indicators on the test provide very useful information about the person's motivations in the evaluation. A recent study by Shores and Carstairs (1998) found that the computer-based interpretive program was effective at detecting fake-good and fake-bad response sets on the test.

When it has been determined that the client's test response approach is valid and cooperative, the clinical and content scales can be interpreted according to the traditional test correlates.

The Case of Alleged Brain Damage

Description

Eva B., a 38-year-old, twice divorced school teacher, filed a lawsuit against an electric power company alleging that toxic materials, which she believed were stored in one of the company's buildings near her home, had caused her brain impairment. She alleged that the toxic material had caused her memory loss, motor difficulty, severe fatigue, loss of energy, and mood shifts. She further alleged that she had been unable to function for the past several months because of these problems and had experienced depressed mood and morale problems because of the toxic materials. Eva had a problematic work history. She was suspended from teaching for 1 year for "excessive" punishment of a child in her class and for becoming embroiled in conflicts with parents and the school administration over her handling of discipline in her classroom.

Eva was evaluated by an osteopathic physician, who thought that her physical and emotional problems likely resulted from brain lesions. Other medical evaluations by two independent neurologists, however, found no evidence of organic impairment. In another evaluation, a neuropsychologist found no credible evidence of cognitive disorder; however, the neuropsychologist did conclude that Eva performed poorly on some testing and that her performance was not consistent with organic impairment. His conclusion was that Eva appeared unmotivated to perform the tasks on the neuropsychological battery administered. He concluded that her performance was more suggestive of a conscious distortion of the tasks on the test. For example, there were long delays in her responding to tasks that required very simple answers. During the discovery stage of the case, Eva became embroiled in a dispute with her attorneys and the case was withdrawn.

Comment

Eva's MMPI-2 profile is valid, although it shows some defensiveness (see Figure 8.1). She presented a moderately favorable picture of herself, as shown by the elevations of the *K* and *S* scales. Her high elevation on the S4 subscale (Denial of Irritability) suggests that she defensively claimed that she never got irritable or grouchy. Eva's MMPI-2 clinical scale pattern (see Figure 8.2) does not reflect evidence of a depressive disorder but is more consistent with severe personality disorder or paranoid disorder.[1] Her high elevation on the *Pa* scale suggests the possibility of personality characteristics centering on suspicion, mistrust, and hypervigilance to other people taking advantage or harming her. People with extreme elevations on Scale 6 tend to use faulty logic and jump to conclusions with insufficient information. Eva was likely to experience a great deal of anger and react toward others with hostility and indignation when she felt "wronged." There is some possibility that her allegations originated from her own personality make-up and interpersonal problems rather than from actual environmental circumstances. There are no practical hypotheses to obtain from the content scales or supplemental scales in her case (see Figure 8.3). Exhibit 8.1 is the narrative report produced by the computer for Eva's diagnosis.

The Use of Assessment With Minorities

Questions have been raised about potential bias that might result with the original MMPI in respect to the assessment of minority clients. Some researchers have noted that some items and the original norms were thought to portray minority clients unfairly, making them appear more pathological than they actually were (Greene, 1987). Such criticisms were taken into account during the revision of the MMPI, and the MMPI Restandardization Committee attempted to provide a more appropriate and effective assessment for minority patients in several ways:

- In the revision of the MMPI-2, some items were reworded to eliminate awkward or provincial wordings.

---

[1]She did not endorse many of the MMPI-2 items associated with head injury. She only endorsed 1 out of the 14 items on the Gass Head Injury Correction Factor (Gass, 1991).

Figure 8.1

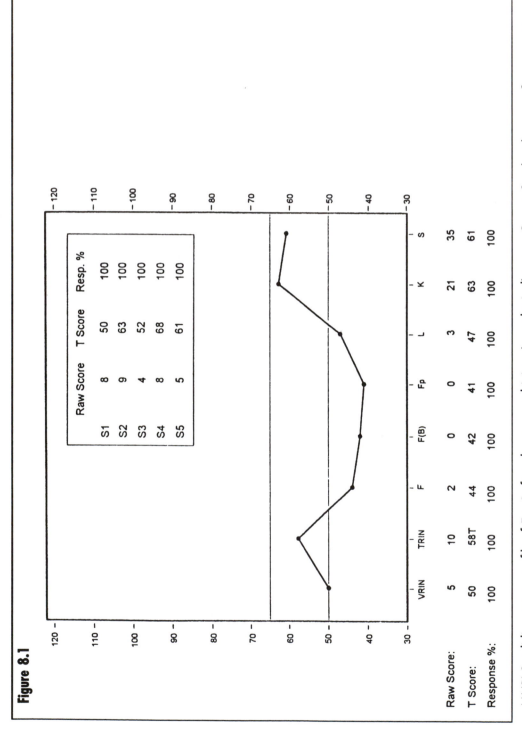

MMPI-2 validity pattern profile of Eva B. from her personal injury (neurological) report. Cannot Say (raw) score = 0; percent true = 35; percent false = 65.

Figure 8.2

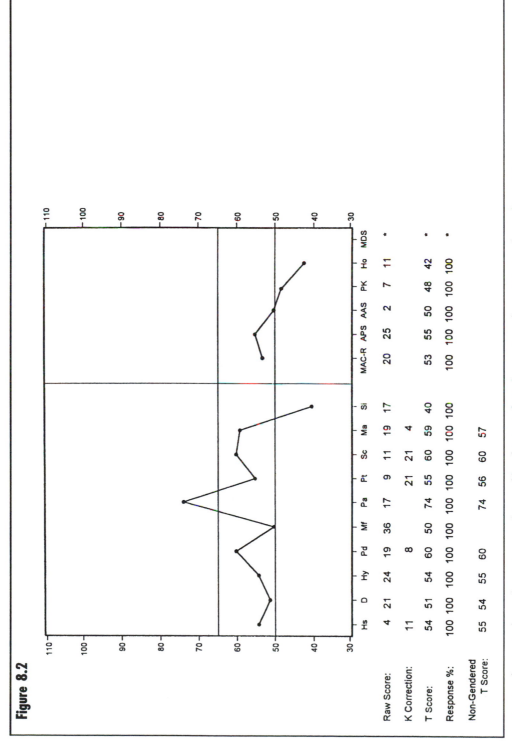

	Hs	D	Hy	Pd	Mf	Pa	Pt	Sc	Ma	Si		MAC-R	APS	AAS	PK	Ho	MDS
Raw Score:	4	21	24	19	36	17	9	11	19	17		20	25	2	7	11	*
K Correction:	11			8			21	21	4								
T Score:	54	51	54	60	50	74	55	60	59	40		53	55	50	48	42	*
Response %:	100	100	100	100	100	100	100	100	100	100		100	100	100	100	100	*
Non-Gendered T Score:	55	54	55	60		74	56	60	57								

MMPI-2 basic and supplementary scales profile of Eva B. from her personal injury (neurological) report.

Figure 8.3

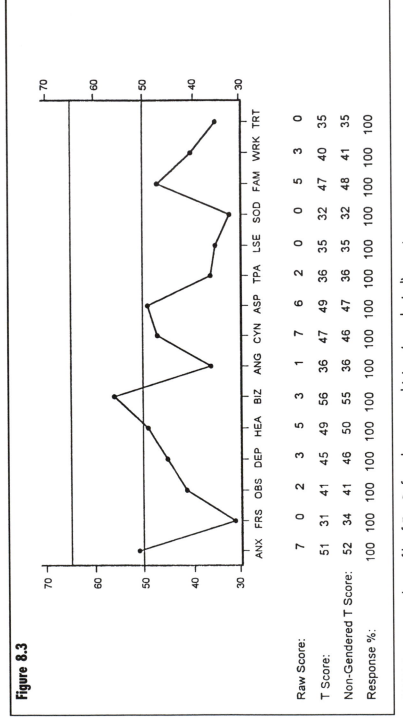

	ANX	FRS	OBS	DEP	HEA	BIZ	ANG	CYN	ASP	TPA	LSE	SOD	FAM	WRK	TRT
Raw Score:	7	0	2	3	5	3	1	7	6	2	0	0	5	3	0
T Score:	51	31	41	45	49	56	36	47	49	36	35	32	47	40	35
Non-Gendered T Score:	52	34	41	46	50	55	36	46	47	36	35	32	48	41	35
Response %:	100	100	100	100	100	100	100	100	100	100	100	100	100	100	100

MMPI-2 content scales profile of Eva B. from her personal injury (neurological) report.

Exhibit 8.1

Personal Injury (Neurological) Report for Eva B.

Profile Validity

This is a valid MMPI-2 profile. The client's responses to the MMPI-2 validity items suggest that she cooperated with the evaluation enough to provide useful interpretive information. The resulting clinical profile is probably an adequate indication of her present personality functioning.

Symptomatic Patterns

Very high profile definition characterizes the MMPI-2 profile code that includes *Pa*. This scale was used as the prototype for this report. This well-defined pattern increases confidence that the following personality correlates apply to this individual. People with this MMPI-2 clinical profile are likely to be experiencing intense problems at this time. Overly sensitive to criticism, the client reacts to even minor problems with anger or hostility. She is highly suspicious of other people and is constantly on guard to prevent being taken advantage of; this touchiness often makes her argumentative.

Individuals with this pattern are usually aloof and distant, and they may be rigid and opinionated. The client's great lack of trust makes her feel particularly wary of others. When she feels threatened, she may react with self-righteous indignation and complain that she has been wronged. Individuals with this profile tend to project and externalize blame. They typically do not assume responsibility for their problems, and they tend to blame others or to rationalize their faults.

This individual is not likely to change significantly, although she may become angry if she feels others are taking advantage of her. On the other hand, she may become less intensely angry and may "clam up" in order to reduce the attention being paid her. Symptom intensity may vary with mood and stress.

Profile Frequency

Profile interpretation can be greatly facilitated by examining the relative frequency of clinical scale patterns in various settings. The client's high-point clinical scale score (*Pa*) occurs in 10.4% of the MMPI-2 normative sample of women. However, only 3.4% of the women have *Pa* as the peak score at or above a *T* score of 65, and only 1.9% have well-defined *Pa* spikes.

The relative frequency of this MMPI-2 high-point *Pa* score is informative. In the large NCS medical sample, this high-point clinical scale score (*Pa*) occurs in 6.9% of the women. Only 5% of the women were found to have this high-point scale spike at or above a *T* score of 65, and only 2.9% have a well-defined *Pa* peak in that range.

continued

Exhibit 8.1, continued

Profile Frequency

In the sample reported by Butcher (1997), the MMPI-2 profile peak score on the *Pa* occurs with modest frequency (13.4%) among individuals involved in personal injury litigation. In addition, 6.4% have well-defined scores at or above a *T* score of 65.

According to Putnam et al. (1995), only 0.6% of patients with mild head injury and 2% with moderate to severe head injury produce this high-point score on *Pa*.

Profile Stability

The relative elevation of the highest scales in her clinical profile shows very high profile definition. Her peak scores are likely to be very prominent in her profile pattern if she is retested at a later date. However, because of the lower test–retest correlation for the *Pa* scale, her high-point score on *Pa* may indicate only modest stability over time. Short-term test–retest studies have shown a correlation of 0.58 for this high-point score.

Interpersonal Relations

She is overly sensitive, rigid, and hostile. She tends to brood a great deal, holds grudges, and may actively work to get even with others when she feels they are doing her wrong. Her lack of trust and inability to compromise often disrupt interpersonal relationships. Her lack of trust may prevent her from developing warm, close relationships. She tends to feel insecure in personal relationships, is hypersensitive to rejection, and may become jealous at times. She tends to need a great deal of reassurance.

Mental Health Considerations

Only tentative diagnoses can be provided for this profile type because factors other than the MMPI-2 should be considered. There is some indication that the client may have a paranoid personality disorder or a paranoid disorder.

Individuals with this profile type tend not to seek psychological help, but more often submit to it at the request or insistence of others. They are often guarded, and it is difficult to gain rapport with them. In psychological treatment, they deny responsibility for their problems, have stormy and unproductive treatment sessions, and may terminate therapy prematurely.

continued

Exhibit 8.1, continued

Personal Injury (Neurological) Considerations

The symptoms or problems she reported in this valid MMPI-2 profile might provide important information about her current situation. Her performance on the MMPI-2 clinical scales should be taken into consideration in any forensic disposition. Her high score on the *Pa* scale could reflect important problem areas that influence the manner in which she relates to others. Some people involved in personal injury litigation experience a heightened state of interpersonal sensitivity and anger that is reflected in this MMPI-2 pattern. However, her score on the *Pa* scale is too high to be accounted for by her anger over the present situation. The possibility that this extreme elevation on *Pa* reflects a paranoid predisposition should be evaluated. She is likely to be hypersensitive and overly responsive to others. She feels she is getting a raw deal from life, and she rationalizes and blames others for her problems. In addition, her suspicious behavior and generally hostile, resentful, and argumentative approach to relationships should be taken into consideration. Her litigious behavior could result from her mistrust and her feeling that others are working against her.

NOTE: This MMPI-2 interpretation can serve as a useful source of hypotheses about clients. This report is based on objectively derived scale indices and scale interpretations that have been developed with diverse groups of people. The personality descriptions, inferences, and recommendations contained herein should be verified by other sources of clinical information because individual clients may not fully match the prototype. The information in this report should be considered confidential and should only be used by a trained, qualified test interpreter.

From a Minnesota Report, National Computer Systems (NCS), Minneapolis, MN.

- In the collection of a normative sample, minority participation was encouraged and solicited.
- Representative samples of African Americans, Hispanics, Native Americans, and Asians were incorporated into the final normative sample.
- Several studies assess the impact of minority status on MMPI-2 responses.

Research on the MMPI-2 confirms that the instrument does not disadvantage ethnic minorities by depicting them differently in terms of measured psychopathology from the White majority population. To illustrate this point, I show below the mean profiles of several published minority group comparisons.

The data from the MMPI-2 normative population shown in Figure 8.4 (Butcher, Dahlstrom, Graham, Tellegen, & Kaemmer, 1989) indicate that the results from the African American and Caucasian research participants of the normative sample do not show any appreciable mean MMPI-2 differences. As noted earlier, the normative sample comprised individuals from across the United States (including different minority group subsamples), randomly recruited at each testing site. Similarly, the data shown in Figure 8.5 contrasting African American and Caucasian individuals tested in a court-ordered evaluation show no group differences (Ben-Porath, Shondrick, & Stafford, 1995). A third comparison of American Indian and Caucasian alcoholic individuals is shown in Figure 8.6 (Tinius & Ben-Porath, 1993).

As in the previous comparisons, the differences between the ethnic groups are minor and result in no practical interpretive differences. Finally, Figure 8.7 shows a study of Chinese American versus Caucasian college students (Keefe, Sue, Enomoto, Durvasula, & Chao, 1996). This study illustrates an important finding, that *acculturation* (how well adapted individuals are to a new culture) is a more pertinent variable than ethnic group membership per se. In this group mean comparison, the acculturated Chinese and White samples showed no practical differences, whereas those Chinese students that were not yet well acculturated to American culture produced more elevated scale scores. This finding that recent immigrants show more measured MMPI-2 psychopathology has been replicated in other studies (Azan, 1989; Deinard, Butcher, Thao, Vang, & Hang, 1996; Tran, 1996) and may reflect the adjustment problems that result when people move to a new and different culture.

A Case of the Likely Psychologically Based Physical Symptoms

Description

Ms. Jeanel D. is a 29-year-old receptionist who is currently separated from her husband of 5 years. She and her husband have two children, ages 2 and 4. She was referred to a clinical psychologist for evaluation and possible psychological treatment. In her medical evaluation the doctor found no organic factors to account for her symptoms. Jeanel initially presented at the health maintenance clinic with complaints of persistent fatigue, sleeping difficulty, and lower back and stomach pains that she suspected might be cancer. She reportedly had been feeling sick for 5 months, beginning over Christmas. She went through a dif-

Figure 8.4

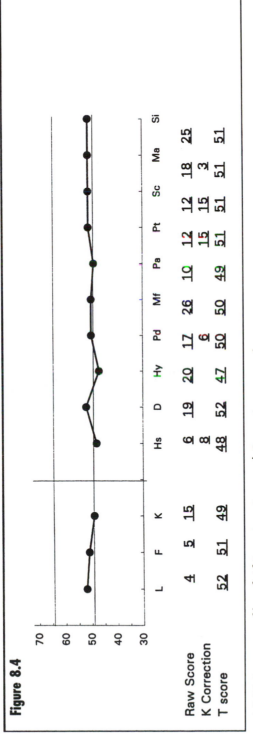

	L	F	K	Hs	D	Hy	Pd	Mf	Pa	Pt	Sc	Ma	Si
Raw Score	4	5	15	6	19	20	17	26	10	12	12	18	25
K Correction				8			6			15	15	3	
T score	52	51	49	48	52	47	50	50	49	51	51	51	51

MMPI-2 mean profiles of African American and Caucasian comparison groups.

Figure 8.5

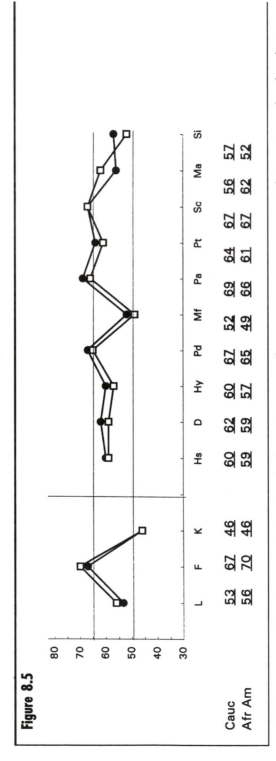

	L	F	K	Hs	D	Hy	Pd	Mf	Pa	Pt	Sc	Ma	Si
Cauc	53	67	46	60	62	60	67	52	69	64	67	56	57
Afr Am	56	70	46	59	59	57	65	49	66	61	67	62	52

MMPI-2 mean profiles of Caucasian (Cauc) and African American (Afr Am) comparison groups tested in a court-ordered evaluation.

Figure 8.6

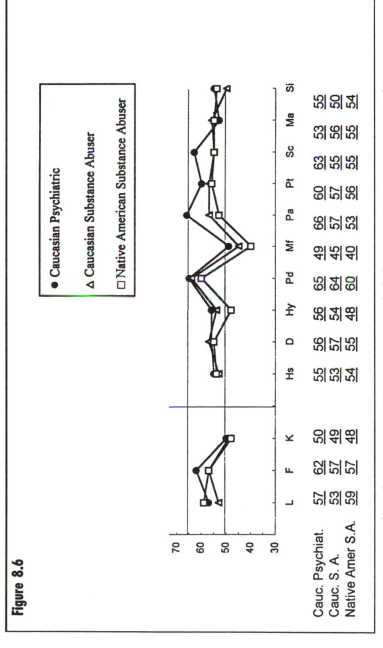

	L	F	K	Hs	D	Hy	Pd	Mf	Pa	Pt	Sc	Ma	Si
Cauc. Psychiat.	57	62	50	55	56	56	65	49	66	60	63	53	55
Cauc. S. A.	53	57	49	53	57	54	64	45	57	57	55	56	50
Native Amer S.A.	59	57	48	54	55	48	60	40	53	56	55	55	54

MMPI-2 mean profiles of Caucasian and Native American alcoholic comparison groups. Cauc. Psychiat. = Caucasian psychiatric (patient); Caus. S. A. = Caucasian substance abuser; Native Amer S. A. = Native American substance abuser.

Figure 8.7

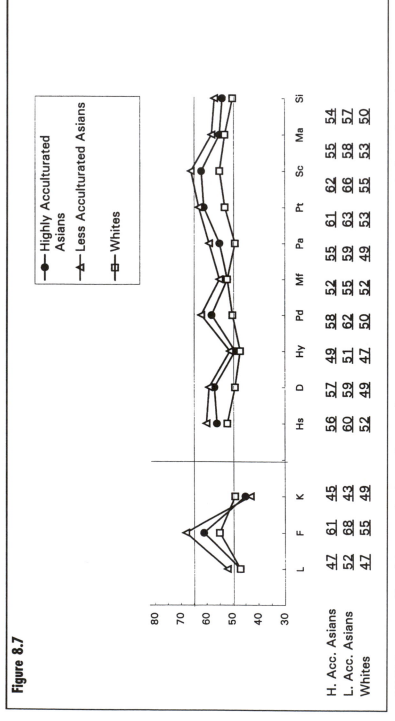

	L	F	K	Hs	D	Hy	Pd	Mf	Pa	Pt	Sc	Ma	Si
H. Acc. Asians	47	61	45	56	57	49	58	52	55	61	62	55	54
L. Acc. Asians	52	68	43	60	59	51	62	55	59	63	66	58	57
Whites	47	55	49	52	49	47	50	52	49	53	55	53	50

MMPI-2 mean profiles of Asian and White college student comparison groups. H. Acc. Asians = high acculturated Asians; L. Acc. Asians = low acculturated Asians.

ficult period when her husband left her for another woman. She had the full responsibility of taking care of her two small children and earning a living. Her husband provided no financial support.

Although her medical tests were negative, she appeared to experience little relief over the news that her physical condition was sound. Instead, she became sad and tearful in her interview with her doctor. Her physician diagnosed that her symptoms were stress related and prescribed Prozac. In addition, her physician thought that she would benefit from stress-management therapy.

Comment

Jeanel's MMPI-2 validity profile (Figure 8.8) shows a valid test performance. She appears to have cooperated with the evaluation and to have produced interpretable scale scores. Her clinical profile (also in Figure 8.8) shows a pattern of depression and an inability to function. She appears to be anxious and tense (see Figure 8.9) and shows a number of physical symptoms. The computer interpretation of her profile, shown in Exhibit 8.2, provides a thorough summary of the personality factors involved in her symptom disorder.

The Use in International Settings

Psychopathological conditions appear to have similar forms across cultures. The major categories of mental disorder are found in most cultures and appear generally similar in symptom expression cross-culturally (Butcher, Narikiyo, & Bemis-Vitousek, 1992). Moreover, extensive research shows that the symptoms and problems included in the MMPI-2 item pool describe many disorders in other countries as well. Patients with similar problems tend to endorse MMPI-2 items in a similar manner (Butcher & Pancheri, 1976). For the MMPI-2 to work effectively in other languages and cultures, it needs to be carefully translated. The typical procedures used in developing an effective test translation are outlined in Exhibit 8.3.

The MMPI-2 has been widely adapted in countries outside the United States. There are over 150 translations of the original MMPI, and it is widely used in over 46 countries (Butcher, 1985). There have also been 22 translations made of the MMPI-2 since 1989 (Butcher, 1996).

Once translated, adapted, and researched in the host country, the

Figure 8.8

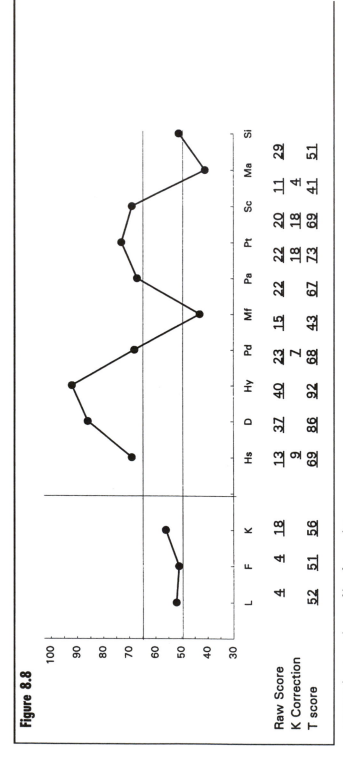

	L	F	K	Hs	D	Hy	Pd	Mf	Pa	Pt	Sc	Ma	Si
Raw Score	4	4	18	13	37	40	23	15	22	22	20	11	29
K Correction				9			7			18	18	4	
T score	52	51	56	69	86	92	68	43	67	73	69	41	51

MMPI-2 basic scales profile of Jeanel D.

Figure 8.9

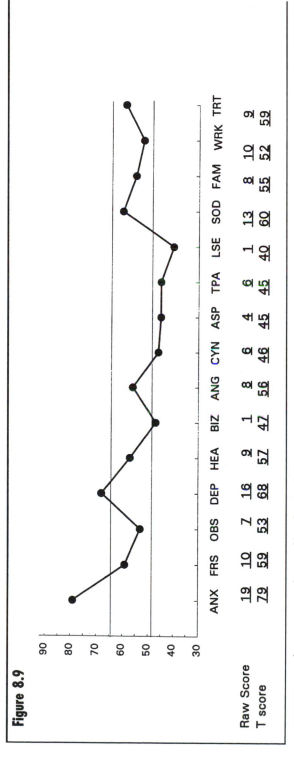

	ANX	FRS	OBS	DEP	HEA	BIZ	ANG	CYN	ASP	TPA	LSE	SOD	FAM	WRK	TRT
Raw Score	19	10	7	16	9	1	8	6	4	6	1	13	8	10	9
T score	79	59	53	68	57	47	56	46	45	45	40	60	55	52	59

MMPI-2 supplementary scales profile of Jeanel D.

Exhibit 8.2

Adult Clinical Interpretive Report for Jeanel D.

Profile Validity

Her MMPI-2 clinical profile is probably valid. The client's responses to the MMPI-2 validity items suggest that she cooperated with the evaluation enough to provide interpretive information. The resulting clinical profile is an adequate indication of her present personality functioning.

She endorsed the items at the end of the booklet in an extreme or exaggerated manner, producing a high score of F(B). This elevated score could result from a number of conditions, such as confusion, exaggerated symptom checking, or consistently misrecording her responses on the answer sheet. The scores on the MMPI-2 content scales, supplementary scales, and content component scales could be influenced by this tendency.

Symptomatic Patterns

The clinical scale prototype used in the development of this narrative included prominent elevations on scales D and Hy. Physical concerns and depressed mood appear to be the primary problems emerging from a somewhat mixed symptom pattern. The client feels nervous, tense, and unhappy, and she is quite worried at this time. She also appears to be quite indifferent to many of the things she once enjoyed and believes she is no longer able to function well in life. Overly sensitive to criticism, she tends to blame herself a great deal and feels that she has not been treated well. Her depressed mood is accompanied by physical complaints and extreme fatigue.

She appears to be inhibited and overcontrolled, relying on denial and repression to deal with anxiety and conflict. She may seek medical attention for her "run-down" condition, but her physical problems are likely to be related to her depressed mood.

In addition, the following description is suggested by the content of the client's item responses. She has endorsed a number of items that suggest that she is experiencing low morale and a depressed mood. She reports a preoccupation with feeling guilty and unworthy. She feels that she deserves to be punished for wrongs she had committed. She feels regretful and unhappy about life, and she seems plagued by anxiety and worry about the future. She feels hopeless at times and feels that she is a condemned person. She has difficulty managing routine affairs, and the items she endorsed suggest a poor memory, concentration problems, and an inability to make decisions. She appears to be immo-

continued

Exhibit 8.2, continued

bilized and withdrawn and has no energy for life. She views her physical health as failing and reports numerous somatic concerns. She feels that life is no longer worthwhile and that she is losing control of her thought processes. She endorsed items that suggest a history of suicidal ideation. It is important to perform a suicide assessment and, if necessary, to take appropriate precautions. She has acknowledged having suicidal thoughts recently. Although she denies suicidal attempts in the past, given her current mood, an evaluation of suicidal potential appears to be indicated. She is rather high strung and believes that she feels things more, or more intensely, than others do. She feels quite lonely and misunderstood at times. Her high endorsement of general anxiety content is likely to be important to understanding her clinical picture.

Profile Frequency

It is usually valuable in MMPI-2 clinical profile interpretation to consider the relative frequency of a given profile pattern in various settings. The client's MMPI-2 high-point clinical scale score (*Hy*) is found in 10.5% of the MMPI-2 normative sample of women. However, only 3.7% of the sample have *Hy* as the peak score at or above a *T* score of 65 and only 2.1% have well-defined *Hy* spikes. This elevated MMPI-2 profile type (2-3/3-2) is very rare in samples of normals, occurring in less than 1% of the MMPI-2 normative sample of women.

The relative freqency of her profile in various medical settings is informative. An extremely large number of women being evaluated in a medical context produce this high-point score. In the NCS medical sample, this MMPI-2 high-point clinical scale score (*Hy*) occurs in 24.4% of the women. Furthermore, 20.9% of the women have the *Hy* scale spike at or above a *T* score of 65, and 12.2% have a well-defined *Hy* peak at or over a *T* score of 65. This elevated MMPI-2 profile configuration (2-3/3-2) is found in many women in medical settings. It occurs in 7.1% of the women in the NCS medical sample.

Profile Stability

The relative elevation of the highest scales in her clinical profile shows very high profile definition. Her peak scores on this testing are likely to be very prominent in her profile pattern if she is retested at a later date. Her high-point score on *Hy* is likely to remain stable over time. Short-term test–retest studies have shown a correlation of 0.76 for this high-point score.

Interpersonal Relations

She is passive dependent in relationships and is easily hurt by others. She is nonassertive and keeps anger bottled up, avoiding confrontation for fear of being rejected or hurt.

continued

Exhibit 8.2, continued

Interpersonal Relations

Her very high score on the Marital Distress Scale suggests that her marital situation is quite problematic at this time. She has reported a number of problems with her marriage that are possibly important to understanding her current psychological symptoms.

Diagnostic Considerations

Many individuals with this profile will present with psychophysiologic symptoms. Possible organic factors should be evaluated because some individuals with this profile pattern eventually develop psychophysiological disorders. The most frequent diagnosis for individuals with this profile is dysthymic disorder. Physically disabling conditions related to psychological stress, such as ulcers or hypertension, may be part of this clinical pattern. Her self-reported tendency toward experiencing depressed mood should be taken into consideration in any diagnostic formulation.

Treatment Considerations

She views herself as having so many problems that she is no longer able to function effectively in day-to-day situations. Her low mood and pessimistic outlook on life weigh heavily on her and seemingly keep her from acting to better her situation. Her negative self-image and sense of frustration may be very detrimental to treatment and will require attention early in therapy.

Individuals with this MMPI-2 clinical profile tend to feel quite tense and depressed and may need relief for their psychological symptoms. Perhaps the most frequent form of treatment given to individuals with this pattern is antidepressant medication. Many patients with this profile require a great deal of reassurance. They tend to lack insight into their behavior and will tolerate a great deal of tension before they will seek help. Some individuals with this profile respond to a direct action-oriented treatment approach and possibly to assertiveness training.

NOTE: This MMPI-2 interpretation can serve as a useful source of hypotheses about clients. This report is based on objectively derived scale indices and scale interpretations that have been developed in diverse groups of patients. The personality descriptions, inferences, and recommendations contained herein need to be verified by other sources of clinical information because individual clients may not fully match the prototype. The information in this report should most appropriately be used by a trained, qualified test interpreter. The information contained in this report should be considered confidential.

From a Minnesota Report, National Computer Systems (NCS), Minneapolis, MN.

Exhibit 8.3

Procedures for Developing an Effective MMPI-2 Translation

1. *An indigenous developer.* Familiarity with the culture in which the test is being translated is required to ensure that taking an MMPI-2 is appropriate for the intended population. The most effective translations of the MMPI-2 are those in which the translator–adapter is native to the culture and has a broad familiarity with the MMPI-2 and its use.

2. *Diverse input into item renderings.* In the initial phase of the translation, it is important to use more than one (usually two or more) translators to convert the items independently. Mirza (1973) noted that translating personality items is like translating poetry. It is important to get both the psychological and linguistic equivalence for each item. Using multiple translators for the initial development ensures that items are not too idiosyncratically translated.

3. *Committee discussion to obtain the final translation.* In this phase, the independent translators should meet to discuss any items on which there might be some disagreement. Once a final version is obtained, then the next step in translation development is to test out the translation.

4. *Backtranslation study.* An independent translator (often a linguist) then back translates the translated version into English. Once this is accomplished, then the back translated version is compared with the original English version to determine if any of the item meanings have been distorted. Usually about 10–15% of the items require additional translation effort.

5. *Bilingual test–retest study.* Once the back translation improvements have been made, it is important next to field test the translation. This study involves administering both the translated and the English versions of the MMPI-2 to a number of people who are fluent in both languages. Their performances on both versions can be compared to determine if they obtain the same scores on both.

6. *Field-test study of known clinical groups.* It is now time to conduct field tests with patients and other samples to determine if their scores are comparable with similar groups in other countries. A number of psychometric studies can be conducted to determine if the MMPI-2 is working similarly in both countries.

7. *Appropriate host country norms.* Researchers so far on translations of the MMPI-2 have found that many of the translations of the MMPI-2 can actually operate using American norms. If research shows that normals in the target country deviate substantially from the American norms, then incountry norms need to be developed to take the cultural differences into account.

Note. Information adapted from Butcher (1996) and Brislin (1986).

MMPI-2 can be an effective tool for assessing patients and making practical decisions in the new culture. Soliman (1996) provided the following case.

The Case of a Psychiatric Inpatient From the United Arab Emirates[2]

Description

A 30-year-old male patient was brought to the psychiatric clinic by his father 3 years ago for the first time. The patient was a Palestinian and was jobless at the time the MMPI-2 was administered. His father complained that his son had always been aggressive toward his mother. He accused her of having affairs with other men. He always sat alone in his room talking loudly to himself. His scholastic performance was deteriorating.

A History of the Disorder

The patient's condition became apparent 4 years ago. At that time, his parents noticed that he isolated himself and that his behavior was inappropriate. He refused to go to school several times without any apparent reason. He expressed several health complaints and was taken several times to the clinic as a result. His behavior increasingly deteriorated, and he was brought to the psychiatric clinic.

When the patient was seen for the first time, the following symptoms were reported by the psychiatrist: delusions of persecution, nonverbal auditory hallucinations, insomnia, faulty emotions with manifest incongruity of affect, and avoidance of eye contact.

Diagnosis and Treatment

The provisional diagnosis for this patient was schizophrenia. Treatment was prescribed, and the patient came to the clinic regularly. The clinic reported that he was improving after he found a job in a drug factory. He did well for a few months, but later he stopped coming to the clinic. One year later, he was brought to the clinic by his father. The father reported that his son had left his job to resume his studies but did not go to school and began to isolate himself again. When he was seen by the psychiatrist, all the previous symptoms were present and more intense. Moreover, he reported that he was hearing voices. He was

---

[2]Information adapted from Soliman (1996).

treated with phenothiazine medication. After a few days, his father returned to the clinic complaining that his son was not taking his medicine.

A few months later, the patient himself came to the clinic, complaining of an inability to sleep and of having strange ideas. Long-acting phenothiazine injections were prescribed every 2 weeks. The patient was under treatment, and his condition was fluctuating. His parents reported that before his illness, he had had few friends. He was careless about how he looked and dressed. He was not willing to take much responsibility. His school achievement had been above average, but he left school in the 12th grade after repeated failures. Failure in 12th grade is a stressful event for Palestinian Arab students, because it determines whether the students will get a grade point average that will enable them to be admitted to a university. A clinical examination revealed no physical illness. No history of mental illness or other related disorders were found in the family. Again, the patient's illness was diagnosed as schizophrenia.

Comment

The MMPI-2 patterns shown in Figure 8.10 and Figure 8.11 match this case history well. The clinical profile, an 8-3 pattern, along with the high elevations on the context scales *BIZ, DEP,* and *LSE,* show a serious mental disorder. The narrative report, shown in Exhibit 8.4, summarizes well the severe psychological problems and likely schizophrenic disorder reflected in this case history.

Summary

The primary goal of this chapter was to illustrate with clinical examples how the MMPI-2 can effectively describe personality and behavior over a broad range of clinical cases. In addition, patients from very different cultural backgrounds tend to produce interpretable MMPI-2 patterns, even though the instrument was not initially developed for those populations. The interpretations generalize well because they are based on a common core of symptoms and behaviors that are central to a number

Figure 8.10

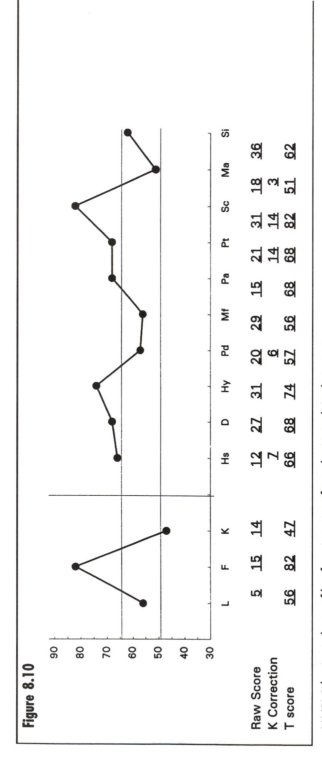

	L	F	K	Hs	D	Hy	Pd	Mf	Pa	Pt	Sc	Ma	Si
Raw Score	5	15	14	12	27	31	20	29	15	21	31	18	36
K Correction				7			6			14	14	3	
T score	56	82	47	66	68	74	57	56	68	68	82	51	62

MMPI-2 basic scales profile of an inpatient from the United Arab Emirates.

Figure 8.11

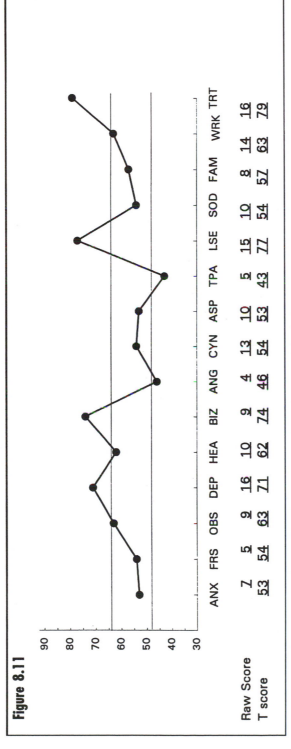

	ANX	FRS	OBS	DEP	HEA	BIZ	ANG	CYN	ASP	TPA	LSE	SOD	FAM	WRK	TRT
Raw Score	7	5	9	16	10	9	4	13	10	5	15	10	8	14	16
T score	53	54	63	71	62	74	46	54	53	43	77	54	57	63	79

MMPI-2 supplementary scales profile of an inpatient from the United Arab Emirates.

Exhibit 8.4

Adult Clinical Interpretive Report of an Inpatient From the United Arab Emirates

Profile Validity

This MMPI-2 profile should be interpreted with caution. There is some possibility that the clinical report is an exaggerated picture of the client's present situation and problems. He is presenting an unusual number of psychological symptoms. This response set could result from poor reading ability, confusion, disorientation, stress, or a need to seek a great deal of attention for his problem.

His test-taking attitudes should be evaluated for the possibility that he has produced an invalid profile. He may be showing a lack of cooperation with the testing, or he may be malingering by attempting to present a false claim of mental illness. Determining the source of his confusion, whether conscious distortion or personality deterioration, is important because immediate attention may be required. Clinical patients with this validity profile are often confused and distractible and have memory problems. Evidence of delusions and thought disorder may be present. He may be exhibiting a high degree of distress and personality deterioration.

The client's responses to items in the latter portion of the MMPI-2 were somewhat exaggerated in comparison to his responses to earlier items. There is some possibility that he became more careless in responding to these later items, thereby raising questions about that portion of the test. Although the standard validity and clinical scales are scored from items in the first two thirds of the test, caution should be taken in interpreting the MMPI-2 content scales and supplementary scales, which include items found throughout the entire item pool.

Symptomatic Patterns

This report was developed using the *Hy* and *Sc* scales as the prototype. A pattern of chronic psychological maladjustment characterizes individuals with this MMPI-2 clinical profile. The client is presenting with a somewhat mixed pattern of complaints. His symptomatic pattern may be unusual, and he may seem quite eccentric. He may cling strongly to delusional or other transcendental beliefs. Apparently rather tense and nervous, the client may have some unusual somatic complaints that he rigidly maintains even when they are challenged. He may also complain of confusion and poor memory. His adjustment is apathetic, immature, and marginal. He is likely to be experiencing delusions, hallucinations, or other symptoms of a thought disorder.

continued

Exhibit 8.4, continued

Profile Frequency

Profile interpretation can be greatly facilitated by examining the relative frequency of clinical scale patterns in various settings. The client's high-point clinical scale score (*Sc*) is the least frequent MMPI-2 peak score in the MMPI-2 normative sample of men, occurring in only 4.7% of the cases. Only 2.6% of the sample have *Sc* as the peak score at or above a *T* score of 65, and less than 1% have a well-defined *Sc* spike. This elevated MMPI-2 profile configuration (3-8/8-3) is very rare in samples of normals, occurring in less than 1.0% of the MMPI-2 normative sample of men.

In the NCS outpatient sample, 5.6% of the men have this high-point clinical scale score (*Sc*). Moreover, 4.8% of the male outpatients have the *Sc* scale spike at or above a *T* score of 65, and 2.4% have well-defined *Sc* scores in that range. This elevated MMPI-2 profile configuration (3-8/8-3) occurs in 0.6% of the men in the NCS outpatient sample.

Profile Stability

The relative scale elevation of the highest scales in his clinical profile reflects high profile definition. If he is retested at a later date, the peak scores on this test are likely to retain their relative salience in his retest profile pattern. His high-point score on *Sc* is likely to show considerable stability over time. Short-term test–retest studies have shown a correlation of 0.87 for this high-point score. Spiro, Butcher, Levinson, Aldwin, and Bosse (1993) reported a test–retest stability of 0.61 in a large study of normals over a 5-year test–retest period.

Interpersonal Relations

His peculiar structure of beliefs is likely to interfere with his social relationships because he tends to withdraw from people and feels distant and alienated from them. He appears to be rigid in interpersonal relationships and may be functioning at a reduced level of social effectiveness. Behavioral deterioration and lowered efficiency seem to characterize his present functioning.

He is somewhat shy, with some social concerns and inhibitions. He is a bit hypersensitive about what others think of him and is occasionally concerned about his relationships with others. He appears to be somewhat inhibited in personal relationships and social situations, and he may have some difficulty expressing his feelings toward others.

continued

Exhibit 8.4, continued

Diagnostic Considerations

The behaviors reflected in this profile may present some diagnostic problems. The client exhibits features of both a severe neurotic disorder (such as somatoform disorder) and a psychotic process (such as schizophrenia). Information from sources other than the MMPI-2 should be taken into account. He is likely to have a schizoid adjustment and will probably be diagnosed as having an Axis II personality disorder of a schizoid or schizotypal form.

Treatment Considerations

Individuals with this MMPI-2 clinical profile may be experiencing much tension and behavioral deterioration. Their symptomatic behavior, because it has an odd quality, might prove difficult for a therapist to understand clearly. Patients with this pattern often receive psychotropic medication for symptom relief. They tend not to respond well to insight-oriented psychotherapy because they resist psychological interpretation and rigidly adhere to unusual thoughts or bizarre beliefs about their health.

Individuals with this profile also find it difficult to relate to others, further reducing the effectiveness of relationship-oriented psychotherapy. Some patients with this profile respond to a direct, supportive therapeutic approach.

NOTE: This MMPI-2 interpretation can serve as a useful source of hypotheses about clients. This report is based on objectively derived scale indices and scale interpretations that have been developed in diverse groups of patients. The personality descriptions, inferences, and recommendations contained herein need to be verified by other sources of clinical information because individual clients may not fully match the prototype. The information in this report should most appropriately be used by a trained, qualified test interpreter. The information contained in this report should be considered confidential.

From a Minnesota Report, National Computer Systems (NCS), Minneapolis, MN.

of clinical problems that appear similar, regardless of culture. I also examined some computer-based interpretive reports on a few patients to illustrate how automated interpretation involves the objective application of standard interpretations to test indices.

In the final chapter, I turn my attention to the crucial task of communicating the results of an MMPI-2 evaluation to others.

The Report: Documenting the Results of MMPI-2 Evaluations

Now that you have learned about the sources of information about clients that are available in the MMPI-2 and have begun to develop some strategies for interpreting various MMPI-2 indices, the next step is to communicate this information clearly to the referral source and, where appropriate, provide feedback to the client. The first part of this chapter is devoted to the task of writing an MMPI-2 report; later in the chapter, I look at a powerful clinical intervention strategy, the provision of MMPI-2-based test feedback to the client.

Developing a Written MMPI-2-Based Report

In this section, I examine the factors important for test interpreters to consider in communicating results of the MMPI-2 in a report. This chapter does not attempt to serve as a complete exploration of all of the factors pertinent to writing psychological test reports—that is a larger task and beyond the scope of this book. A number of useful resources provide students with general guidelines and suggestions for writing psychological reports (see, e.g., Harvey, 1997; Ownby, 1987; and Tallent, 1992, 1993). Those interested in communicating test results and developing specific reports for various clinical settings should also refer to Beutler (1995) and for forensic assessments refer to the discussion by Weiner (1987).

A model outline of suggested sections for an MMPI-2 interpretive report in a clinical setting is provided in Exhibit 9.1 as an example to

---

Exhibit 9.1

Outline Structure for an MMPI-2-Based Report

Referral question
Relevant observations
Validity considerations
Clinical symptom patterns
Profile stability
Interpersonal relationships
Clinical diagnostic considerations
Treatment planning information

---

follow in this discussion. Keep in mind that this is only one suggested approach for a particular setting (i.e., an outpatient mental health facility). If one were developing a report for a different setting, for example, a domestic court evaluation or a health care facility, then the headings would change and a somewhat different approach would be taken because the referral questions and circumstances would differ.

Referral Question

What is the purpose of the requested evaluation? It is important to ensure that the questions of interest to the referral source are actually addressable with the measures available in the MMPI-2. What is the purpose of this MMPI-2 evaluation? Is the evaluation designed to provide a personality description of the patient? Does the purpose of the evaluation include making projections or predictions about the patient's likely future behavior? For example, will the patient have problems establishing a relationship in psychotherapy? Vague referrals can be problematic, and it might be necessary, before attempting to answer particular referral questions, to talk with the referring professional to get a more explicit idea of what they are interested in knowing from the test. An example of a vague and generally useless referral comes from a psychiatric resident when the author was a clinical intern. The referral was a request for a psychological evaluation written in a hurried scrawl: "Psychology: a 33-year-old male, trombone player—please evaluate." This referral was certainly not specific enough for a psychological assessment, and the writer did not have the necessary musical background to comply with the request as it was written.

Does the MMPI-2 possess relevant measures to fulfill the goals of the referral question? In determining whether to include the MMPI-2 in the assessment study, the clinician should examine whether the test possesses indexes that can address the referral problems. For example, if the referral problem centers on determining if the client's physical complaints are genuine or if the individual is likely to experience an organic brain syndrome, then the MMPI-2 would not be the measure of choice. The MMPI-2 does not possess scales to address these questions (nor does any known personality measure).

Observations

Early in the report, there needs to be a discussion that informs the clinician about the structure of the testing situation. Were there any special considerations in the administration of the MMPI-2 with this patient? For example, was the test administered using a tape-recorded version? Was the test administered in more than one sitting? (There is no problem with splitting the administration over more than one session, but this should be noted in the report.) Did the client have difficulty understanding the items? Did the client use a foreign language version of the MMPI-2?

What was the "mental set" under which the client took the MMPI-2? This is a key consideration for "framing" in psychological test interpretations. Although it is possible to formulate personality descriptions on the basis of the MMPI-2 profile alone, one's conclusions can be more specific and focused if the conditions under which the individual took the test are known. For example, it is important to note whether the person took the test under court order or as a self-referral to mental health treatment. It is a good idea to specify in the observations section of the report any clues as to what is known about the client's test-taking attitudes. For example, did the client take the test as part of a court case? Was the test administered in an outpatient clinic? Was the individual physically handicapped in ways that required special administrative procedures?

Validity Considerations

An early section of the MMPI-2 report should be devoted to a description of the most salient validity considerations. All of the validity scales should be considered to provide the reader of the report with your determination as to whether the client cooperated sufficiently with the evaluation. In this section of the report, a conclusion as to whether you consider the individual's test protocol to be valid and interpretable should be made. A few sample summarizing statements about test validity are provided below to illustrate the type of description that can "set the stage" for the clinical interpretation, which comes later in the report:

- This is a valid MMPI-2 protocol based on the client's normal range performance on all of the validity scales. The client appears to have been cooperative with the appraisal. The personality descriptions provided are likely a good indication of the client's personality functioning.
- His performance on the MMPI-2 *L, K,* and *S* indicates an extreme tendency to present himself in a favorable light and to minimize problems. His defensive test performance results in an invalid protocol; his clinical and content scales do not provide credible information about his personality functioning.
- On the basis of her extremely elevated scores on the *F* and *F(B)*, it is likely that she produced an invalid profile. Her extremely high ranging scores on *F* suggests the possibility of a malingered MMPI-2 protocol.
- Given the fact that he omitted an excessive number of items on the MMPI-2, his clinical and content scale profiles should not be interpreted. It is likely that he has attenuated his test performance on the symptom-oriented scales of the MMPI-2.

Clinical Symptom Patterns

A Summary of Clinical Symptom Patterns

Develop this section of the report from the empirical correlate literature on the MMPI-2 clinical scales. Describe the patient's likely symptoms, attitudes, and problems by reference to MMPI-2 code books. Stick to the data in making interpretations and personality descriptions by using well-established scale and code-type correlates.

In developing this section of the clinical report, the interpreter may refer to one of the well-established MMPI-based code books or texts, such as Graham's (in press) or Butcher and William's (1992) book that lists likely correlates for various MMPI-2 patterns.

Ordering the Correlates Into a Hierarchy of the Most Likely Descriptions

Which of the possible correlates for a particular scale are incorporated into the report? Do you include them all? If not, which ones should be prominently noted in the report? One helpful way for determining which correlates to emphasize for a particular scale elevation, as discussed in chapter 3, is to use the Harris–Lingoes subscales to determine which item relationships are most likely prominent. For example, if the Harris–Lingoes *Pd* 1 subscale (Family Problems) is the only elevated subscale for a patient who has an elevated *Pd* score, then the correlates that address family problems should be considered more central to the personality and given more prominence in the description. Similarly, if the MMPI-2 Content Family Problem Scale is prominently elevated, the elevation on *Pd* would more likely be considered the result of present family turmoil than of more long-standing psychopathic tendencies.

Integrating the MMPI-2 Content Scales Into the Symptom Description

In addition to using the empirical correlates for describing the symptom picture in the report, the clinician should incorporate the most prominent content scales that provide symptom themes acknowledged by the patient. For example, if the patient scored highest on the *OBS* (above $T = 65$), the obsessive quality of the individual's thinking should be highlighted in the symptom pattern section of the report. For example, a man who scored high on *OBS* would be characterized as the following: This client is likely experiencing a great deal of indecisiveness and pathological rumination at this time. Irrational thinking and obsessive thoughts are likely to characterize his thinking. He is also likely to show compulsive thinking and behavior in his everyday activities.

Interpersonal Relationships

This section is designed to provide a description of the patient's interpersonal relationships and social functioning. The MMPI-2 contains a number of indexes that address this important area of personality functioning. For example, the elevations on *Si* and the content scale Social Maladjustment (*SOD*) are initial indexes to consider. However, social behavior factors are also prominent correlates in many high scores or code types. For example, people with high *Sc* scores tend to be isolated and withdrawn and may show eccentric behavior in social situations. High-scoring *Pd* people are viewed as manipulative in relationships.

The extent of coverage devoted to interpersonal behavior depends on the referral problem. For example, if the referral problem centers on whether the individual can develop a therapeutic relationship in pretreatment planning, this section might be given more prominence in the report.

It is important to keep in mind as you develop this section of the report that the personality characteristics assessed by the Social Introversion–Extraversion Scale tend to be very stable characteristics over time. Therefore, relatively long-range predictions about the client's social effectiveness can be made with confidence. More is said below about assessing profile stability over time.

Profile Stability

Providing a projection of the likely stability of the client's profile over time can add to the utility of an MMPI-2 report. The likely stability of a profile over time, as noted in chapter 3, can be estimated using the concept of *profile definition*: very well-defined profiles, that is, those that have at least a 10-point difference between the scale or profile interpreted and the next scale in the profile. The reference to highly stable scores over time might also be relevant to include in this section of the report. For example, as noted above, the *Si* has been shown to have very high stability over long periods of time. For example, Spiro, Butcher, Levenson, Aldwin, and Bosse (1993) found that this score had a stability coefficient of .86 over a 5-year period, and Leon, Gillum, Gillum, and Gouze (1979) found the 30-year stability of the *Si* to be .73.

Clinical Diagnostic Considerations

Depending on the interest and needs of the referring source, differential clinical diagnosis is likely to be an important consideration that needs to be addressed—not simply to arrive at a *Diagnostic and Statistical Manual of Mental Disorders* (4th ed.; *DSM-IV*) classification but to provide descriptive diagnostic behavior that can be incorporated into the clinical picture. The MMPI-2 and current nosological systems are different ways of describing behavior in clinical settings. Originally, the MMPI was devised in hopes of arriving at an objective clinical diagnosis. Applications of the instrument in real-world clinical settings have shown that the MMPI is not the most effective means of arriving at a clinical diagnosis. As it is practiced, clinical diagnosis requires external information (history, observations, etc.), which are not completely addressed by self-report instruments. Moreover, much of the behavior addressed by the MMPI-2 that is valuable in clinical settings is not included in most diagnostic classification schema. Thus, arriving at a *DSM-IV* or *International Classification of Diseases–10* diagnosis does not use all that is available from the MMPI-2. Although some MMPI-2 patterns have been shown to have high correspondence to some *DSM* codes, using it is usually not considered a desirable goal to try to arrive at psychiatric diagnoses with the MMPI-2 alone.

The MMPI-2 is most suitable for providing information related to descriptive personality assessment. Some of the inferences that can be obtained from the MMPI-2 should be valuable in developing clinical diagnostic pictures. A sample of possible diagnostic inferences from clinical or content scale profiles or supplementary scales is as follows:

- An extremely high score on the clinical scale *D* or the *DEP* content scale suggests that the individual is likely experiencing symptoms of an affective disorder. Marked evidence of depression is prominent in the self-report.
- Elevated scores on *APS, MAC-R,* or *AAS* suggest that the presence of a substance abuse disorder is likely.
- An extremely elevated peak score on *Pt* suggests that the patient is experiencing a severe anxiety-based disorder.
- High elevation on *Pa* as the peak score on the clinical profile suggests that the possibility of a paranoid disorder should be considered.
- An extremely elevated peak score on *Sc* or *BIZ* suggests that the patient is likely experiencing symptoms of a thought disorder, including delusions and hallucinations.
- A high score on the *ASP* content scale suggests that the patient's clinical picture is likely to reflect antisocial features that need to be accounted for on Axis II of *DSM-IV.*

Treatment Planning Information

In clinical or counseling contexts, people often take the MMPI-2 for the clinician to obtain pretreatment planning information. The MMPI-2 report in these settings should provide a description of the client's personality and behavior and list conclusions as to their amenability to psychological treatment. The validity pattern should be the first point of reference when determining if a client is open to psychological treatment. A great deal of information can be gleaned from the configuration and elevation ranges of the validity scales to address the client's openness and willingness to participate in the treatment process. For example, individuals with extremely high *L* or *K* scores are likely to be highly resistant to discussing their problems in psychological treatment (Butcher, 1990).

High scores also provide useful information as to how a client will likely interact in a treatment situation. Substantial research literature exists on the clinical scale scores and engagement in psychotherapy. Many of the published correlates that can be found described in standard interpretive textbooks report treatment-related descriptors. The MMPI-2 content scales are of great use in treatment planning. Recall that the MMPI-2 content scales represent "summary scores," describing themes that the client willingly shared in the assessment. Significant elevations on symptom scales like *DEP* and *ANX* can be viewed as likely important focal symptoms to address in treatment.

Sharing MMPI-2 Data With Patients

People who take psychological tests in clinical settings usually anticipate that the psychologist will, at some point in the clinical contact, go over the results of their test with them. Learning about one's personality from an objective, supportive therapist can often be an important part of psychotherapy (Miller & Rollnick, 1991). Patients need to be provided a clear, understandable summary of their test information. Furthermore, the provision of test feedback can be one of the most therapeutic aspects of the patient's clinical contact. Several researchers have demonstrated that sensitive test feedback can have powerful effects. Finn and Tonsager (1992), Finn and Martin (1997), and Newman and Greenway (1997), in what has been called *therapeutic assessment*, have shown that patients in psychological treatment can gain substantial self-esteem, understanding of their problems, and reduced adjustment difficulties if they have a clear picture of their MMPI-2-measured personality factors.

Butcher (1990) suggested a practical strategy for providing MMPI-2 feedback to the patients entering psychological treatment to facilitate the clinical process and to provide the client with pertinent personality information. The following outline, adapted from Butcher's volume, might be useful for the test interpreter to consider in conducting an MMPI-2 test-feedback session.

Explain Why the MMPI-2 Was Administered

The practitioner should provide the patient a clear reason why he or she was administered the MMPI-2. The therapist can explain that he or she would like to use every effective means available to try to understand the client fully. (It is interesting to note that patients actually appreciate that the therapist used scientific means to understand their problems.) The therapist may indicate that he or she used the MMPI-2 for this purpose because it contains extensive external sources of information about their client's problems.

Describe What the MMPI-2 Is and How Widely It Is Used

Most people are unfamiliar with psychological testing or the MMPI-2; in some communities where the MMPI-2 is widely used, there may be preconceived ideas about the test or misconceptions about its use. It is important to establish the credibility of the feedback procedure and to indicate the objective nature of the MMPI-2 by providing the client with background on the instrument: its length of service to the mental health profession (about 60 years), its extensive application (the most widely used psychological test; see Lubin, Larsen, & Matarazzo, 1984), and its respected status as the major personality–clinical test in the majority of clinical settings in the United States and in many other countries, with adaptations in many other languages.

Describe How the MMPI-2 Works

Briefly describe how the scales were developed and highlight the extent of the empirical scale development and validation. Emphasize that the MMPI-2 is an objective and valid instrument that provides the patient with a problem review (clinical and content scales profiles) as well as a view of test-taking attitudes (validity scale profile) using the following:

1. Point out what an "average" or typical performance on each scale is by referring to the "normal" range on a profile sheet.
2. Point out where the elevated score range is and what a score of $T = 65$ or 80 means in terms of the number of people falling above and below that score.

It is useful to point out that the MMPI-2 patterns have been widely studied among diverse groups of patients. It is also helpful to use the client's own profile to serve as an illustration of the scale score average range, elevation differences and their meaning, and so forth.

Describe How the Validity Scales Work

Briefly describe how the validity indicators can provide important information about the client's strategies in approaching the test items. It is useful to focus on how the client presented himself or herself on the test and how he or she viewed the problem situation at the time. Discussion of the client's validity pattern is a crucial aspect of the test feedback process because it provides the therapist with an opportunity to explore the patient's motivation for treatment and his or her initial accessibility to treatment. For example, patients who omit a lot of items or obtain high elevations on L or K ($T > 60$) are seen as defensive and self-protective and are not likely to enter into the treatment process with the goal of self-revelation. In cases of high initial treatment resistance, the therapist can explore with the patient possible factors influencing this reluctance and can discuss the potentially negative outcomes from such resistance.

Point Out the Most Salient Problems

It is important to give the patient a clear understanding that his or her responses are compared with those of thousands of other individuals who have taken the MMPI-2 under different conditions. Describe their highest ranging clinical scores in terms of prevailing attitudes, symptoms, problem areas, and so forth, as shown by any significant departures from the norms on the clinical scales. It is also valuable to discuss the individual's low points on the profile to provide a contrast with other personality areas in which he or she does not seem to be having problems. Avoid making rare predictions. MMPI-2 correlates or descriptions that are low in occurrence (i.e., having a low base rate) should not be included in the feedback. It is often useful and desirable in treatment-feedback sessions to use the psychological test indices to base predictions about future behavior of the patient. Avoid using psychological jargon when providing personality feedback; translate the technical terms into language the patient can understand. The personality descriptions and symptoms presented by the patient through the item content are important concepts to communicate.

Communicate the Information in Segments

Be selective and choose the most pertinent features to share with the client. It is possible that the client might have low insight into his or her own contribution to the problems and might not "see" or accept some feedback on some issues or characteristics. In this case, the therapist should avoid getting into a disagreement with the client to win the point. The goal for providing feedback should be to present tentative findings from the test that have high validity and generalizability and that might prove useful in the individual's treatment.

Seek Questions During the Feedback Session

Give the client an opportunity to ask questions about his or her scores, and clear up any points of concern. Sometimes a person will become fixed on an irrelevant or inconsequential point or an incorrect interpretation. It is important to ensure that the misconceptions are cleared up and that the individual becomes aware of the most salient elements of his or her test performance. Providing an active interchange over issues raised by the test can promote a treatment-oriented atmosphere that encourages self-knowledge on the part of the client.

Evaluate How the Test Feedback Was Accepted

Before you end the feedback session, it is important to get a "closing summary" from the client as to how he or she feels the test characterized his or her problems. The clinician can evaluate whether any aspects of the test results were particularly surprising or distressing and whether the patient disagreed with or disclaimed any aspects of the interpretation. (This does not mean that the test interpretation is wrong, only that it does not agree with the individual's self-perception at the moment. That might change as therapy proceeds.) The information exchange in the feedback session may actually provide excellent material and foci with which to proceed directly in the treatment process.

Depending on the patient, it may be necessary to schedule more than one test feedback session to ensure that the feedback is incorporated by the client. It is important to evaluate whether the individual has accepted, rejected, or elaborated on the feedback. Some clients, particularly those with high elevations on the *Pd,* may not incorporate feedback well. They do not appear to accept outside opinion well but may distort the information provided in an effort to minimize their problems. Having a second feedback session allows the therapist an opportunity to reiterate points that have been deleted or to correct inaccurate perceptions. Having a second feedback session allows the person to ask questions he or she might have had (after a few days consideration) but were hesitant to ask before.

Should Patients Be Able to Keep Their Reports and Profiles?

Providing patients with technical information, such as profiles or narrative computer reports, to keep is not a good idea. The clinical report, described in chapter 8, and MMPI-2 profiles were not developed for nonpsychologists. These are essentially "raw data" from which psychologists draw their conclusions and make their interpretations. Such technical test materials require psychological training to understand, and most people do not have that background.

Computer-based narratives are recommended as a professional-to-professional communication and are not meant as reports to be given to clients to keep. This is not to say that patients should not receive written feedback on their MMPI-2 results. On the contrary, it is valuable in some clinical contexts that patients receive a summary of their test results. In the event that clients need to have a written summary of their MMPI-2-based performance, a very brief summary written in lay language can be provided. It is not recommended, however, that they receive the professionally oriented report or be provided with the psychometric aspects of their test results, such as clinical profiles.

Summary

In this chapter, I addressed the process of communication between the MMPI-2 interpreter and the referral source and between the therapist and client. I examined ways of describing MMPI-2 information for other professionals and sharing test results with clients. With this task completed, I have come to the end of the trail that has wound its way through a labyrinth of MMPI-2 indices, interpretive lore, and strategies for incorporating the instrument into a clinical assessment. The introduction provided in this book serves as a starting point for using the most versatile and effective clinical assessment instrument available to the psychological practitioner.

What else is there to learn about the MMPI-2? The mission of this volume was to introduce the beginner to the concepts and strategies of MMPI-2 interpretation, with the understanding that there is considerably more to learn before you reach the level of expertise of feeling comfortable evaluating profiles and making clinical decisions about people on the basis of their response to the MMPI-2's 567 items. Although the scope of this introductory book did not allow the exploration of a number of pertinent topics and applications, you might encounter with the MMPI-2 that the path to further study is well marked. In Appendix B, readers can find a number of guides that take one a step further toward MMPI-2 expertise.

Appendix A:
Correlates of Selected
MMPI-2 Code Types

1-2/2-1

These patients report somatic problems and pain, have complaints of being physically ill, and are overly concerned about health and bodily functions. They overreact to minor physical dysfunction; their symptoms are likely to be in their digestive system. They report weakness, fatigue, and dizziness but resist psychological interpretations of their symptoms. They appear anxious, tense, nervous, restless, irritable, and dysphoric, with signs of brooding and unhappiness; they often show a loss of initiative. They may report a depressed mood.

These patients are self-conscious, introverted, and shy in social situations. They may be withdrawn and seclusive, have doubts about their ability, and show vacillation and indecision about even minor matters. They tend to be hypersensitive and passive dependent. They harbor hostility toward those who are perceived as not offering enough attention and support.

Excessive use of alcohol or prescription drugs may occur as these patients' tension reducers. This profile type is usually diagnosed as neurotic (hypochondriacal, anxiety, or depressive). They may not be a good risk for traditional psychotherapy, can tolerate high levels of discomfort before becoming motivated to change, and use repression and somatization. They lack insight and self-understanding and resist accepting responsibility for their own behavior. Short-lived symptomatic changes often occur.

1-3/3-1

This profile code typically describes patients diagnosed with psycho-physiologic or neurotic (hysterical, hypochondriacal) disorders. The classic conversion syndrome may be present. Severe anxiety and depression are usually absent. This type of person functions at a re-duced level of efficiency and develops physical symptoms under stress that may disappear when the stress subsides. In terms of their basic personality characteristics, patients with this profile pattern tend to be overly optimistic and superficial in social situations. They tend to be immature, egocentric, and selfish. They feel insecure and have strong needs for attention and affection. They frequently tend to seek sympathy from others. In addition, they often show a pattern of dependency.

High 1-3/3-1 patients are usually found to be outgoing and socially extraverted, but their interpersonal relationships are superficial. They tend to lack genuine involvement with people and may be exploitive in social relationships. They are reportedly naïve and lacking in skills to deal with the opposite sex. Many patients with this code type appear low in sexual drive but may be flirtatious. They seek attention and may show resentment and hostility toward those who do not offer enough attention and support to them. They are overcontrolled and passive–aggressive and have occasional angry outbursts. They are mostly conventional and conforming in attitudes and beliefs.

These patients are usually not motivated for psychotherapy, and when there they expect definite answers and solutions to their problems. They may terminate their therapy prematurely if their therapist fails to respond to their demands. Individuals who fall into this code-type group tend to prefer medical explanations for their symptoms and to resist psychological interpretations for their problems. They tend to deny and rationalize their behavior and to be uninsightful. They may see themselves as normal, responsible, and without fault. They tend to be "Pollyanna"-ish about their symptoms and lack appropriate concern, even though their symptoms and problems, if genuine, are extremely disabling.

1-4/4-1

Severe hypochondriacal symptoms are present, especially nonspecific headaches and stomach distress. These patients are indecisive and anxious; they are socially extraverted but lack skills to relate to the opposite sex. They feel rebellious toward home and parents but do not express these feelings. Excessive use of alcohol is likely. They lack drive and have poorly defined goals. They are often dissatisfied, pessimistic, demanding, grouchy, aggressive, and resistant to traditional psychotherapy.

1-8/8-1

These patients tend to harbor feelings of hostility and aggression but cannot express them in a modulated, adaptive manner. Reporting as either inhibited and "bottled up" or overly belligerent and abrasive, they feel socially inadequate and do not trust other people. They live an isolated, alienated, and nomadic life style, in which they are unhappy and depressed. They often show a flat affect and may be confused and distractible. These patients are usually diagnosed as schizophrenic.

1-9/9-1

Extreme distress is present. These patients are anxious, tense, and restless. They have somatic complaints and are reluctant to accept psychological explanations for such complaints. They are aggressive and belligerent but actually passive dependent; however, they try to deny it. They tend to be ambitious and have a high drive level but lack clear goals. They are often frustrated by their inability to achieve at such a high level. Sometimes, this profile is found in people with brain damage who experience difficulty coping with such deficits.

2-3/3-2

The 2-3/3-2 patients usually do not experience disabling anxiety, but they do feel nervous, tense, worried, sad, depressed, fatigued, exhausted, and weak. They lack interest and involvement in life situations and cannot get started on things. They have a decreased physical activity level, and often report gastrointestinal complaints.

In terms of personality features, these patients are passive, docile, and dependent; they often have self-doubts and feel inadequate, insecure, and helpless. They elicit nurturance from others; they are driven but afraid to place themselves directly in competitive situations. They seek increased responsibility but dread pressure associated with such responsibility. They feel that they do not get adequate recognition for their accomplishments and are hurt by even minor criticism. They tend to be overcontrolled; they cannot express their feelings or feel "bottled up." They deny unacceptable impulses and avoid social involvement. They often feel especially uncomfortable around the opposite sex. Sexual maladjustment, including frigidity and impotence, is common.

These patients tend to function at a lowered level of efficiency for long periods. They appear to tolerate a great deal of unhappiness. They are usually diagnosed with depressive neurosis and are not very responsive to psychotherapy. They are not introspective, lack insight, and resist psychological formulations of their problems.

2-4/4-2

These patients may have a history of legal problems. They are impulsive and unable to delay gratification of their impulses. They have little respect for social standards and values, and often act out. Excessive drinking is likely. They appear frustrated by a lack of their own accomplishments and are resentful of demands placed on them by others. After their acting out behavior, these patients may express guilt and remorse, but they are not sincere. Suicide ideation and attempts are possible, especially if both scales are grossly elevated.

They tend to appear sociable and outgoing, making a favorable first impression. Their tendency to manipulate others causes resentment in their long-term relationships. Beneath the facade of competent and comfortable is self-conscious, self-dissatisfied, and passive dependent. They may express a need for help and a desire to change, but the prognosis for psychotherapy is poor. They are likely to terminate therapy prematurely when their stress subsides or when they are extracted from legal difficulties.

2-7/7-2

People with this profile type typically present with mood symptoms, such as depression, anxiety, and tension. They reportedly feel nervous a great deal of the time and worry to excess. They tend to be vulnerable to real and imagined threats and tend to anticipate problems before they occur. They reportedly overreact to minor stress with feelings of "catastrophic doom."

Symptomatically, they report a variety of physical problems, centering on fatigue and exhaustion. They usually report that they feel unhappy and sad. They often acknowledge that they feel sluggish in their actions and speech and may display a slowness of their thought processes. In conversations, they are usually very pessimistic about overcoming their problems. They usually report that their daily activities are filled with dull and uninteresting activities. Others typically view them as brooding, moody, and ruminative.

People with the 2-7/7-2 code type tend to be overly conscientious and reportedly have a strong need to do what is right. They may have high and unrealistic expectations of themselves. They often report feeling guilty at times, without having done anything wrong. Clinically, they report being indecisive and feeling inadequate, insecure, and inferior to others. They are viewed as intropunitive and rigid in their thinking and problem-solving styles. In addition, they are often meticulous, perfectionistic, and somewhat compulsive. Many with this pattern are excessively religious and extremely moralistic. They tend to be docile, passive, and dependent in their relationships. They have difficulty asserting themselves in social situations.

They show a high capacity for forming deep, emotional ties and actively tend to seek nurturance and reassurance from others. They usually are highly motivated for psychotherapy and tend to remain in therapy for a long time. Individuals with this pattern tend to show considerable improvement in therapy. They are variously diagnosed as depressive, obsessive–compulsive, or having an anxiety disorder.

2-8/8-2

These patients appear anxious, agitated, tense, and jumpy. They have sleep disturbances and are unable to concentrate. They have forgetfulness and confused thinking. They are inefficient in carrying out responsibilities and are unoriginal and stereotyped in thinking and problem solving. They experience somatic symptoms but often underestimate the seriousness of their problems, hence they have an unrealistic self-appraisal.

Personality features include dependent, unassertive, irritable, and resentful. They fear a loss of control and do not express their emotions. They deny their impulses. Dissociative periods of acting out may occur. They are sensitive to others' reactions and are suspicious of others' motivations. They have a history of being hurt emotionally and fear being hurt more; hence they avoid close interpersonal relationships. Feelings of despair and worthlessness are usually present.

Serious maladjustment is likely; the most common diagnoses are manic-depressive psychosis and schizophrenia, schizoaffective type. They often have chronic, incapacitating symptomatology, and are guilt ridden and clinically depressed. They have soft and reduced speech and a retarded stream of thought. They are often tearful and show apathy and indifference toward most activities. They often have a preoccupation with suicidal thoughts and may have specific plans for doing away with themselves.

2-9/9-2

These patients are likely to be self-centered and narcissistic; they ruminate about their self-worth. They often express concern about achieving at a high level but set themselves up for failure. In younger people, this may suggest an identity crisis.

They may be anxious and tense; their somatic complaints are in their gastrointestinal tract. They are not particularly depressed but may have a history of serious depression. They use alcohol as an escape from stress and pressure. These patients often deny their feelings of inadequacy and worthlessness and defend against depression through excessive activity, with alternating periods of increased activity and fatigue. The most common diagnosis is manic-depressive disorder. This profile is sometimes found in patients with brain damage who have lost control or who are trying to cope with their deficits through excessive activity.

3-4/4-3

Chronic and intense anger may be present; these patients harbor hostile and aggressive impulses but cannot express them appropriately. They are usually overcontrolled but often have occasional, brief episodes of assaultive, violent acting out. They lack the insight into the origins and consequences of their behavior. They are extrapunitive and do not see their own behavior as problematic.

These patients are free of disabling anxiety and depression but may have somatic complaints. Occasional upset does not seem to be related directly to their external stress.

They show deep, chronic feelings of hostility toward family members and demand attention and approval from others; however, they are sensitive to rejection and feel hostile when criticized. They appear outwardly conforming but are inwardly rebellious. Sexual maladjustment and promiscuity are common. Suicidal thoughts and attempts may follow acting-out episodes. The most common diagnoses are passive–aggressive personality and emotionally unstable personality.

3-6/6-3

These patients' presenting problems may not seem incapacitating and include moderate tension, anxiety, and physical complaints. They often show deep, chronic feelings of hostility toward their family members. They do not express negative feeling directly and may not recognize hostile feelings within themselves. They are often defiant, uncooperative, and hard to get along with. They report being mildly suspicious and resentful, self-centered, and narcissistic. They deny serious psychological problems and have a naive and gullible attitude toward the world.

3-8/8-3

These patients show intense psychological turmoil. They appear anxious, tense, nervous, fearful, and worried and have phobias, depression, and feelings of hopelessness. They cannot make even minor decisions. They often report a wide variety of physical complaints. They appear vague and evasive when they are talking about their complaints and difficulties.

They are likely to be immature and dependent; they have strong needs for attention and affection. They are intropunitive, apathetic, and pessimistic. They are not actively involved in life situations and have an unoriginal, stereotyped approach to problems. Insight-oriented therapy is not effective with these patients, but supportive therapy is.

They may show disturbed thinking and have concentration problems, lapses of memory, unusual unconventional ideas, loose ideational associations, obsessive ruminations, delusions, and hallucinations. Irrelevant, incoherent speech may be present; the most common diagnosis for these patients is schizophrenia.

4-5/5-4

Usually present in only men, these patients are immature, narcissistic, and emotionally passive. They have strong, unrecognized dependency needs and a difficulty in incorporating societal values. They are nonconforming and defy convention through their dress, speech, and behavior. They usually have adequate control, but brief periods of acting out in an aggressive manner may occur; temporary guilt and remorse may follow such behavior. They are usually diagnosed with a passive–aggressive personality. They experience great difficulty with their sex role identity, and overt homosexuality is possible, especially if both scales are grossly elevated. They often fear being dominated by women.

4-6/6-4

These patients are likely to be immature, narcissistic, self-indulgent, and passive dependent. They often make excessive demands on others for attention and sympathy; but they are resentful of demands made on them. Women with this profile overly identify with the traditional female role and are very dependent on men. These patients do not get along well with others, especially members of the opposite sex. They are suspicious of others' motivations. They avoid deep emotional involvement and have repressed hostility and anger. They are often irritable, sullen, argumentative, and generally obnoxious as well as resentful of authority.

These patients will probably deny their serious psychological problems; instead they rationalize and transfer the blame. They cannot accept responsibility for their own behavior and are unrealistic and grandiose in their self-appraisals. These patients are unreceptive to psychotherapy and are usually diagnosed with a passive–aggressive personality or schizophrenia, paranoid type.

4-7/7-4

Patients with this profile may alternate between periods of gross insensitivity to the consequences of their own actions and excessive concern about the effects of their own behavior. They often have episodes of acting out, followed by temporary guilt and self-condemnation. Characteristics include vague somatic complaints, tense, fatigued, exhausted, dependent, and insecure. They require almost constant reassurance of their self-worth. In therapy, they respond symptomatically to support and reassurance.

4-8/8-4

These patients do not seem to fit into their environment; they appear odd or peculiar and are nonconforming and resentful of authority.

They may espouse radical religious or political views. They are often erratic and unpredictable and have problems with impulse control. These patients are angry, irritable, and resentful and act out in asocial ways, such as delinquency and criminal acts. Sexual deviation may be present. They often partake in excessive drinking and drug abuse, especially hallucinogens. They show underachievement and marginal adjustment.

These patients show deep feelings of insecurity and have exaggerated needs for attention and affection. They have a poor self concept and often set themselves up for rejection and failure. They have periods of suicidal obsessions. They are distrustful and avoid close relationships. They have impaired empathy and lack basic social skills. They are withdrawn and isolated and tend to see the world as threatening and rejecting. They often withdraw into a fantasy world or strike out in anger as a defense against being hurt. They accept little responsibility for their own behavior, instead they rationalize and blame others for their own difficulties. They harbor strong concerns about masculinity or femininity and are obsessed with sexual thoughts. They are afraid of being unable to perform sexually and may indulge in antisocial sexual acts in an attempt to demonstrate sexual adequacy. The most common diagnosis for this profile type is schizophrenia (paranoid type, asocial personality, schizoid personality, and paranoid personality).

4-9/9-4

Individuals with this profile type tend to show marked disregard for social standards and values. They are usually viewed as antisocial; they appear to have a poorly developed conscience, easy morals, and fluctuating ethical values. It is not unusual to find that they have legal difficulties or work problems. They tend to have a wide array of problem behaviors, such as alcoholism, fighting, and sexual acting out.

In terms of personality features, the 4-9/9-4 patient is likely to be narcissistic, selfish, self-indulgent, and impulsive. These individuals tend to be viewed as irresponsible. They cannot delay gratification of impulses and show poor judgment. They also reportedly act out, without considering the consequences of their behavior. People with this pattern tend to fail to learn from punishing experiences. When in trouble, they rationalize their shortcomings and failures, blame their difficulties on others, and lie to avoid responsibility. They reportedly have a low frustration tolerance and are seen as moody, irritable, and having a caustic manner. They are often angry and hostile and may have occasional emotional outbursts.

These patients are also energetic, restless, and overactive. They tend to seek out emotional stimulation and excitement. They are uninhibited, extraverted, and talkative in social situations. They often create a good first impression because they are glib and spontaneous; however, their relationships are usually superficial. They appear to avoid deep emotional ties. They are considered "loners" who keep others at an emotional distance. They usually present as self-confident and secure but are quite immature. The usual diagnosis for this profile type is antisocial personality.

6-8/8-6

Patients with this profile type usually experience severe mental disorder and are diagnosed as having schizophrenia, paranoid type. They manifest clearly psychotic behavior; their thinking is autistic, fragmented, tangential, and circumstantial. They usually experience bizarre thought content and have difficulties in concentrating, attention, and memory. They usually have poor judgment, delusions of persecution or grandeur, and feelings of unreality. They typically show a preoccupation with unusual, abstract thoughts. Delusions and blunted affect are often present. These individuals may have rapid and incoherent speech. They tend to lack effective defense mechanisms and show extreme anxiety at times. They are likely to react to stress and pressure by withdrawing into fantasy and daydreaming. They tend to have difficulty in differentiating between fantasy and reality.

Feelings of inferiority and insecurity are common in this type of patient, as is a lack self-confidence and self-esteem. People with this pattern often feel guilty about perceived failures. Social withdrawal from activity and emotional apathy are likely to be prominent in their clinical pattern. These patients are usually not involved with other people and are suspicious and distrustful, usually avoiding deep emotional ties. Their poor social skills are likely to limit efforts at rehabilitation. They are most comfortable when they are alone. They resent interpersonal demands placed on them, and they become moody, irritable, unfriendly, and negative. They tend to have a long-term pattern of maladjustment and usually a schizoid life style. They are typically treated with phenothyzianes to control their psychotic thought patterns and behaviors.

6-9/9-6

These patients are likely to be overly sensitive and mistrustful. They may show a strong need for affection, feel vulnerable to real or imagined threats, and feel anxious much of the time. They may be tearful and trembling, overreact to minor stress, respond to severe stress by withdrawing into fantasy, and cannot express emotions in adaptive, modulated way. They may alternate between overcontrolled and direct, uncontrolled emotional outbursts.

Psychiatric inpatients with this code may be diagnosed as schizophrenia, paranoid type, or a mood disorder. They are likely to show signs of thought disorder and complain of difficulties in thinking and concentrating. They appear to have stream of consciousness problems and are ruminative or overideational and obsessional. They may have delusions and hallucinations, and their speech may be irrelevant and incoherent. They often are disoriented and perplexed and have poor judgment.

7-8/8-7

Patients with this profile code typically show a great deal of turmoil. They do not hesitant to admit to having psychological problems. They lack the defenses to keep themselves comfortable; hence, they are depressed, worried, tense, and nervous. They may be confused and in a state of panic. They have poor judgment and do not profit from experience. They are introspective, ruminative, and overideational.

Chronic feelings of insecurity, inadequacy, inferiority, and indecisiveness are likely to occur. They lack socialization experiences and are not socially poised or confident. They withdraw from social interactions and are passive dependent. They cannot take dominant roles in relationships and have difficulties with mature heterosexual relationships. They often feel inadequate in a traditional sex role; their sexual performance is poor; and they engage in rich sexual fantasies.

Patients with this profile may be diagnosed with anxiety disorder; however, anxiety-based disorder diagnoses decrease, as Scale 8 becomes greater than Scale 7, as the likelihood of psychotic diagnosis increases. Even when they are diagnosed as psychotic, blatant psychotic symptoms may not be present.

8-9/9-8

Individuals with this profile code are viewed as self-centered and infantile in their expectations of others; they demand much attention and become resentful and hostile when their demands are not met. However, they fear emotional involvement and avoid close relationships; hence, they are socially withdrawn and isolated and are especially uncomfortable in heterosexual relationships. They also tend to have poor sexual adjustment.

They are hyperactive and emotionally labile, appearing agitated and excited. They demonstrate loud, excessive talk and have unrealistic self-appraisal. Their thoughts are grandiose and boastful, resulting in vague and evasive statements. They are fickle. They avoid talking about their difficulties and may not state a need for professional help. They have a high need to achieve and may feel pressured to do so; however, their performance tends to be mediocre. They often feel inferior and inadequate and have a low self-esteem. They show limited involvement in competitive or achievement-oriented situations.

A serious psychological disturbance is likely. The most common diagnosis is schizophrenia (catatonic, schizoaffective, or paranoid). A severe thinking disturbance may also be present, resulting in the patients feeling confused, perplexed, and disoriented. They also have feelings of unreality and a difficulty in thinking and concentrating. They are unable to focus on issues and experience odd, unusual, autistic, circumstantial thinking. Bizarre speech (clang associations, neologisms, echolalia), delusions, and hallucinations may be symptoms of these patients. This profile is sometimes found in adolescent drug users.

Appendix B: Selected References for the MMPI-2

Surveys of Test Usage

Ackerman, M. J., & Ackerman, M. C. (1997). Custody evaluation practices: A survey of experienced professionals (revisited). *Professional Psychology: Research and Practice, 28,* 137–145.

Borum, R., & Grisso, T. (1995). Psychological test use in criminal forensic evaluations. *Professional Psychology: Research and Practice, 26,* 465–473.

Lees-Haley, P. R. (1992). Psychodiagnostic test usage by forensic psychologists. *American Journal of Forensic Psychology, 10,* 25–30.

Lees-Haley, P. R., Smith, H. H., Williams, C. W., & Dunn, J. T. (1996). Forensic neuropsychological test usage: An empirical survey. *Archives of Clinical Neuropsychology, 11,* 45–51.

Lubin, B., Larsen, R. M., & Matarazzo, J. (1984). Patterns of psychological test usage in the United States: 1935–1982. *American Psychologist, 39,* 451–454.

General MMPI and MMPI-2

Ben-Porath, Y. S. (1994). The MMPI and MMPI-2: Fifty years of differentiating normal and abnormal personality. In S. Strack & M. Lorr (Eds.), *Differentiating normal and abnormal personality* (pp. 361–401). New York: Springer.

Ben-Porath, Y. S., & Butcher, J. N. (1995). Personality assessment. In L. A. Heiden & M. Hersen (Eds.), *Introduction to clinical psychology* (pp. 141–169). New York: Plenum Press.

Ben-Porath, Y. S., Graham, J. R., Hall, G. C., Hirschman, R. D., & Zaragoza, M. S. (Eds.). (1995). *Forensic applications of the MMPI-2*. Thousand Oaks, CA: Sage.

Butcher, J. N. (1990). *Use of the MMPI-2 in treatment planning*. New York: Oxford University Press

Butcher, J. N. (Ed.). (1997). *Personality assessment, psychological treatment, and managed care*. New York: Oxford University Press.

Butcher, J. N., Dahlstrom, W. G., Graham, J. R., Tellegen, A. M., & Kaemmer, B. (1989).

Minnesota Multiphasic Personality Inventory–2 (MMPI-2): Manual for administration and scoring. Minneapolis: University of Minnesota Press.

Butcher, J. N., Graham, J. R., & Ben-Porath, Y. S. (1995). Methodological problems and issues in MMPI/MMPI-2/MMPI-A research. *Psychological Assessment, 7,* 320–329.

Butcher, J. N., Graham, J. R., Williams, C. L., & Ben-Porath, Y. S. (1990). *Development and use of the MMPI-2 content scales.* Minneapolis: University of Minnesota Press.

Butcher, J. N., & Williams, C. L. (1992). *MMPI-2 and MMPI: Essentials of clinical interpretation.* Minneapolis: University of Minnesota Press.

Butcher, J. N., Williams, C. L., Graham, J. R., Tellegen, A., Ben-Porath, Y. S., Archer, R. P., & Kaemmer, B. (1992). *Manual for administration, scoring, and interpretation of the Minnesota Multiphasic Personality Inventory for Adolescents: MMPI-A.* Minneapolis: University of Minnesota Press.

Dahlstrom, W. G. (1993). *MMPI-2: Manual supplement.* Minneapolis: University of Minnesota Press.

Graham, J. R. (in press). *The MMPI-2: Assessing personality and psychopathology* (3rd ed.). New York: Oxford University Press.

Greene, R. L. (1991). *MMPI-2/MMPI: An interpretive manual.* Boston: Allyn & Bacon.

Hathaway, S. R., & McKinley, J. C. (1940). A multiphasic personality schedule (Minnesota): 1. Construction of the schedule. *Journal of Psychology, 10,* 249–254.

Pope, K. S., Butcher, J. N., & Seelen, J. (1993). *The MMPI, MMPI-2, & MMPI-A in court: A practical guide for expert witnesses and attorneys.* Washington, DC: American Psychological Association.

Williams, C. L., Butcher, J. N., Graham, J. R., & Ben-Porath, Y. S. (1992). *Assessing adolescent personality: Development and use of the MMPI-A content scales.* Minneapolis: University of Minnesota Press.

Normative Issues

Butcher, J. N. (Ed.). (1972). *Objective personality assessment: Changing perspectives.* New York: Academic Press.

Butcher, J. N. (1994). Psychological assessment of airline pilot applicants with the MMPI-2. *Journal of Personality Assessment, 62,* 31–44.

Butcher, J. N., Aldwin, C., Levenson, M., Ben-Porath, Y. S., Spiro, A., & Bosse, R. (1991). Personality and aging: A study of the MMPI-2 among elderly men. *Psychology of Aging, 6,* 361–370.

Butcher, J. N., Graham, J. R., Dahlstrom, W. G., & Bowman, E. (1990). The MMPI-2 with college students. *Journal of Personality Assessment, 54,* 1–15.

Butcher, J. N., Jeffrey, T., Cayton, T. G., Colligan, S., DeVore, J., & Minnegawa, R. (1990). A study of active duty military personnel with the MMPI-2. *Military Psychology, 2,* 47–61.

Pancoast, D. L., & Archer, R. P. (1989). Original adult MMPI norms in adult samples: A review with implications for future developments. *Journal of Personality Assessment, 53,* 376–395.

Parkison, S., & Fishburne, F. (1984). MMPI normative data for a male active duty Army population. In *Proceedings of the psychology in the Department of Defense: Ninth Symposium* (USAFA-TR-84-2, pp. 570–574). Colorado Springs, CO: U.S. Air Force Academy, Department of Behavioral Sciences and Leadership.

Tellegen, A., & Ben-Porath, Y. S. (1992). The new uniform T scores for the MMPI-2: Rationale, derivation, and appraisal. *Psychological Assessment, 4,* 145–155.

Tellegen, A., & Ben-Porath, Y. S. (1993). Code-type comparability across MMPI and

MMPI-2 norms: Some necessary clarifications. *Journal of Personality Assessment, 61,* 489–500.

Equivalence of the MMPI-2 With the Original MMPI

Ben-Porath, Y. S., & Butcher, J. N. (1989). The comparability of MMPI and MMPI-2 scales and profiles. *Psychological Assessment: A Journal of Consulting and Clinical Psychology, 1,* 345–347.

Ben-Porath, Y. S., & Tellegen, A. (1995). How (not) to evaluate the comparability of MMPI and MMPI-2 profile configurations: A reply to Humphrey and Dahlstrom. *Journal of Personality Assessment, 65,* 52–58.

Chojnacki, J. T., & Walsh, W. B. (1992). The consistency of scores and configural patterns between the MMPI and MMPI-2. *Journal of Personality Assessment, 59,* 276–289.

Chojnacki, J. T., & Walsh, W. B. (1994). The consistency between scores of the Harris–Lingoes subscales of the MMPI and MMPI-2. *Journal of Personality Assessment, 62,* 157–165.

Graham, J. R., Timbrook, R., Ben-Porath, Y. S., & Butcher, J. N. (1991). Code-type congruence between MMPI and MMPI-2: Separating fact from artifact. *Journal of Personality Assessment, 57,* 205–215.

Harrell, T. H., Honaker, L. M., & Parnell, T. (1992). Equivalence of the MMPI-2 with the MMPI in psychiatric patients. *Psychological Assessment, 4,* 460–465.

Tellegen, A., & Ben-Porath, Y. S. (1993). Code type comparability of the MMPI and MMPI-2: Analysis of recent findings and criticisms. *Journal of Personality Assessment, 61,* 489–500.

Vincent, K. R. (1990). The fragile nature of MMPI codetypes. *Journal of Clinical Psychology. 46,* 800–802.

Ward, L. C. (1991). A comparison of *T* scores from MMPI and MMPI-2. *Psychological Assessment: A Journal of Consulting and Clinical Psychology, 3,* 688–690.

Reliability

Ben-Porath, Y. S., & Butcher, J. N. (1989). Psychometric stability of rewritten MMPI items. *Journal of Personality Assessment, 53,* 645–653.

Leon, G. R., Gillum, B., Gillum, R., & Gouze, M. (1979). Personality stability and change over a 30-year period—Middle age to old age. *Journal of Consulting and Clinical Psychology, 47,* 517–524.

Spiro, R., Butcher, J. N., Levenson, M., Aldwin, C., & Bosse, R. (1993, August). *Personality change over five years: The MMPI-2 in older men.* Paper presented at the 101st Annual Convention of the American Psychological Association, Toronto, Ontario, Canada.

Van Cleve, E., Jemelka, R., & Trupin, E. (1991). Reliability of psychological test scores for offenders entering a state prison system. *Criminal Justice and Behavior, 18,* 159–165.

MMPI-2 Validity

Archer, R. P., Griffin, R., & Aiduk, R. (1995). MMPI-2: Clinical correlates for ten common code types. *Journal of Personality Assessment, 65,* 391–408.

Ben-Porath, Y. S., Butcher, J. N., & Graham, J. R. (1991). Contribution of the MMPI-2 content scales to the differential diagnosis of psychopathology. *Psychological Assessment, 3,* 634–640.

Ben-Porath, Y. S., McCully, E., & Almagor, M. (1993). Incremental validity of the MMPI-2 content scales in the assessment of personality and psychopathology by self-report. *Journal of Personality Assessment, 61,* 557–575.

Blake, D. D., Penk, W. E., Mori, D. L., Kleespies, P., Walsh, S. S., & Keane, T. (1992). Validity and clinical scale comparisons between the MMPI and MMPI-2 with psychiatric patients. *Psychological Reports, 70,* 323–332.

Brems, C., & Lloyd, P. (1995). Validation of the MMPI-2 Low Self-Esteem Content Scale. *Journal of Personality Assessment, 65,* 550–556.

Butcher, J. N., Rouse, S., & Perry, J. (in press). *Empirical correlates of MMPI-2 scales in an outpatient psychotherapy population: Foundation sources for the MMPI-2.* Minneapolis: University of Minnesota Press.

Egeland, B., Erickson, M., Butcher, J. N., & Ben-Porath, Y. S. (1991). MMPI-2 profiles of women at risk for child abuse. *Journal of Personality Assessment, 57,* 254–263.

Faull, R., & Meyer, G. J. (1993, March). *Assessment of depression with the MMPI-2: Distinctions between Scale 2 and the* DEP. Paper presented at the midwinter meeting of the Society for Personality Assessment, San Francisco, CA.

Flamer, S. (1992, May). *Differential diagnosis of post traumatic stress disorder in injured workers: Evaluating the MMPI-2.* Paper presented at the 27th Annual Symposium on Recent Developments in the Use of the MMPI (MMPI-2), Minneapolis, MN.

Gass, C. S. (1991). MMPI-2 interpretation and closed head injury: A correction factor. *Psychological Assessment: A Journal of Consulting and Clinical Psychology, 3,* 27–31.

Gass, C. S. (1992). MMPI-2 interpretation of patients with cerebrovascular disease: A correction factor. *Archives of Neuropsychology, 7,* 17–27.

Graham, J. R. (1988, August). *Establishing validity of the revised form of the MMPI.* Symposium presented at the 96th Annual Convention of the American Psychological Association, Atlanta, GA.

Graham, J. R., Ben-Porath, Y. S., & McNulty, J. (in press). *Using the MMPI-2 in outpatient mental health settings.* Minneapolis: University of Minnesota Press.

Greene, R. L., Weed, N. C., Butcher, J. N., Arrendondo, R., & Davis, H. G. (1992). A cross-validation of MMPI-2 substance abuse scales. *Journal of Personality Assessment, 58,* 405–410.

Hills, H. A. (1995). Diagnosing personality disorders: An examination of the MMPI-2 and MCMI-II. *Journal of Personality Assessment, 65,* 21–34.

Hjemboe, S., Almagor, M., & Butcher, J. N. (1992). Empirical assessment of marital distress: The Marital Distress Scale (*MDS*) for the MMPI-2. In C. D. Spielberger & J. N. Butcher (Eds.), *Advances in personality assessment* (Vol. 9, pp. 141–152). Hillsdale, NJ: Erlbaum.

Hjemboe, S., & Butcher, J. N. (1991). Couples in marital distress: A study of demographic and personality factors as measured by the MMPI-2. *Journal of Personality Assessment, 57,* 216–237.

Khan, F. I., Welch, T., & Zillmer, E. (1993). MMPI-2 profiles of battered women in transition. *Journal of Personality Assessment, 60,* 100–111.

Keane, T. M., Weathers, F. W., & Kaloupek, D. G. (1992). Psychological assessment of post-traumatic stress disorder. *PTSD Research Quarterly, 3,* 1–3.

Keller, L. S., & Butcher, J. N. (1991). *Use of the MMPI-2 with chronic pain patients.* Minneapolis: University of Minnesota Press.

Kurman, R. G., Hursey, K. G., & Mathew, N. T. (1992). Assessment of chronic refractory headache: The role of the MMPI-2. *Headache, 32,* 432–435.

Lilienfeld, S. O. (1991). Assessment of psychopathy with the MMPI and MMPI-2. *MMPI-2 News & Profiles, 2,* 2.

Litz, B. T., Penk, W., Walsh, S., Hyer, L., Blake, D. D., Marx, B., Keane, T. M., & Bitman, D. (1991). Similarities and differences between Minnesota Multiphasic Personality Inventory (MMPI) and MMPI-2 applications to the assessment of posttraumatic stress disorder. *Journal of Personality Assessment, 57,* 238–254.

Schill, T., & Wang, T. (1990). Correlates of the MMPI-2 Anger Content Scale. *Psychological Reports, 67,* 800–804.

Sieber, K. O., & Meyers, L. (1992). Validation of the MMPI-2 Social Introversion subscales. *Psychological Assessment, 4,* 185–189.

Strassberg, D. S., Clutton, S., & Korboot, P. (1991). A descriptive and validity study of the Minnesota Multiphasic Personality Inventory–2 (MMPI-2) in an elderly Australian sample. *Journal of Psychopathology and Behavioral Assessment, 13,* 301–312.

Weed, N. C., Butcher, J. N., McKenna, T., & Ben-Porath, Y. S. (1992). New measures for assessing alcohol and drug abuse with the MMPI-2: The *APS* and *AAS*. *Journal of Personality Assessment, 58,* 389–404.

Determining Profile Validity

Adelman, R. M., & Howard, A. (1984). Expert testimony on malingering: The admissibility of clinical procedures for the detection of deception. *Behavioral Sciences & the Law, 2,* 5–19.

Arbisi, P., & Ben-Porath, Y. S. (1995). An MMPI-2 infrequency scale for use with psychopathological populations: The Infrequency-Psychopathology Scale, $F(p)$. *Psychological Assessment, 7,* 424–431.

Arbisi, P., & Ben-Porath, Y. S. (1997). Characteristics of the MMPI-2 $F(p)$ scale as a function of diagnosis in an inpatient sample of veterans. *Psychological Assessment, 9,* 102–105.

Austin, J. S. (1992). The detection of fake good and fake bad on the MMPI-2. *Educational and Psychological Measurement, 52,* 669–674.

Baer, R. A., Wetter, M. W., & Berry, D. T. (1992). Detection of underreporting of psychopathology on the MMPI: A meta-analysis. *Clinical Psychology Review, 12,* 509–525.

Baer, R. A., Wetter, M. W., Nichols, D., Greene, R., & Berry, D. T. (1995). Sensitivity of MMPI-2 validity scales to underreporting of symptoms. *Psychological Assessment, 7,* 419–423.

Ben-Porath, Y. S., & Tellegen, A. (1992). Continuity and changes in MMPI-2 validity indicators: Points of clarification. *MMPI-2 News & Profiles, 3,* 6–8.

Berry, D. T. (1995). Detecting distortion in forensic evaluations with the MMPI-2. In Y. S. Ben-Porath, J. R. Graham, G. C. N. Hall, R. D. Hirschman, & M. S. Zaragoza (Eds.), *Forensic applications of the MMPI-2* (pp. 82–103). Thousand Oaks, CA: Sage.

Berry, D. T. R., Adams, J. J., Smith, G. T., Greene, R. L., Sekirnjak, G. C., Wieland, G., & Tharpe, B. (1997). MMPI-2 clinical scales and two-point code types: Impact of varying levels of omitted items. *Psychological Assessment, 9,* 158–160.

Berry, D. T., Baer, R. A., & Harris, M. J. (1991). Detection of malingering on the MMPI: A meta-analysis. *Clinical Psychology Review, 11,* 585–591.

Berry, D. T. R., & Butcher, J. N. (1997). Detection of feigning of head injury symptoms on the MMPI-2. In C. R. Reynolds (Ed.), *Detection of malingering during head injury litigation* (pp. 209–238). New York: Plenum Press.

Berry, D. T., Wetter, M. W., Baer, R. A., Larsen, L., Clark, C., & Monroe, K. (1992). MMPI-2 random responding indices: Validation using a self-report methodology. *Psychological Assessment: A Journal of Consulting and Clinical Psychology, 4,* 340–345.

Berry, D. T., Wetter, M. W., Baer, R. A., Widiger, T. A., Sumpter, J. C., Reynolds, S. K.,

& Hallam, R. A. (1991). Detection of random responding on the MMPI-2: Utility of *F,* back *F,* and *VRIN* scales. *Psychological Assessment: A Journal of Consulting and Clinical Psychology, 3,* 418–423.

Berry, D. T. R., Wetter, M. W., Baer, R., Youngjohn, J. R., Gass, C., Lamb, D. G., Franzen, M., MacInnes, W. D., & Bucholz, D. (1995). Overreporting of closed-head injury symptoms on the MMPI-2. *Psychological Assessment, 7,* 517–523.

Butcher, J. N., & Han, K. (1995). Development of an MMPI-2 scale to assess the presentation of self in a superlative manner: The *S* scale. In J. N. Butcher & C. D. Spielberger (Eds.), *Advances in personality assessment* (Vol. 10, pp. 25–50). Hillsdale, NJ: Erlbaum.

Graham, J. R., Watts, D., & Timbrook, R. (1991). Detecting fake-good and fake-bad MMPI-2 profiles. *Journal of Personality Assessment, 57,* 264–277.

Lees-Haley, P. R., English, L. T., & Glenn, W. T. (1991). A fake-bad scale on the MMPI-2 for personal injury claimants. *Psychological Reports, 68,* 203–310.

Lim, J., & Butcher, J. N. (1996). Detection of faking on the MMPI-2: Differentiation between faking-bad, denial, and claiming extreme virtue. *Journal of Personality Assessment, 67,* 1–26.

Rogers, R. (1984). Towards an empirical model of malingering and deception. *Behavioral Sciences and the Law, 2,* 93–111.

Rogers, R. (1988). *Clinical assessment of malingering and deception.* New York: Guilford Press.

Rogers, R., Bagby, R. M., & Chakraborty, D. (1993). Feigning schizophrenic disorders on the MMPI-2: Detection of coached simulators. *Journal of Personality Assessment, 60,* 215–226.

Rogers, R., Dolmetsch, R., & Cavanaugh, J. L. (1983). Identification of random responders on MMPI protocols. *Journal of Personality Assessment, 47,* 364–368.

Rogers, R., Gillis, J. R., McMain, S., & Dickens, S. E. (1988). Fitness evaluations: A retrospective study of clinical, criminal, and sociodemographic characteristics. *Canadian Journal of Behavioral Science, 20,* 192–200.

Rogers, R., Harris, M., & Thatcher, A. A. (1983). Identification of random responders on the MMPI: An actuarial approach. *Psychological Reports, 53,* 1171–1174.

Roman, D. D., & Gerbing, D. W. (1989). The mentally disordered criminal offender: A description based on demographic, clinical, and MMPI data. *Journal of Clinical Psychology, 45,* 983–990.

Roman, D. D., Tuley, M. R., Villanueva, M. R., & Mitchell, W. E. (1990). Evaluating MMPI validity in a forensic psychiatric population. *Criminal Justice and Behavior, 17,* 186–198.

Schretlen, D. (1988). The use of psychological tests to identify malingered symptoms of mental disorder. *Clinical Psychology Review, 8,* 451–476.

Sivec, H. J., Hilsenroth, M. J., & Lynn, S. J. (1995). Impact of simulating borderline personality disorder on the MMPI-2: A costs–benefits model of employing base rates. *Journal of Personality Assessment, 64,* 295–311.

Timbrook, R. E., Graham, J. R., Keiller, S. W., & Watts, D. (1993). Comparison of the Wiener–Harmon Subtle–Obvious Scales and the standard validity scales in detecting valid and invalid MMPI-2 profiles. *Psychological Assessment, 5,* 53–61.

Wasyliw, O. E., Grossman, L. S., Haywood, T. W., & Cavanaugh, J. L. (1988). The detection of malingering in criminal forensic groups: MMPI validity scales. *Journal of Personality Assessment, 52,* 321–333.

Weed, N., Ben-Porath, Y. S., & Butcher, J. N. (1990). Failure of the Weiner–Harmon MMPI subtle scales as predictors of psychopathology and as validity indicators. *Psychological Assessment, 2,* 281–283.

Wetter, M. W., Baer, R. A., Berry, D. T., Robison, L. H., & Sumpter, J. (1993). MMPI-2 profiles of motivated fakers given specific symptom information. *Psychological Assessment, 5,* 317–323.

Wetter, M. W., Baer, R. A., Berry, D. T., Smith, G. T., & Larsen, L. (1992). Sensitivity of MMPI-2 validity scales to random responding and malingering. *Psychological Assessment, 4,* 369–374.

Wetter, M. W., & Deitsch, S. E. (1996). Faking specific disorders and temporal response consistently on the MMPI-2. *Psychological Assessment, 8,* 39–47.

Ethnic Cultural Considerations

Azan, A. (1989). The MMPI Version Hispana: Standardization and cross-cultural personality study with a population of Cuban refugees (Doctoral dissertation, University of Minnesota, 1988). *Dissertation Abstracts International, 50,* 2144B.

Ben-Porath, Y. S., Shondrick, D. D., & Stafford, K. (1994). MMPI-2 and race in a forensic diagnostic sample. *Criminal Justice & Behavior, 22,* 19–32.

Butcher, J. N. (Ed.). (1996). *International adaptations of the MMPI-2: A handbook of research and clinical applications.* Minneapolis: University of Minnesota Press.

Butcher, J. N., Berah, E., Ellertsen, B., Miach, P., Lim, J., Nezami, E., Pancheri, P., Derksen, J., & Almagor, M. (1998). Objective personality assessment: Computer-based MMPI-2 interpretation in international clinical settings (pp. 277–312). In C. Belar (Ed.), *Comprehensive clinical psychology: Sociocultural and individual differences.* New York: Elsevier.

Butcher, J. N., & Pancheri, P. (1976). *Handbook of cross-national MMPI research.* Minneapolis: University of Minnesota Press.

Dahlstrom, W. G., Lachar, D., & Dahlstrom, L. E. (Eds.). (1986). *MMPI patterns of American minorities.* Minneapolis: University of Minnesota Press.

Derksen, J., De Mey, H., Sloore, H., & Hellenbosch, G. (1993). *MMPI-2: Handeleiding bij afname, scoring en interpretatie* [*MMPI-2: Handbook of scoring and interpretation*]. Nijmegen, The Netherlands: PEN Test.

Lucio, E. (1994). *Manual para la administracion y calificacion del MMPI-2* [*Manual for administration and scoring of the MMPI-2*]. Mexico City: El Manual Moderno. (Original work published 1989)

Lucio, E., Reyes-Lagunes, I., & Scott, R. L. (1994). MMPI-2 for Mexico: Translation and adaptation. *Journal of Personality Assessment, 63,* 105–116.

Mo, W., Zhang, J., & Song, W. (1992). The trial application of the MMPI-2 among Chinese college students. *Psychological Science* (China), *6,* 29–32.

Pancheri, P., & Sirgatti, S. (1996). MMPI-2: Manuale de italiano [*MMPI-2: Italian manual*]. Florence, Italy: Organazziani Espacali (OS). (Original work published 1989)

Sirigatti, S., Pancheri, P., Narbone, G., & Biondi, M. (1994). L'adattamento italiano del MMPI-2 al vaglio del test–retest con bilingui [Italian adaptation of the MMPI-2 by test–retest study of bilinguals]. *Bollettino di Psicologia Applicata, 211,* 23–27.

Sirigatti, S., & Stefanile, E. C. (1994). Il questionario è leggibile? Il caso del MMPI-2 [Questionnaire legibility: The case of the MMPI-2]. *Bollettino di Psicologia Applicata, 211,* 49–51.

Stevens, M. J., Kwan, K., & Graybill, D. F. (1993). Comparison of MMPI-2 scores of foreign Chinese and Caucasian-American students. *Journal of Clinical Psychology, 49,* 23–27.

Strassberg, D. S., Clutton, S., & Korboot, P. (1991). A descriptive and validity study of the Minnesota Multiphasic Personality Inventory–2 (MMPI-2) in an elderly Australian sample. *Journal of Psychopathology and Behavioral Assessment, 13,* 301–311.

Use of Computer-Based Reports

Allard, G., Butler, J., Faust, D., & Shea, M. T. (1995). Errors in hand scoring objective personality tests: The case of the Personality Diagnostic Questionnaire–Revised (PDQ-R). *Professional Psychology: Research and Practice, 26,* 304–308.

Butcher, J. N. (Ed). (1987). *Computerized psychological assessment.* New York: Basic Books.

Butcher, J. N. (1994). Psychological assessment by computer: Potential gains and problems to avoid. *Psychiatric Annals, 20,* 20–24.

Butcher, J. N. (1995a). Clinical use of computer-based personality test reports. In J. N. Butcher (Ed.), *Clinical personality assessment: Practical approaches* (pp. 78–94). New York: Oxford University Press.

Butcher, J. N. (1995b). *User's guide for the Minnesota Report: Revised personnel report.* Minneapolis, MN: National Computer Systems.

Eyde, L., Kowal, D. M., & Fishburne, J. E. (1987, August–September). *Clinical implications of validity research on computer-based test interpretations of the MMPI.* Paper presented at the 95th Annual Convention of the American Psychological Association, New York, NY.

Eyde, L., Kowal, D., & Fishburne, F. J. (1991). The validity of computer-based test interpretations of the MMPI. In T. B. Gutkin & S. L. Wise (Eds.), *The computer and the decision making process* (pp. 75–123). Hillsdale, NJ: Erlbaum.

Roper, B., Ben-Porath, Y. S., & Butcher, J. N. (1991). Comparability of computerized adaptive and conventional testing with the MMPI-2. *Journal of Personality Assessment, 57,* 278–290.

Roper, B., Ben-Porath, Y. S., & Butcher, J. N. (1995). Comparability and validity of computerized adaptive testing with the MMPI-2. *Journal of Personality Assessment, 65,* 358–371.

MMPI-2 Forensic

Butcher, J. N., & Pope, K. S. (1993). Seven issues in conducting forensic assessments: Ethical responsibilities in light of new standards and new tests. *Ethics and Behavior, 3,* 267–288.

Heilbrun, K. (1995). Risk assessment with the MMPI-2. In Y. S. Ben-Porath, J. R. Graham, G. C. N. Hall, R. D. Hirschman, & M. S. Zaragoza (Eds.), *Forensic applications of the MMPI-2* (pp. 160–178). Thousand Oaks, CA: Sage.

Ogloff, J. R. P. (1995). The legal basis of forensic application of the MMPI-2. In Y. S. Ben-Porath, J. R. Graham, G. C. N. Hall, R. D. Hirschman, & M. S. Zaragoza (Eds.), *Forensic applications of the MMPI-2* (pp. 18–47). Thousand Oaks, CA: Sage.

Ziskin, J. (1981). Use of the MMPI in forensic settings. In J. N. Butcher, G. Dahlstrom, M. Gynther, & W. Schofield (Eds.), *Clinical notes on the MMPI* (pp. 1–16). Minneapolis, MN: National Computer Systems.

Family Custody

Bathurst, K., Gottfried, A. W., & Gottfried, A. E. (1997). Normative data for the MMPI-2 in child litigation. *Psychological Assessment, 9,* 205–211.

Butcher, J. N., & Pope, K. S. (1992). Forensic psychology: Psychological evaluation in family custody cases—Role of the MMPI-2 and MMPI-A. *Family Law News, 15,* 25–28.

Khan, F. I., Welch, T., & Zillmer, E. (1993). MMPI-2 profiles of battered women in transition. *Journal of Personality Assessment, 60,* 100–111.

Otto, R., & Butcher, J. N. (1995). Computer-assisted psychological assessment in child custody evaluations. *Family Law Quarterly, 29,* 79–96.

Otto, R., & Collins, R. P. (1995). Use of the MMPI-2/MMPI-A in child custody evaluations. In Y. S. Ben-Porath, J. R. Graham, G. C. N. Hall, R. D. Hirschman, & M. S. Zaragoza (Eds.), *Forensic applications of the MMPI-2* (pp. 222–252). Thousand Oaks, CA: Sage

Personal Injury Litigation

Butcher, J. N. (1995). Personality patterns of personal injury litigants: The role of computer-based MMPI-2 evaluations. In Y. S. Ben-Porath, J. R. Graham, G. C. N. Hall, R. D. Hirschman, & M. S. Zaragoza (Eds.), *Forensic applications of the MMPI-2* (pp. 179–201). Thousand Oaks, CA: Sage.

Butcher, J. N., & Miller, K. (in press). Psychological assessment in personal injury cases. In A. Hess & I. Weiner (Eds.), *Handbook of forensic psychology* (2nd ed.). New York: Wiley.

Keller, L. S., & Butcher, J. N. (1991). *Use of the MMPI-2 with chronic pain patients.* Minneapolis: University of Minnesota Press.

Lees-Haley, P. R. (1997). MMPI-2 base rates for 492 personal injury plaintiffs: Implications and challenges for forensic assessment. *Journal of Clinical Psychology, 53,* 745–756.

Nelson, L. (1995). Use of the MMPI and MMPI-2 in forensic neurological evaluations. In Y. S. Ben-Porath, J. R. Graham, G. C. N. Hall, R. D. Hirschman, & M. S. Zaragoza (Eds.), *Forensic applications of the MMPI-2* (pp. 202–221). Thousand Oaks, CA: Sage.

Strassberg, D. S., Tilley, D., Bristone, S., & Tian, P. S. (1992). The MMPI and chronic pain: A cross-cultural view. *Psychological Assessment, 4,* 493–497.

Felon Classification

Megargee, E. I. (1994). Using the Megargee MMPI-based classification system with the MMPI-2 of male prison inmates. *Psychological Assessment, 6,* 337–344.

Megargee, E. I. (1995). Use of the MMPI-2 in correctional settings. In Y. S. Ben-Porath, J. R. Graham, G. C. N. Hall, R. D. Hirschman, & M. S. Zaragoza (Eds.), *Forensic applications of the MMPI-2* (pp. 127–159). Thousand Oaks, CA: Sage.

Assessment of Murderers

Holcomb, W. R., Adams, N. A., Ponder, H. M., & Anderson, W. P. (1984). Cognitive and behavioral predictors of MMPI scores in pretrial psychological evaluations of murderers. *Journal of Clinical Psychology, 40,* 592–597.

Parwatikar, S. D., Holcomb, W. R., & Menninger K. A., (1985). The detection of malingered amnesia. I. Accused murderers. *Bulletin of American Academy of Psychiatry and Law, 13,* 97–103.

Glossary

Many of the technical terms and abbreviations relevant to using the MMPI-2 are included in this glossary. No attempt has been made to include all of the technical MMPI-2 terms; only those general technical terms or statistical concepts needed for understanding the MMPI-2 scores are addressed.

Acting out: A defense mechanism (psychoanalytic or psychodynamic) in which the individual expresses painful or "unacceptable" emotions through behavior as a way to keep such emotions out of his or her conscious awareness.

Acquiescence: The tendency on the part of people to respond to questions by "going along" with what they think is appropriate; the tendency to "yeasay" or agree with others.

Actuarial approach: The application of probability statistics to predict human behavior, as in the use of insurance mortality tables to predict events.

Acute posttraumatic stress disorder: A disorder in which symptoms develop from an extremely stressful or traumatic experience (occurring within 6 months of the incident).

Adaptive testing: An approach to test administration, usually by computer, using a "branching" approach. Rather than the administration of all items for each person, a different set of items is administered for each person, depending on the person's previous responses.

α coefficient: A statistical index assessing homogeneity of items on a scale. This index assesses the extent to which the items of a scale are intercorrelated.

Antisocial personality: A personality disorder involving a marked lack of ethical or moral development.

ANX: Abbreviation for the Anxiety Content Scale on the MMPI-2 (see chapter 5).

ASP: Abbreviation for the Antisocial Practices Content Scale on the MMPI-2 (see chapter 5).

Automated assessment: Psychological test interpretation by computer or some other mechanical means of combining test results.

Base rate: The number of cases occurring in a particular population. The probabilities of the cases occurring are usually expressed in a percentage. Base rates are often calculated in clinical settings. For example, if 5 out of every 100 clients in a hospital try to commit suicide, the base rate of suicide attempts in this setting is 5%. To put it another way, as one of this book's reviewers noted, If you are at Churchill Downs and hear hoof beats, look for horses, not zebras.

BIZ: Abbreviation for the Bizarre Mentation Content Scale on the MMPI-2 (see chapter 5).

Cannot say score: An MMPI validity score (often shown as "?"; see chapter 2). It is the number of unanswered items on the MMPI.

Control group: A comparison group used in research that allows the effect(s) of one or more independent variables to be assessed (e.g., to provide "normal" responses to a test when a clinical population is studied).

Construct validity: The theory surrounding a particular test construct that provides information as to how high and low scorers differ on the scale. Research on a construct provides the "network" of information for interpreting a scale's measurement of the quality assessed.

Correlation coefficient: A statistic indicating the degree of association between two variables. The coefficient falls somewhere on the continuum running from -1 (*perfectly negatively correlated*) to 0 (*no relationship whatsoever*) to $+1$ (*perfectly positively correlated*).

Critical items: Sets of items (e.g., the Koss–Butcher or the Lachar–Wrobel) that have been determined to suggest the presence of specific problems. These items are used to provide cues to psychopathology. They are not used as predictor scales.

CYN: Abbreviation for the Cynicism Content Scale on the MMPI-2 (see chapter 5).

D: Abbreviation for the Depression Clinical Scale (i.e., Scale 2) on the MMPI (see chapter 5).

DEP: Abbreviation for the Depression Content Scale on the MMPI-2 (see chapter 5).

Empirical scale construction: The development of scales by selecting items that contrast a group known to possess particular qualities (e.g., depressed patients) with another group of individuals without such problems (e.g., the normative sample).

F: An MMPI-2 validity scale (see chapter 2) created to measure exaggeration (infrequency) of symptoms.

F(b): An MMPI-2 validity scale (see chapter 2) created to measure exaggeration of symptoms (infrequency) on the items that appear at the end (or back) of the MMPI.

F(p): An MMPI-2 validity scale (see chapter 2) created to measure exaggeration of symptoms or infrequent responding in a psychiatric sample (a measure of malingering of psychiatric symptoms).

FAM: Abbreviation for the Family Problems Content Scale on the MMPI-2 (see chapter 5).

FRS: Abbreviation for the Fears Content Scale on the MMPI-2 (see chapter 5).

HEA: Abbreviation for the Health Concerns Content Scale on the MMPI-2 (see chapter 5).

Ho: Abbreviation for the Cooke–Medley Hostility Scale that assesses the personality characteristics of competitiveness and hostility associated with the development of coronary disease.

Hs: Abbreviation for the Hypochondriasis Clinical Scale (i.e., Scale 1) on the MMPI (see chapter 3), measuring somatic concerns.

Hy: Abbreviation for the Hysteria Clinical Scale (i.e., Scale 3) on the MMPI (see chapter 3). This scale measures the tendency to overuse repression and denial and to develop vague physical complaints.

K: Abbreviation for an MMPI-2 validity scale (see chapter 2) created to measure test defensiveness and problem denial.

L: Abbreviation for an MMPI validity scale (see chapter 2) created to measure the tendency to claim excessive virtue.

Linear scores: A statistical term (see *T* score in which the *M* of the distribution = 50 and the *SD* = 10); the type of scaling used by the original MMPI (see chapter 1).

LSE: Abbreviation for the Low Self-Esteem Content Scale on the MMPI-2 (see chapter 5).

Ma: Abbreviation for the Mania Scale of the MMPI-2 (Scale 9) that measures unrealistically elevated mood.

Mf: Abbreviation for the Masculinity–Femininity Scale (i.e., Scale 5) on the basic MMPI-2 profile (see chapter 3).

Normative population: The MMPI-2 normative sample was a random selection of individuals (1,138 men and 1,462 women, balanced for ethnic group membership) from seven regions of the United States who were administered the MMPI-2 items in a controlled setting. These item response data were used for the MMPI-2 test norms.

OBS: Abbreviation for the Obsessiveness Content Scale on the MMPI-2 (see chapter 5).

Pa: Abbreviation for the Paranoia Clinical Scale (i.e., Scale 6) on the MMPI (see chapter 3).

Percentile rank: Shows what proportion of the group falls below a particular point.

Percentile score: The rank from the bottom of a scale is expressed in percentage form.

Profile: A chart that graphically shows several scale score results of a test taker.

Profile definition: A construct used in MMPI-2 interpretation to convey the relative "uniqueness" of a particular test score or code type. A very well-defined scale score or code type differs from the next scale in the profile by at least 10 points.

Pd: Abbreviation for the Psychopathic Deviate Clinical Scale (i.e., Scale

4) on the MMPI (see chapter 3) that measures personality disorder problems.

Pk: Abbreviation for a personality measure that assesses posttraumatic stress symptoms and was developed by Keane.

Profile stability: The extent to which a test score is similar to the re-testing score.

Protocol validity: A measure of the extent to which a particular performance on a psychological test is credible.

Pt: Abbreviation for the Psychasthenia Clinical Scale (i.e., Scale 7) on the MMPI created to measure anxiety (see chapter 3).

Raw score: A measure of performance (e.g., the total number of scored answers) for a particular scale. These raw scores are typically converted to scale scores using a test distribution, referred to as a *norm*.

Random sample: A subgroup selected from a larger group (termed the *population*) in such a way that each member of the larger group has an equal probability of being chosen on a random draw.

Rational scale development: Scale construction strategy based on the combination of similar content items, for example, the MMPI-2 content scales.

Reliability: The degree to which a test or other form of measurement is consistent in producing the same result every time it is used to assess or measure a particular person who has not changed significantly between testings.

Sc: Abbreviation for the Schizophrenia Clinical Scale (i.e., Scale 8) on the MMPI (see chapter 3).

Scale: A group of items in a personality inventory that is assumed to measure a particular personality construct.

Self-report questionnaire: A questionnaire or inventory designed to obtain self-descriptions from an individual.

Social desirability: A test construct that suggests that people respond to test items in the same direction as other people, that is, in a direction that is socially desirable.

SOD: Abbreviation for the Social Discomfort Content Scale on the MMPI-2 (see chapter 5).

Standard deviation: A statistical measure of the spread or dispersion of scores (or other measures) around the mean; the square root of the variance (see chapter 1).

Standard profile: (Traditional clinical scales) A chart that plots the traditional MMPI (or MMPI-2) clinical scales, *Mf,* and *Si* scores.

Standard score: A score (e.g., on a standardized psychological test) calculated in terms of standard deviations from the statistical mean of scores.

***T* score:** *See* Standard score. Scores falling along a distribution in which $M = 50$ and the $SD = 10$ (see chapters 1 and 5).

TPA: Abbreviation for the Type A Personality Content Scale on the MMPI-2 (see chapter 5).

TRIN: Abbreviation for the True Response Inconsistency Scale, one of the validity scales of the MMPI-2 (see chapter 2).

TRT: Abbreviation for the Negative Treatment Indicators Content Scale on the MMPI-2 (see chapter 5).

Uniform *T* score: A statistical term (see *T* score); the type of scaling used by the MMPI-2 and MMPI-A, resulting in comparable percentile values for a given *T* score across various clinical or content scales (see chapter 1).

Validity: The degree to which a test or other form of measurement actually assesses or measures what it is designed to assess or measure (see chapter 1).

VRIN: Abbreviation for the Variable Response Inconsistency Scale, one of the validity scales of the MMPI-2 (see chapter 2).

WRK: Abbreviation for the Work Interference Content Scale on the MMPI-2 (see chapter 2).

References

Allard, G., Butler, J., Faust, D., & Shea, M. T. (1995). Errors in hand scoring objective personality tests: The case of the Personality Diagnostic Questionnaire–Revised (PDQ-R). *Professional Psychology: Research and Practice*, 26, 304–308.

American Psychological Association. (1986). *American Psychological Association guidelines for computer-based tests and interpretations*. Washington, DC: Author.

Arbisi, P., & Ben-Porath, Y. S. (1995). An MMPI-2 infrequency scale for use with psychopathological populations: The Infrequency-Psychopathology Scale, *F(p)*. *Psychological Assessment*, 7, 424–431.

Arbisi, P., & Ben-Porath, Y. S. (1997). Characteristics of the MMPI-2 *F(p)* scale as a function of diagnosis in an inpatient sample of veterans. *Psychological Assessment*, 9, 102–105.

Archer, R. P., Griffin, R., & Aiduk, R. (1995). Clinical correlates for ten common code types. *Journal of Personality Assessment*, 65, 391–408.

Azan, A. A. (1989). The MMPI version Hispana: Standardization and cross-cultural personality study with a population of Cuban refugees (Doctoral dissertation, University of Minnesota, 1988). *Dissertation Abstracts International*, 50, 2144B.

Barefoot, J. C., Dahlstrom, W. G., & Williams, R. B. (1983). Hostility, CHD incidence, and total mortality: A 25 year follow-up study of 255 physicians. *Psychosomatic Medicine*, 45, 58–63.

Ben-Porath, Y. S., Hostetler, K., Butcher, J. N., & Graham, J. R. (1995). New subscales for the MMPI-2 Social Introversion (*Si*) Scale. *Psychological Assessment: A Journal of Consulting and Clinical Psychology*, 1, 169–174.

Ben-Porath, Y. S., Shondrick, D. D., & Stafford, K. P. (1995). MMPI-2 and race in a forensic diagnostic sample. *Criminal Justice & Behavior*, 22, 19–32.

Berah, E., Butcher, J., Miach, P., Bolza, J., Colman, S., & McAsey, P. (1993, October). *Computer-based interpretation of the MMPI-2: An Australian evaluation of the Minnesota Report*. Paper presented at the Australian Psychological Association Meetings, Melbourne, Australia.

Berry, D. T. R., Adams, J. J., Smith, G. T., Greene, R. L., Sekirnjak, G. C., Wieland, G., & Tharpe, B. (1997). MMPI-2 clinical scales and two-point code types: Impact of varying levels of omitted items. *Psychological Assessment*, 9, 158–160.

Berry, D. T., Baer, R. A., & Harris, M. J. (1991). Detection of malingering on the MMPI: A meta-analysis. *Clinical Psychology Review*, 11, 585–591.

Beutler, L. E. (1995). Integrating and communicating findings. In L. E. Beutler & M. B. Berren (Eds.), *Integrative assessment of adult personality* (pp. 25–64). New York: Guilford Press.

Block, J. (1965). *The challenge of response sets.* New York: Appleton-Century-Crofts.

Brislin, R. (1986). The wording and translation of research instruments. In W. J. Lonner & J. W. Berry (Eds.), *Field methods in cross-cultural research* (pp. 137–164). Beverly Hills, CA: Sage.

Butcher, J. N. (Ed.). (1972). *Objective personality assessment: Changing perspectives.* New York: Academic Press.

Butcher, J. N. (1985). Current developments in MMPI use: An international perspective. In J. N. Butcher & C. D. Spielberger (Eds.), *Advances in personality assessment* (Vol. 4, pp. 83–94). Hillsdale, NJ: Erlbaum.

Butcher, J. N. (1990). *Use of the MMPI-2 in treatment planning.* New York: Oxford University Press.

Butcher, J. N. (1993). *User's guide for the Minnesota Clinical Report.* Minneapolis, MN: National Computer Systems.

Butcher, J. N. (1995). Clinical use of computer-based personality test reports. In J. N. Butcher (Ed.), *Clinical personality assessment: Practical approaches* (pp. 78–94). New York: Oxford University Press.

Butcher, J. N. (1996). (Ed.). *International adaptation of the MMPI-2: A handbook of research and clinical applications.* Minneapolis: University of Minnesota Press.

Butcher, J. N. (1997). Base-rate information for the personal injury samples in the Minnesota Forensic Study. *MMPI-2 News & Profiles, 8,* 2–4.

Butcher, J. N., Berah, E., Ellertsen, B., Miach, P., Lim, J., Nezami, E., Pancheri, P., Derksen, J. & Almagor, M. (1998). Objective personality assessment: Computer-based MMPI-2 interpretation in international clinical settings (pp. 277–312). In C. Belar (Ed.), *Comprehensive clinical psychology: Sociocultural and individual differences.* New York: Elsevier.

Butcher, J. N., Dahlstrom, W. G., Graham, J. R., Tellegen, A. M., & Kaemmer, B. (1989). *Minnesota Multiphasic Personality Inventory-2 (MMPI-2): Manual for administration and scoring.* Minneapolis: University of Minnesota Press.

Butcher, J. N., Graham, J. R., Williams, C. L., & Ben-Porath, Y. S. (1990). *Development and use of the MMPI-2 content scales.* Minneapolis: University of Minnesota Press.

Butcher, J. N., & Han, K. (1995). Development of an MMPI-2 scale to assess the presentation of self in a superlative manner: The *S* scale. In J. N. Butcher & C. D. Spielberger (Eds.), *Advances in personality assessment* (Vol. 10, pp. 25–50). Hillsdale, NJ: Erlbaum.

Butcher, J. N., Narikiyo, T., & Bemis-Vitousek, K. (1992). Understanding abnormal behavior incultural context. In P. Sutker & H. Adams (Eds.), *Handbook of psychopathology* (2nd ed., pp. 83–108). New York: Plenum.

Butcher, J. N., & Pancheri, P. (1976). *Handbook of cross-national MMPI research.* Minneapolis: University of Minnesota Press.

Butcher, J. N., & Rouse, S. (1996). Clinical personality assessment. *Annual Review of Psychology, 47,* 87–111.

Butcher, J. N., & Williams, C. L. (1992). *Essentials of MMPI-2 and MMPI-A.* Minneapolis: University of Minnesota Press.

Butcher, J. N., Williams, C. L., Graham, J. R., Archer, R., Tellegen, A., Ben-Porath, Y. S., & Kaemmer, B. (1989). *MMPI-A manual for administration, scoring, and interpretation.* Minneapolis: University of Minnesota Press.

Cook, W. W., & Medley, D. M. (1954). Proposed hostility and pharisaic-virtue scales for the MMPI. *Journal of Applied Psychology, 38,* 414–418.

Cronbach, L. J. (1942). Studies of acquiescence as a factor in the true–false test. *Journal of Educational Psychology, 33,* 401–415.

Cronbach, L. J., & Meehl, P. E. (1955). Construct validity in psychological tests. *Psychological Bulletin, 52,* 281–302.

Dahlstrom, W. G. (1972). Whither the MMPI? In J. N. Butcher (Ed.), *Objective personality assessment: Changing perspectives* (pp. 85–116). New York: Academic Press.

Deinard, A., Butcher, J. N., Thao, U. D., Vang, S. H. M., & Hang, K. (1996). Development of a Hmong translation of the MMPI-2. In J. N. Butcher (Ed.), *International adaptation of the MMPI-2* (pp. 194–205). Minneapolis: University of Minnesota Press.

Edwards, A. L. (1957). *The social desirability variable in personality assessment and research.* New York: Holt.

Finn, S., & Kamphuis, J. H. (1995). What a clinician needs to know about base rates. In J. N. Butcher (Ed.), *Clinical personality assessment: Practical approaches* (pp. 214–235). New York: Oxford University Press.

Finn, S., & Martin, H. (1997). Therapeutic assessment with the MMPI-2 in managed care settings. In J. N. Butcher (Ed.), *Personality assessment in managed health care* (pp. 131–152). New York: Oxford University Press.

Finn, S., & Tonsager, M. (1992). Therapeutic effects of providing MMPI-2 test feedback to college students awaiting therapy. *Psychological Assessment, 4,* 278–287.

Fowler, R. D. (1985). Landmarks in computer-assisted psychological test interpretation. *Journal of Consulting and Clinical Psychology, 53,* 748–759.

Gallagher, R. W., Ben-Porath, Y. S., & Briggs, S. (1997). Inmate views about the purpose and use of the MMPI-2 at the time of correctional intake. *Criminal Justice and Behavior, 24,* 360–369.

Gass, C. S. (1991). MMPI-2 interpretation and closed head injury: A correction factor. *Psychological Assessment: A Journal of Consulting and Clinical Psychology, 3,* 27–31.

Gillet, I., Simon, M., Guelfi, J. D., Brun-Eberentz, A., Monier, C., Seunevel, F., & Svarna, L. (1996). The MMPI-2 in France. In J. N. Butcher (Ed.), *International adaptation of the MMPI-2* (pp. 395–415). Minneapolis: University of Minnesota Press.

Gottesman, I. I., & Prescott, C. A. (1989). Abuses of the MacAndrew MMPI Alcoholism Scale: A critical review. *Clinical Psychology Review, 9,* 223–242.

Graham, J. R. (in press). *MMPI-2: Assessing personality and psychopathology* (3rd ed.). New York: Oxford University Press.

Graham, J. R., Ben-Porath, Y. S., & McNulty, J. (in press). *Using the MMPI-2 in outpatient mental health settings.* Minneapolis: University of Minnesota Press.

Graham, J. R., Smith, R. L., & Schwartz, G. F. (1986). Stability of MMPI configurations for psychiatric inpatients. *Journal of Consulting and Clinical Psychology, 54,* 375–380.

Graham, J. R., & Strenger, V. E. (1988). MMPI characteristics of alcoholics: A review. *Journal of Consulting and Clinical Psychology, 56,* 197–205.

Graham, J. R., Timbrook, R., Ben-Porath, Y. S., & Butcher, J. N. (1991). Code-type congruence between MMPI and MMPI-2: Separating fact from artifact. *Journal of Personality Assessment, 57,* 205–215.

Grayson, H. M. (1951). *Psychological admission testing program and manual.* Los Angeles, CA: Veterans Administration Center, Neuropsychiatric Hospital.

Greene, R. (1987). Ethnicity and MMPI performance: A review. *Journal of Consulting and Clinical Psychology, 55,* 497–512.

Han, K., Weed, N., Calhoun, R. F., & Butcher, J. N. (1995). Psychometric characteristics of the MMPI-2 Cook-Medley Hostility Scale. *Journal of Personality Assessment, 65,* 567–585.

Harris, R. E., & Lingoes, J. C. (1955). *Subscales for the MMPI: An aid to profile interpretation*

[Mimeographed materials]. Los Angeles: University of California, Department of Psychiatry. (Reprinted in 1968)

Harvey, V. S. (1997). Improving readability of psychological reports. *Professional Psychology: Research and Practice, 28*, 271–274.

Hathaway, S. R. (1972). Where have we gone wrong? The mystery of missing progress. In J. N. Butcher (Ed.), *Objective personality assessment: Changing perspectives* (pp. 21–43). New York: Academic Press.

Hathaway, S. R., & McKinley, J. C. (1940). A multiphasic personality schedule (Minnesota): I. Construction of the schedule. *Journal of Psychology, 10*, 249–254.

Hathaway, S. R., & McKinley, J. C. (1943). *The Minnesota Multiphasic Personality Schedule.* Minneapolis: University of Minnesota Press.

Hjemboe, S., Almagor, M., & Butcher, J. N. (1992). Empirical assessment of marital distress: The Marital Distress Scale (*MDS*) for the MMPI-2. In C. D. Spielberger & J. N. Butcher (Eds.), *Advances in personality assessment* (Vol. 9, pp. 141–152). Hillsdale, NJ: Erlbaum.

Hjemboe, S., & Butcher, J. N. (1991). Couples in marital distress: A study of demographic and personality factors as measured by the MMPI-2. *Journal of Personality Assessment, 57*, 216–237.

Jackson, D., & Messick, S. (1962). Acquiescence and desirability as response determinants of the MMPI. *Educational and Psychological Measurement, 22*, 771–790.

Keane, T. M., Malloy, P. F., & Fairbank, J. A. (1984). Empirical development of an MMPI subscale for the assessment of combat-related posttraumatic stress disorder. *Journal of Consulting and Clinical Psychology, 52*, 888–891.

Keefe, K., Sue, S., Enomoto, K., Durvasula, R. S., & Chao, R. (1996). Asian American and White college students' performance on the MMPI-2. In J. N. Butcher (Ed.), *International adaptations of the MMPI-2* (pp. 206–218). Minneapolis: University of Minnesota Press.

Kelly, C. K., & King, G. D. (1978). Behavioral correlates for within-normal limit MMPI profiles with and without elevated *K* in students at a university mental health center. *Journal of Clinical Psychology, 34*, 695–699.

Koss, M. P., & Butcher, J. N. (1973). A comparison of psychiatric patients' self-report with other sources of clinical information. *Journal of Research in Personality, 7*, 225–236.

Lachar, D., & Wrobel, T. A. (1979). Validating clinicians' hunches: Construction of a new MMPI critical item set. *Journal of Consulting and Clinical Psychology, 47*, 227–284.

Lees-Haley, P. R., Smith, H. H., Williams, C. W., & Dunn, J. T. (1995). Forensic neuropsychological test usage: An empirical survey. *Archives of Clinical Neuropsychology, 11*, 45–51.

Leon, G. R., Gillum, B., Gillum, R., & Gouze, M. (1979). Personality stability and change over a 30-year period—Middle age to old age. *Journal of Consulting & Clinical Psychology, 47*, 517–524.

Lubin, B., Larsen, R. M., & Matarazzo, J. (1984). Patterns of psychological test usage in the United States, 1935–1982. *American Psychologist, 39*, 451–454.

MacAndrew, C. (1965). The differentiation of male alcoholic outpatients from nonalcoholic psychiatric outpatients by means of the MMPI. *Quarterly Journal of Studies on Alcohol, 26*, 238–246.

Meehl, P. E., & Hathaway, S. R. (1946). The *K* factor as a suppressor variable in the MMPI. *Journal of Applied Psychology, 30*, 525–564.

Miller, W. R., & Rollnick, S. (1991). Using assessment results. In W. R. Miller & S. Rollnick (Eds.), *Motivational interviewing* (pp. 89–99). New York: Guilford Press.

Mirza, L. (1973). *Cultural adaptation, validation, and standardization of the Minnesota Multiphasic Personality Inventory (MMPI)*. Doctoral dissertation, University of Punjab, Pakistan.

Newman, M. L., & Greenway, P. (1997). Therapeutic effects of providing MMPI-2 test feedback to clients at a university counseling service: A collaborative approach. *Psychological Assessment, 9,* 122–131.

Ownby, R. L. (1987). *Psychological reports: A guide to report writing in professional psychology.* Brandon, VT: Clinical Psychology.

Pearson, J. S., Swenson, W. M., Rome, H. P., Mataya, P., & Brannick, T. L. (1965). Development of a computer system for scoring and interpreting the Minnesota Multiphasic Personality Inventory in a medical setting. *Annals of the New York Academy of Sciences, 126,* 682–692.

Putnam, S. H., Kurtz, J. E., Millis, S. R., & Adams, K. (1995, March). *Prevalence and correlates of MMPI-2 codetypes in patients with traumatic brain injury.* Paper presented at the 30th Annual Symposium on Recent Developments in the Use of the MMPI/MMPI-2, St. Petersburg, FL.

Rome, H. P., Swenson, W. M., Mataya, P., McCarthy, C. E., Pearson, J. S., Keating, F. R., & Hathaway, S. R. (1962). Symposium on automation techniques in personality assessment. *Proceedings of the Staff Meetings of the Mayo Clinic, 37,* 61–82.

Schretlen, D. (1988). The use of psychological tests to identify malingered symptoms of mental disorder. *Clinical Psychology Review, 8,* 451–476.

Shores, A., & Carstairs, J. R. (1998). Accuracy of the MMPI-2 computerized Minnesota Report in identifying fake-good and fake-bad response sets. *The Clinical Neuropsychologist, 12,* 101–106.

Soliman, A. M. (1996). Development of an Arabic version of the MMPI-2: With clinical applications. In J. N. Butcher (Ed.), *International adaptation of the MMPI-2* (pp. 463–487). Minneapolis: University of Minnesota Press.

Spiro, R., Butcher, J. N., Levinson, M., Aldwin, C., & Bosse, R. (1993, August). *Personality change over five years: The MMPI-2 in older men.* Paper presented at the 101st Annual Convention of the American Psychological Association, Toronto, Ontario, Canada.

Tallent, N. (1992). *The practice of psychological assessment.* Englewood Cliffs, NJ: Prentice-Hall.

Tallent, N. (1993). *Psychological report writing* (4th ed.). Englewood Cliffs, NJ: Prentice-Hall.

Tellegen, A., Butcher, J. N., & Hoeglund, T. (1993, March). *Are unisex norms for the MMPI-2 needed?* Paper presented at the 28th Annual Symposium on Recent Developments in the Use of the MMPI/MMPI-2/MMPI-A, St. Petersburg, FL.

Tinius, T., & Ben-Porath, Y. S. (1993, March). *A comparative study of Native Americans and Caucasian Americans undergoing substance abuse treatment.* Paper presented at the 28th Annual Symposium on Recent Developments in the Use of the MMPI/MMPI-2/MMPI-A, St. Petersburg, FL.

Tran, B. C. (1996). Vietnamese translation and adaptation of the MMPI-2. In J. N. Butcher (Ed.), *International adaptation of the MMPI-2* (pp. 175–193). Minneapolis: University of Minnesota Press.

Weed, N. C., Butcher, J. N., McKenna, T., & Ben-Porath, Y. S. (1992). New measures for assessing alcohol and drug abuse with the MMPI-2: The *APS* and *AAS. Journal of Personality Assessment, 58,* 389–404.

Welsh, G. S. (1951). Some practical uses of MMPI profile coding. *Journal of Consulting Psychology*, 15, 82–84.

Weiner, I. B. (1987). Writing forensic reports. In I. B. Weiner & A. Hess (Eds.), *Handbook of forensic psychology* (pp. 511–528). New York: Wiley.

Wiggins, J. S. (1966). Substantive dimensions of self-report in the MMPI item pool. *Psychological Monographs*, 80(22, Whole No. 630).

Wiggins, J. S. (1969). Content dimensions in the MMPI. In J. N. Butcher (Ed.), *MMPI: Research developments and clinical applications* (pp. 127–180). New York: McGraw-Hill.

Woodworth, R. S. (1920). *The personal data sheet.* Chicago: Stoelting.

Index

About the Author

James N. Butcher, PhD, earned advanced degrees in experimental and clinical psychology from the University of North Carolina at Chapel Hill. Currently a professor of psychology at the University of Minnesota and former editor of the APA journal *Psychological Assessment,* he was awarded Doctor Honoris Causa by the Free University of Brussels, Belgium, and was selected by the University of Minnesota Press to serve on the committee to revise and restandardize the MMPI. He founded both the annual Symposium on Recent Developments in the Use of the MMPI and the International Conference on Personality Assessment. Recent books include *Clinical Personality Assessment* (Oxford University Press, 1995), *Essentials of MMPI-2 and MMPI-A Interpretation* (with Carolyn L. Williams; University of Minnesota Press, 1992), and *International Adaptations of the MMPI-2* (University of Minnesota Press, 1996). He also consults and testifies as an expert witness in trials involving the MMPI.